THE EMERGENT MANAGER

THE EMERGENT MANAGER

Tony Watson and Pauline Harris

SAGE Publications
London · Thousand Oaks · New Delhi

First published 1999

SAGE Publications Ltd
6 Bonhill Street
London EC2A 4PU

SAGE Publications Inc
2455 Teller Road
Thousand Oaks, California 91320

SAGE Publications India Pvt Ltd
32, M-Block Market
Greater Kailash - I
New Delhi 110 048

British Library Cataloguing in Publication data

A catalogue record for this book is
available from the British Library

ISBN 0 7619 5841 X
ISBN 0 7619 5842 8 (pbk)

Library of Congress catalog record available

Typeset by Type Study, Scarborough, North Yorkshire
Printed in Great Britain by The Cromwell Press,
Trowbridge, Wiltshire

CONTENTS

PREFACE

We all have to manage our lives. And some of us are also paid by employers to 'manage' at work. *The Emergent Manager* is a study of both these things – and of how they relate to each other. It focuses on the ways in which people come to be managers in work organisations and how they learn to do managerial work. What it shows is that there is no clear point at which one becomes a manager and that there is no clear formal learning process which prepares people for a managerial career. Indeed, for many, the process of becoming a manager can be traced back into their earlier lives. And, for everyone, the 'becoming' process continues long after they are first given a managerial title.

At a more general level, *The Emergent Manager* is a study of how people in managerial work shape their personal identities and their working lives – at the same time as being shaped by the world around them. Great emphasis is placed on managers' own words in considering how forty of them, working in a variety of settings, make sense of their work and their lives. These settings range from a construction company to a bingo hall, a hospital ward to a retailing company, a university department to a prison wing, a courtroom to a civil service department, a restaurant to an engineering company, a social work department to a building society, a school to a bank. Within this variety of organisational settings and this variety of human personalities there are some fascinating similarities as well as some intriguing differences.

The book is written to be meaningful to any reader who is curious about how managers in a variety of work contexts talk about and make sense of what they do. Readers who are themselves involved in managerial work should, however, find it especially helpful to reflect on what other managers say about the challenges they face and how they handle the pleasures, pressures and pains of shaping their lives – at home and at work. But the book is also addressed to an academic audience who will be interested in how it relates these issues to methodological, theoretical and substantive debates about what is going on in the world of management and work organisation and how we might most effectively understand it.

At the heart of the book is a notion of the human being as always in a process of 'becoming'. Every one of us is continually changing, adapting and learning, it is argued. This can be experienced as something frightening and unfulfilling. Alternatively, it can be exciting and rewarding. Our book is about managers and their ongoing *emergence* – something which, as the study shows, has both fulfilling and frustrating aspects to it. But the book has been written by two people who are also 'emergent' – as researchers, writers, teachers and private individuals. In the same way that researching and writing the book has played its part in our emergence as academics and human beings, we hope that it may be of value to everybody who reads it. We have learned a lot from doing the research and we hope that you, the reader, will enjoy the book and will also find that it plays a part in how your thinking and your practices – be they academic or managerial – go on to emerge.

We dedicate this book to all of those who gave us so much of their time and of their selves in contributing to this research.

CHAPTER I

MAKING SENSE OF MANAGING

What is it all about?

I think that I am only now really beginning to see what it is all about – actually thinking about what my management philosophy is. For years I was probably doing things without really thinking out what I was doing. I was learning without really being conscious of learning. I was managing things but I don't think I had . . . I . . . I don't think I thought about being a MANAGER, you know, in big letters. It's only looking back that I can see how I was changing.

Kevin Berry is a manager in a private coal mining company. He was originally a mining engineer in the nationalised coal industry and is finding it difficult to say at what point he moved into a managerial role. When pressed on whether he could possibly identify the point at which he actually 'became' a manager, he went on,

I didn't. Daft in't it? But I am now: Mr management man. Look at me – the suit, the mobile phone. But the accent and the [patting his middle] shape don't change. The rough bit's there, but meetings, targets, paperwork, budgets, it's meat and ale to me.

So you've changed, yet you haven't changed?
That's it. I can put my finger on one thing – I think. You see I as I rose up through the ranks so to speak I wasn't called 'the manager' – it weren't written on my door, like. There was only one manager and he was the Colliery Manager. I was an engineer. I still am – I still get the wellies and gear on you know. But anyway, I was going to say about this day when I – like it was all of a sudden, well sort of – when I actually noticed that people, some of the lads, younger ones that is – were calling me Mr Berry. I thought to me'sen 'Ay up, how long's this been going on?' That was it. Actually, most people these days, the lads and all that, still call me Kev. But this made me think.

This was a transitional point, then. You saw yourself as different because others were speaking to you differently?
Yes.

And did you think of this in terms of now being a manager?
No. You see I think of managing as involving yourself more than others in getting things done – you know, organising the blokes around you. I've always tended to do that. I sort of used to say, when I was with others of the same level – and even higher level, 'Come on, lads, let's move this along'.

So you were 'managing' even when there was no question of your having the formal status of a manager?
Or of a senior bloke in any sense.

So what was the significance of noticing people calling you mister?
I got them to stop that.

But you implied it made you think that . . .
Yeah. Something was going on. Perhaps I saw myself as becoming *management* [*coughs and sits up as if about to salute*], you know, part of *the management*. It couldn't be that I was starting to manage people. I'd been doing that – I even did it at school. I was going over some line somewhere. I didn't like it.

And where are you now with regard to that line?
No problem at all. My approach to people hasn't changed. But with privatisation and the complete culture changes that this entails, I really am part of that. I'm still an engineer but it's the business side of it that . . . I've read the books, been on the courses. I am a, ahem, a *manager of change*. No problem . . .

No problem?
Well, you know. I do ask whether I can keep up with the terrifying pace of what's going on. But I just say, 'Use the old head, Kev, like you always did. And deal fairly with folks.' There's nowt new.

You're the same but different.
Different but the same.

This conversation with Kevin Berry touches on a number of the key themes with which we are concerned. It can be read as a joint exploration of issues of identity, biography and the nature of managerial work. The interviewer is looking for insights into the process whereby people 'become' managers and the interviewee is not only helping the researcher with their project but is also making sense *for himself* of who and what he is. A key notion that we ourselves are using to make sense of these processes is that of the *emergent manager*. We think that this is a useful way of thinking about all people who are engaged in managerial work but Kevin, in an especially clear manner, talks along lines very close to our own. He articulates, in his own way and with reference to his own unique biography, a notion of the individual never fully *being* a particular thing – a manager in this case – but in some process of *continually becoming*. There is not a point when one actually and unambiguously *becomes* something. There is never a point when one has actually emerged. Instead there is an ongoing process of *becoming*; one is forever *emergent*.

This way of looking at humans as emergent beings is something we will shortly explain more fully. It is central to our conceptual position. Our story will interweave our own conceptual work as social scientists with the story-telling work of the people we have been in dialogue with, and, in that spirit, we will turn back, for the moment, to the relatively specific case of Kevin and the account he gave us.

Let us contrast the account Kevin gives us with the one that we might expect if we were thinking about someone entering an occupation as if this were the relatively uncomplicated and straightforward process we often and conventionally take it to be. Following this, we would tend to think of someone growing up and eventually settling on – *choosing* – an occupation they wished to enter. They would then pursue the appropriate educational programmes and, once in a post, would systematically train themselves and develop specific skills. They would be able to say to others, 'I am a pharmacist' or 'I am a firefighter'. But this is not what happened to Kevin, he suggests. His formal occupational identity was that of a mining engineer. He calls himself a manager nowadays, and indeed relishes the idea of it. Yet he was doing such work long before either he or others used the title. He was even doing it, he suggests, when he was at school. Not only this, he talks of learning without being conscious of learning and his awareness of changes in himself and in his work, he says, came after the event: 'It's only looking back that I can see how I was changing.'

Being a manager appears to have several different aspects to it, for Kevin. There is a *social* dimension, in which he becomes part of what he calls 'the management' – a process which at an early stage led certain young employees to address him as Mr Berry. This demands an adjustment at a *personal* level. He has, in some way, to come to terms with seeing himself as a manager. And there is also the *task* dimension. There appears to be something potentially frightening about this (the reference to the 'terrifying pace of what's going on') and there is a process of engaging with the special knowledge to be found in books and courses. On the one hand, the activity sounds rather grand and as if it involves a lot of expertise: Kevin is a 'manager of change'. But, on the other hand, he is doing 'nowt new'. To 'manage' one has to 'use the old head' and 'deal fairly with folks'. One is different and the same at the same time!

This messiness in the process of becoming a manager and the ambiguities surrounding the nature of managerial work make the notion of *emergence* especially appropriate for studying processes of entry into managerial work and the development of managerial roles and careers. Such a concept is valuable for looking at many other aspects of human life. It is not the case, for example, that the process of becoming a firefighter or pharmacist is anything like as straightforward as the conventional assumptions referred to earlier would imply. All careers and lives can be looked at as processes of continuous emergence in which people are continuously making sense of what they are doing and where they are going in the light of how they make sense of where they have been. But it is especially valuable to look at management and managing in this way. If Kevin Berry's case has any typicality at all, managing is something which one can do in one's work, and indeed in one's non-work life, long before one takes on an occupational identity or a job title of 'manager'. A great of deal of the research which precedes and has inspired the present study took as its starting point a fascination with the way the different meanings of the words management and managing 'bounce off each other':

> When we talk of management or managing in the context of business and other work organisations we think of the work of initiating and organising tasks so that goods and services get produced. But there is an echo of another sense of managing: that of managing as coping, as 'getting by' (Watson 1994c).

Kevin Berry was implying that he engaged in 'managing' at school, as he did when he was simply doing his basic occupational work alongside peers. This fits with Collinson's observation that 'managing' in the workplace is not a prerogative of an 'elite and highly privileged minority' (Collinson 1992). Kevin alludes here to 'organising the blokes' and 'getting things done'. But everyone also organises themselves and others in their non-work lives. We manage events and families. We manage our identities, our relationships and our biographies. But is this to build too much on the fact that we use a similar word for managing in a formal authoritative organisational position and for the process of coping with the shaping by life's exigencies of our personal biographies? It is not. Following the analysis in *In Search of Management* (Watson 1994a), it is argued that formal managerial activities entail skills and practices which are essentially no different from those which human beings use in all sorts of contexts when they are trying to get things done – at home, at school or wherever. Managerial work can usefully be made sense of in this way. In the present study we are interested in the extent to which managers themselves who are relatively new to formal managerial roles make sense of their work and lives in a similar way and we are concerned with how they see their experiences from other areas of their lives translating to their changed situation at work. As 'managers', they are using these skills and performing managerial activities in very particular social relationships where they are separated out and labelled in a way which implies that they possess a special form of expertise.

A key research question, we might say, was that of how people coming to terms with a work role which has central importance for society and economy see the relationship between their formal managerial work and the rest of their lives. How they make sense of such matters is highly relevant to how they perform. As we shall argue later, there is a close relationship between how people act, think and talk. But, at this stage, we switch our focus for a while away from the individual manager making sense of their work and lives to the sorts of expectations of 'the manager' which appear to exist in contemporary culture.

What is expected? The discursive context of managing

It was suggested by one recently appointed manager that to understand the size of what she saw as 'the gap between how things are portrayed and how they really are' we might compare the jobs that people do with the description of those jobs provided when they were advertised:

I got this job from reading an advertisement. It sounded really intimidating. But it sort of invited one to rise to a challenge. It has certainly been that. But what is really striking is how much more bloody and messy the reality is compared to the picture they hook you with. I was recruited, if I remember properly, to 'lead a team of dedicated professionals' and something like 'taking the service forward into the next century'. But in practice – phew.

It is interesting, though, that you remember these words.
Yes, I suppose . . . uhm.

Why do you then? If it is simply a . . .
I think those words stick in my mind because in some sense I think I feel that this is how it should be. I suppose, yes, I think that these are the aims I'm meant to have. Perhaps this is where the challenge lies – turning the bunch of people I manage into a 'dedicated team'. Yeah.

And the next century?
Well, it's just hype in one way. But I do think it's to do with me looking at the section strategically. I ought to be doing more on the strategic side – looking at where we are going. Yes, this is what they recruited me for.

What Jenny Holly is suggesting here is that there is a language which is used in advertisements for managerial jobs and which cannot too easily be dismissed as simple hyperbole, as empty rhetoric. Even though one takes with a 'pinch of salt' the high-flown terminology, there are expectations being set for people taking such jobs. And such expectations 'stick in the mind', Jenny says. The cumulative effect of reading the language used in management advertisements, we would argue, gives a strong impression of there having developed a particular *discourse* about managerial activity. This *frames* – but does not determine – the predispositions which recruits to management are likely to take into that activity. Management advertisements are just one small contributor to the *discursive framing* which plays a part in the emergence of the contemporary manager.

Discursive framing is *a process whereby human beings draw on sets of linguistic resources, categories, and concepts made available in their culture to make sense of a particular aspect of their lives and are thereby influenced in the way they conduct themselves in that part of their life.* When we are unsure of how to conduct ourselves on entering a new area of activity we turn to the cultural cues which are available to us. These are inevitably mediated through language and act as what has been called a 'linguistic repertoire' (Potter and Wetherell 1987) or a set of 'discursive resources' which play a part in the way we mentally and 'dialogically' *argue* with ourselves and relevant cultural others about what *should be* (Bahktin 1981; Billig 1995; Watson 1994a; Watson 1996). Our actions are not *determined* by the cues and categories which are culturally available to us: we are continually 'arguing with ourselves' as we 'weigh up' the different 'messages' culturally available to us. The cues and categories play a key part, however, in how we shape our 'selves' and our actions.

What is available to us, and what is not available, by way of discursive or cultural resources is enormously significant. Imagine, for example, that in every article that we read about management, every job advertisement that we saw, every film, play or novel in which we encountered managers and in every conversation with and about managers, the talk was predominantly of 'caring', 'persuading', 'cooperating', 'facilitating', 'listening' and that the stories told were framed in, and were consistent with, these terms. If this were the case, we would approach any managerial situation we might come across with a *frame of reference* or a *mind-set* which would predispose us to act in certain ways. The cues to action to which we would look would shape certain predispositions. These predispositions would be quite different from the ones we might have, however, if the key discursive resources and the *narratives* we drew on in making sense of managerial activity were along the lines of 'commanding', 'utilising', 'competing', 'winning' and so on.

If we treat all the talk and writing about management which we come across as a broad *text* then we can regard it in a similar way to which media scholars have treated the texts they study. These, says Hay (1996), 'effectively construct an empty story board which recruits readers as *dramatis personae* upon an expansive stage created within the text itself'. This storyboard comprises 'a basic set of characters, plot relationships, minimal relevant aspects of context and a variety of interdiscursive cues, intended associations and connotations'. It invites us as readers or 'active decoders' to identify with a particular 'preferred' subject position. In our case, this might be the brilliant dominating entrepreneurial managerial figure found in certain parts of the text. Alternatively, it might be a gentle, nurturing, supportive figure to be found in another part of the narrative. We can choose to deny the relevance of the text, of course (if we have somewhere else to turn for sense-making resources and cues to action). But insofar as we do not, then, as Hay puts it, 'we actively position ourselves as subjects within the narrative ... as we locate ourselves within a subject position inscribed by the text' (1996: 262). In terms close to those of Foucault (1980), who argues that our personal subjectivities are created through the discourses current in our society, Hay says that 'in this instant we are constituted as subjects *through* the text, as we are simultaneously subjected *to* it.'

Taking our own cue from Jenny Holly, let us examine some excerpts from advertisements found in a management periodical. She implies that the way she is currently making sense of her work situation is in part within some of the terms that she remembers from the advertisement which drew her attention to the post she now occupies. And we must recognise that the way we make sense of things is inextricably related to how we act with regard to those things. We act in the light of the sense we have previously made of things and we make sense anew in light of the actions in which we are involved (Weick 1995: 13). Jenny's current sense-making about her managerial work involves *looking back* to the advertisements she read some time ago. For our own purposes at present we can look at a selection of job advertisements to consider what kind of discursive cues they contain – remembering that these are only the raw material which people *draw on* in their own sense-making.

The following excerpts are from advertisements for posts in a range of different types of organisation (public and private sector) and they are for jobs which are above 'first appointment' level but which will typically be taken by people in their first or second managerial appointment.

Create an immediate impact

The number one company in its market, our client – a household name – is committed to excellence across all aspects of its business operations ... To succeed in this highly commercial organisation you will need to call upon your proven management and motivational skills. In addition, you will have the determination to achieve outstanding results and have high personal expectations. This is an excellent opportunity for an individual seeking the scope and freedom to make their mark and provide imaginative solutions in a demanding environment.

Expert at managing change?

Highly developed interpersonal and negotiation skills are essential together with experience gained in a fast moving manufacturing environment. You will also need to be highly organised and resilient, dependable and an approachable team player with the drive to achieve results. A willingness to travel throughout the UK is also required.

Do you have what it takes to meet this challenge ?

Operating in a dynamic and innovative environment this challenging role will provide solutions to business units through support, consultancy and contribution to strategy.
Personal criteria:
A commitment to excellence
A customer focus
High energy levels
Strong interpersonal skills.

Take up the challenge of change in brewing

We operate in a highly competitive business that meets the continuing challenge of continuous improvement, cost reduction and increased quality.

Outstanding opportunities for career progression

In addition to the specific roles outlined above you will be actively encouraged to input fresh ideas, analyse problem areas, initiate solutions and contribute to overall policy formulation. This is an exciting challenge offering excellent opportunities for broadening your skills and advancing your career.

Can you deliver?

You must be able to demonstrate several years' successful experience within a fast moving, volume product manufacturing organisation. Multi-site exposure and evidence of successfully initiating and facilitating/delivering step-change improvements in key areas will add weight to your application. Key personal pre-requisites include the intellect, energy, tenacity and sheer enthusiasm to identify and see through implementation of policies and practices which will make a recognisable contribution to performance: first class communication and leadership skills are also essential.

We need gifted people

You should not underestimate either the breadth of the role or what it means to the future of a business noted for its vitality and entrepreneurship. This is a rare opportunity to develop your own role and that of a department committed to adding value at every level of the company.

Looking for leading edge experience?

As someone who enjoys a challenge, thrives on variety and is not afraid of responsibility, you will be able to balance the demands of day-to-day operational issues with project work and have the ability and confidence to influence at the highest level.

Blue chip career move

Your ability to develop initiatives that add value and deliver results will be critical to your success. You are already respected for your persuasive and influencing skills as well as your tough minded resilience.

We believe that you will have a major impact on the business and confidently expect you to be managing increasingly complex challenges in your career in what is, of course, a truly world class company.

Tackle the challenges of growth

Tenacious, resourceful and imaginative, your strength of character will have been developed in a hard working role within a distributed service business. A persuasive communicator, sensitive to culture, you are adept at juggling numerous issues whilst maintaining a clear set of priorities. Travel within the UK can be extensive.

A rewarding change

A bright mind, business acumen, and a customer-focused approach are among the key qualities looked for.

What story are we being told here, then, about what one needs to be like to obtain one of these managerial posts? These advertisements are only one tiny part of the overall discursive context of contemporary managerial work, but if one reads texts like these, week in and week out as an aspiring manager might do, one sees a quite clear framing of the world managers are said to operate in. And the advertisements' contents are, we believe, quite consistent with the broader pattern of discursive construction.

The organisations seeking to recruit managers are portrayed in managerial advertisements in terms of a series of superlatives. 'Excellence' is a favourite one and we see it here in the typical form 'committed to excellence across all aspects of its ... operations'. But excellence is never taken-for-granted or finally achieved. Things are changing all the time. We see reference in our small sample to a 'fast moving manufacturing environment', a 'fast moving volume product ... organisation' and a 'dynamic and innovative environment'. The environment is often 'highly competitive' and the way this is linked in one of our examples with the 'continuing challenge of continuous improvement, cost reduction and increased quality' is quite typical of the genre.

What sort of person is wanted in these 'number one' or 'truly world class' or 'vital' and 'entrepreneurial' organisations? Is it someone with an advanced knowledge of management science, with a technical or professional expertise, with postgraduate qualifications in business administration, corporate strategy, marketing, personnel or logistics? Qualifications tend to be mentioned in the more detailed part of those advertisements which are recruiting for particular functional special- isms like personnel management. But far outweighing such matters in the texts and almost completely taking the place of any notion of tech- nical or professional managerial knowledge is the stress on personal qualities. The manager is a type of person. The manager is a rather special human being. The story is almost one of the manager as super- woman or superman. The manager is portrayed as someone with great energy, with intellect, enthusiasm, tenacity, resilience, resourcefulness and imagination. They initiate and lead but are also dependable and operate as team players. They thrive on variety, communicate well, are persuasive and can persuade and influence others. Research on the cri- teria that management recruiters work with has shown that this pattern of stressing broad personal qualities is common and the study by Hirsch and Bevan (1988) also shows that the meanings attached to these terms varied considerably when they were discussed with those actu- ally involved in the recruitment and development of managers' careers. However, we are not in the present research concerned with what the writers of these texts *meant* when they wrote them. We are interested in the role such texts play in discursively setting a framework of expectations for people entering and doing managerial work.

The advertisements do more than simply set up separate images of, on the one hand, the dynamic, vital and innovative organisation and, on the other, the exceptionally 'gifted' individual who might join the enterprise. The two are skilfully linked in a way which recognises both the *emergent* nature of the organisation and the *emergent* nature of the manager. The master trope, or key rhetorical device, used throughout these texts is one which makes great use of the notion of *challenge*. The organisation, in its fast-changing and competitive environment, is facing a challenge. It cannot stay still, it cannot stay as it is. It always has to become something else in order to survive. And it does this through employing managers who are themselves attracted by chal- lenge. The managerial recruit is to be someone who wants to become something else – or rather, something more. The individual is directly asked in one case, 'Do you have what it takes to meet this challenge?' In another case the challenge is said to be an 'exciting' one offering excellent opportunities for 'broadening your skills' and, of course, 'advancing your career'. A promise (if you are up to the challenge) of growth and development of self through career opportunities is implicit throughout these texts. The manager is someone who has 'high personal expectations' and these will be met by what they achieve organisationally. This is where the person and the organisation really come together. The individual is looking for the 'scope and freedom' to 'make their mark' to have an 'influence at the highest level' and to 'have a major impact on the business'. Remembering that our sample of advertisements are not for 'top jobs' it is interesting to note that the managers here are not mere functionaries, administrators or heads of sectional territories within organisations. They are contributors to the general direction – the policy or strategy of the organisation. There is, in fact, direct reference in these texts to making a 'contribution to strategy' or contributing to 'overall policy formulation'.

A fascinating rhetorical device which links to and reinforces the theme of personal and corporate challenge in many of these advertisements is the direct address to the reader: 'You will have', 'you will expect', 'you are adept'. The corporation speaks It is looking you directly in the eye. It is flattering *you*. It is challenging *you*. It is challenging you to construct yourself and your experience to show that you are made of the 'right stuff'. If you are someone who wants a challenge, who wants to become something more in your life and career, you are asked 'Can *you* resist the challenge?' Many readers will, of course. In which case there is no problem; you are not wanted. You would not be helpful to the organisation in meeting the challenges it faces.

It all makes sense: the nature of management

The advertisements we have looked at as a sample of the discursive framing of managerial life are written in a style in which the hyperbole is almost compulsive. Not only is every organisation of 'blue chip' standing, or is in some way a world leader, but every corporate environment is one of turbulence and fast change. And, accordingly, every management recruit is a super human. People enter a contract in which they are given the delight of satisfying their desire for challenge in return for helping the corporation meet its challenges. At times this seems to be almost a Faustian contract – in which one exchanges one's immortal soul for occupational fulfilment.

Is this sort of hyperbole just a matter of the literary preferences of management recruitment copywriters? No, it is unlikely that corporate clients would pay people to indulge themselves quite so pointlessly. Colourful and exaggerated the texts may be, but they relate to aspects of contemporary managerial work which are more than in the minds of the writers of texts. Such a point was made to one of us by Rick Prince, a manager in a large public sector organisation who had listened to a talk in which the dangers inherent in what was called 'all the super hero hype of popular management literature' were pointed to. A theme of the talk was that the expectations created in managers about what they can achieve *as individuals* can be too high and that the 'real manager' on recognising that they, unlike the super heroes of the texts, have feet of clay can be demoralised and turn to all kinds of superficial tricks and pseudo techniques to get an effect. Rick spoke along the following lines (notes were scribbled as he spoke):

I don't want to disagree with you entirely. But all this that you say is superman crap, super-hero hype, or whatever you called it, is not as daft as it seems. In some ways it is sensible. It has got to do with realities. The way our new chief executive plays it, I am actually *up for it*. It is up to me. I have got to deliver. And what have I got to put into this. Blood, sweat and tears, I could say. In fact I will be a ruddy super hero if I succeed with the objectives I have got.

You refer to 'what you have got to put into this'. Is it just blood, sweat and tears?
No, I have just got to be pro-active, think up new ways of doing things and get people to own these new ways. Day and night, its cajoling, persuading, selling, doing deals. I am just using every-thing I have got to crack it.

The language here is slightly different from that of the advertise-ments. But being 'pro-active', 'up for it' and 'cracking it' are part of the same discursive realm as the somewhat more polished prose looked at earlier. And in a similar way, Rick Prince ties this notion of deploying personal qualities or interpersonal skills and energy to corporate per-formance. When asked what 'cracking it' was, he replied,

We now have agency status. This could mean that we go out of business. That has been made clear to us. It is clear to us. The competition which we face is real – that was the whole point of the exercise. We have got to turn around the whole operation. At the end of the day that is what as managers we are all about.

The word 'challenge' does not appear in the notes of this brief encounter. But the message of this man telling us about what he called the 'real world' is very similar to that of the copywriting rhetoricians who make much use of that word. Rick's rhetoric is only slightly differ-ent. The story is still one of managers using basic human skills to achieve something corporate, something strategic for the organisation as a whole. There is challenge at the personal level and challenge at the corporate level.

At this stage it is helpful to put alongside these 'lay' and practical attempts to make sense of managerial work some academic attempts to make sense of it. This is done in the spirit of the principle mentioned earlier – that of our text interweaving social science conceptual work with the ideas and accounts of the people with whom we have had dialogues in our research.

For the largest part of the present century – the historical period in which the occupational activity of management has become a major and significant one – writing about management focused on what as an overall activity it would achieve. In the most famous of the 'classical' formulations management was 'planning, organising, staffing, directing, co-ordinating, reporting and budgeting' (Gulick 1937) or to manage was 'to forecast and plan, to organise, to command, to co-ordinate and control' (Fayol 1916). Doubts were later raised about whether this was a helpful way to talk and write about management when researchers began systematically to observe managers at work and built up an impressive cumulative account of managers at every level *behaving* in ways which did not fit with these verbs. From the early studies of Carlson (1951) and Burns (1955), to later ones by Mintzberg (1973) and Stewart (1976) among others, an image emerged of people who were rarely seen to be coolly and rationally planning work activities on the basis of carefully collected and full information, directly commanding people or coordinating work activities. In fact there was very little impression of managers being even remotely in control of their own activities, let alone the activities of others. They were constantly on the move, bargaining, compromising, working on hunches, gossiping, influencing and persuading. At first it seemed that management was turning out to be something different from what had previously been thought. The planning and controlling dimension of management was being discounted, being replaced by the Machiavellian 'fixer' dimension (Reed 1984). In the influential account of Mintzberg (1975), the 'myths' about management were falling as empirical investigation uncovered the day-to-day realities.

There were two seemingly contrasting images of management as, on the one hand, a matter of systematic, rational, neutral and pre-planned control and coordination and, on the other, a matter of a rather anarchic, opportunist, seat-of-the-pants, political and interactive 'getting things done'. However, there has been a reaction to the earlier tendency to reject the classical formulation in the light of empirical research (Carroll and Gillen 1987). It may not be a good describer of the *practices* of managers but it helps us to see what the studies of those practices were discouraging people from doing – setting the observed practices in the context of the broader *function* of management in organisations

(Hales 1986). What we are seeing, then, is that it is helpful to recognise that managerial work is highly political, rarely involves direct and formalised planning on the basis of full information, and so on. But, at the same time, the effect or outcome of all this messy and ambiguous activity is that work, in the final analysis, is coordinated within some general planning and that a degree of control is achieved.

To help us handle this it is helpful to differentiate between *management* as a function, *managers* as people occupationally involved in fulfilling this function and *managing* as the activities engaged in by people to fulfil the function of directing the organisation.

Management

This is something that has to be achieved. It is an outcome. It is a functional requirement of that modern institution, the work organisation. Work organisations are patterns of ongoing human relationships utilising various technologies in which people cooperate to achieve tasks which would otherwise not be possible at all (because of their complexity – say in designing and building a supersonic airliner) or at anything like a comparable cost (providing university education, say, for a high proportion of a whole generation). These organisations could not perform without some planning, coordination, control and the rest. Indeed there has to be a degree of management in any society. As Alvesson and Willmott (1996) put it, 'In all societies, whether primitive or advanced, capitalist or socialist, productive processes are coordinated or "managed".' The issue, they say, is not whether or not management needs to occur – it is one of 'what *kind* of management there will be'. By this, they particularly point to the ways in which this 'management' is implicated in the pattern of social divisions and political economy which prevail in society. But the issue is even broader than this. Just because we have management does not mean there is only one way in which it is carried out – or that it has to be carried out by any particular people.

Managers

These, for present purposes, are those people formally employed to concentrate on carrying out the functions of 'management'. It is a modern form of occupation which has grown with the growth of the modern bureaucratised work organisation. We need to recognise, here, that there is the logical possibility of either a single person doing all the 'managing' (say, the owner/manager of a small enterprise 'running' it without managerial help) or of all members contributing to it (a worker-managed cooperative).

Managing

This, then, is the set of activities which bring about 'management' – the directing or steering of the organisation as a whole to enable it to continue in its environment. It often looks messy, confused and fragmentary and it involves all sorts of conflicts and rivalries. But the outcome (unless it is done so ineffectually that the organisation collapses) is one where enough shaping of activities has occurred and enough cooperation in task achievement has been achieved to keep the enterprise running. It is this activity of *managing* that has been observed by researchers. And just because managers are not visibly all the time formally planning, directly commanding and explicitly coordinating it does not mean that everything is random or 'unplanned' or that sufficient control and coordination within the division of labour has not occurred.

But what are these activities which managers engage in like? This question takes us back to a point made earlier in this chapter; that the activities of managing are not essentially different from those in which people engage in other parts of their lives. This point is very well made by Grint (1995) who starts with Hales's (1986) list of management tasks: 'to lead, liaise, monitor, allocate resources, maintain production, maintain peace, innovate, plan and control'. He goes on to observe, 'Yet parents lead their families ('this way you lot'), liaise with various people about them ('it couldn't have been our children, officer'), monitor their actions ('I'm still watching you'), allocate resources ('it cannot be pocket-money day already'), maintain 'production' ('what do you mean you don't like fish fingers?'), maintain peace ('stop arguing!'), innovate ('let's change the room round'), plan and control ('go to bed')'. Indeed, as Grint observes, it would be difficult to find many people who did not undertake these activities at some time in their normal day.

What this analysis does, in effect, is to demystify managerial work by pointing out that we all do it. But to point out that every parent, every socially involved person almost, does it is in no way to deny that it is a skilled activity. Some people are much better than others at managing their households, for example. Managing, wherever it occurs, is always challenging, involving as it does influencing the thinking and behaviour of other people. Also, to recognise that managing in a broad sense is a quite mundane activity – rather than a science-based professional specialism – is not to deny that those undertaking management tasks in complex work organisations where there are very difficult environmental pressures are going to have to be highly accomplished and sophisticated performers.

It is argued, then, that *to manage* as part of a work organisation's 'management' is not essentially different from managing in the rest of one's life. A highly skilled manager is a highly skilled social actor – a socially accomplished human being. This, presumably, is what the writers of the managerial advertisements were recognising. And in tying the challenges offered to individuals to the challenges facing the work organisations who were to employ them, they were recognising that successful organisational performance, in the sense of ensuring that the organisation survives into the long term, is dependent on people exercising at a high level the basic human skills and qualities that they were calling for. This is perhaps what Rick Prince was getting at when he said the superwoman and superman 'hype' about management had 'to do with realities'.

Meeting the challenge: the job and the person

One of the major purposes of the *In Search of Management* project (Watson 1994a) was to get closely involved, through participant observation research, with managers in a contemporary work organisation to learn more about the day-to-day activities of managing and, especially, to find out how managers cope with (*manage!*) the challenges that their work roles entail. An outcome of this was the argument that the expectations which the discursive framing of managerial work (as it is being called here) creates for managers are problematic. Managers may pick up cues from popular images of hero managers, from senior people in their own organisation or from a business training which portrays managers as the rational planners and unemotional builders of organisational systems. This puts them in constant in danger, it was observed, of 'setting themselves above and apart from the core work of the organisation' so that they end up 'knowing less and less about what is going on'. Yet, 'to justify their being above and apart, they have to put forward an impression of knowing it all'. And this impossible situation not only leads them to outbursts of bad temper and screaming frustration, but leads to a descent into attempts to manage through systems, structures, rules, 'new initiatives', fads and techniques (Watson 1994a: 179–80). Much of the management by 'remote control' which can be seen in work organisations is thus to be understood as a reflection of managers' handling of the anxieties associated with their occupational role.

The basic angst which is part of the normal human condition is exacerbated by the expectations which many managers feel others have of them. They already have the pressures of having to manage or control their own lives and to have added to this a requirement to control the activities and commitments of others at work to achieve particular results can create massive stress. The pressure of this 'double control problem' (Watson 1994b) can be seen as encouraging a fondness for managerial panaceas, quick fixes and a fondness for trying to convince themselves and the world that they are 'special people' through the use of a special language of bottom lines, learning curves, missions, process re-engineering and all the rest of the gruesome jargon of modern 'corporate-speak'. It can also be seen in organisational rituals and procedures which define and reward performance in a way that may reinforce (or possibly relieve) these pressures.

In the present study we wish to understand more about this potentially problematic relationship between the manager, as a private human being with all the normal anxieties, emotions and feelings of the human species, and the role they have to fill in the employing organisation. Where *In Search of Management* took the organisation as a starting point and then looked at how individual managers coped with the particular exigencies of that enterprise, we are here taking the individual as the starting point and looking at how they make sense of the processes whereby they come into, adjust to and, indeed, *manage* their organisational roles as managers. These roles inevitably involve them in all the tensions and contradictions of obtaining cooperation and commitment from others in a setting characterised by divisions and conflicts between employer and employed, managers and managed, senior and junior, highly paid and lowly paid. This is the world which makes the manager. But it is also a world that managers make.

Making and being made by the world: the emergent manager

When we talk about the emergent manager we are, at one level, simply recognising that there is no obvious point at which one suddenly 'becomes' a manager and that even when the individual accepts the status or role of manager they will inevitably continue to learn about managing and will go on through their career to modify or develop their understandings and practices. But there is another level to our thinking. This is to do with the whole way we think about human beings and the social world in which they operate. Put very simply, our position is that we can make better progress in our attempts to understand the human world if we turn away from more orthodox styles of thinking towards a more processual, relational, discursive or constructionist style of thinking about human beings and their social worlds.

The orthodox style of thinking has dominated psychological analysis at the level of the individual and characterised the way human activity at the level of organisations is typically analysed. It looks at the person or at the organisation as a 'thing' or an entity which has various properties – characteristics, goals, motives and so on. This emphasis on 'thingness' or *entitativeness* (Dachler and Hosking 1995) when applied to individuals sees them as relatively fixed beings, each with a certain personality, each holding certain attitudes and each propelled into action by various motives. When applied to the work organisation, this perspective presents a picture of a relatively coherent system which possesses a certain culture and which is propelled towards a certain level of performance by a set of organisational goals or strategies. Goals, motives, strategies, cultures, personalities and so on are *properties* of these entities, whether they be persons or organisations.

Significant trends have occurred in psychology which provide an alternative to this view of the person (Edwards and Potter 1992; Gergen 1993; Harré and Gillet 1994; Shotter 1993, for example). Related to this has been a trend of applying this new thinking to people in organisational contexts (Gergen 1992; Hosking and Morley 1991; Hosking et al. 1995; Weick 1995). And theorising about organisations at a sociological rather than a psychological level has seen a parallel movement (Chia 1996; Cooper and Burrell 1988; Czarniawska -Joerges 1993; Hassard and Parker 1993). Instead of seeing individuals or social groupings as entities, organisations or societies, groups and human identities are seen within the new perspective as the *ongoing achievements* of human interaction. Nothing is fixed, everything is moving. Persons and their worlds are continuously *in process*. Through interacting – and through institutionalising much of that interaction in cultures and discourses – humans are constantly creating (or 'socially constructing') a knowledge or 'sense' of who they are, of what they are doing and of where they are going.

The point of these methodological departures is that they can be helpful to our understanding of the social world in a way that can helpfully inform our practices in that world. They require us to put to one side from time to time the quite reasonable 'everyday' assumptions – Schutz's (1972), 'natural attitude' – in which we understand ourselves as psychological entities possessing a given personality, a given set of attitudes and a given set of motivations who 'enter' organisations to contribute, sometimes as part of a 'management', to the fulfilment of the goals or strategies of that organisation. To get a different type of purchase on our personal and social 'realities', it is helpful to play up the other side of our existence. It is helpful to focus on the extent to which, as individuals, we are forever in the process of 'becoming'. It is insightful to recognise that we are continuously negotiating both cooperatively and in conflict with others to bring about 'organisation'.

The position we are taking is one which moves away from an emphasis on 'being' to one of 'becoming'. None of us has a fixed inner 'self' existing separately from the way we relate to and talk with other people. We are always' becoming'. And the same applies to the organisational dimension. There 'is' no organisation. There is 'organising' – brought about through relating and talking. There is no 'management'. There is 'managing' – brought about, just the same, through talking and relating.

To argue for thinking about the world in this way is to adopt a certain philosophical position with regard to the nature of existence – to take a position on *ontology*. The position being adopted is one which, in Chia's words, 'privileges an ontology of movement, emergence and becoming in which the transient and ephemeral nature of what is "real" is accentuated' (1996: 581). And what are real for us if we think in this way, continues Chia, 'are not so much social states, or entities, but emergent relational interactions and patterns that are recursively intimated in the fluxing and transforming of our life-worlds' (1996: 581–2). Putting this more simply and relating it to the present study, we are interested here in the way that people engaged in *managing* as a kind of work are making their worlds at the same time as their worlds are making them. We see these people as involved in 'emergence' both in shaping their personal sense of 'self' and in shaping their work through 'organising'. In a sense, what it is to be a manager at any particular time in history is 'made up' – it is a sort of fiction. The term, 'making up' in this way, as du Gay points out, 'serves to highlight the way in which conceptions of the person and conceptions of activities are inextricably linked' (1996: 20).

This relational or processual way of thinking about people and their worlds relates to a growing intellectual movement away from the modernist 'dualistic' tendency, typically traced back to Descartes, which unrealistically separates mind from body and individual from society. It is also part of an important shift away from a related 'representationalist' view of language. This is a view of speech or writing as simply a device which the independently existing human being uses to describe, to report or to *represent* the 'reality' which exists outside and separately from him or her. Philosophical assaults on this position (Austin 1962; Derrida 1978; Foucault 1980; Rorty 1989 in their different ways; Wittgenstein 1953) have increasingly come together with contributions in the social sciences to weaken this dominant view (Berger and Luckmann 1971; Giddens 1984; Mead 1962; Potter and Wetherell 1987; Schutz 1972; Weber 1968). There is a shift away from a representationalist (Rorty 1982) philosophy of 'knowing' or *epistemology*, which parallels the shift away from a static *ontology* or philosophy of 'being' discussed above. The movement is towards a view of human beings as creatures who actively use language to make their world.

The idea of language as a tool for world-making was explained earlier in our explanation of our notion of discursive framing (p. 6). And in referring back to that discussion we would reiterate that we are not saying that our actions and our notions of 'what we are' are *determined* by the discourses which we use and which are used with reference to us. Neither are we saying that we can make the world into whatever we want it to be simply by the way we speak and write about it. Human beings, over history and in the processes of cultural activity, are continually creating meanings which are linguistically transmitted. Discourses come to have something of an existence outside of us, yet we are at the same time producers of those discourses (some people more than others, of course). All of us are both givers and receivers in this process – we both 'do' and are 'done to'.

One way of simplifying these matters is to think of humans as storytelling creatures. This was implicit in our earlier notion of management talk and writing as offering managers 'story boards' which they, each in their own way, use to make sense of what they are doing (pp. 6–7). And the present study is based on a process where, through the device of the interview, we have worked with people employed in managerial work to create a narrative about the life and work of each individual. Unlike the traditional social scientist, we do not regard the words spoken in response to our questions as simple 'reports' either of their personal histories or of their 'attitudes', 'motives' and the rest. We believe that the *accounts* which they offer in discussion with us and the *narratives* which unfold as we talk together, are socially achieved constructions which are created in that context of the interview. These narratives are not outcomes of the interview situation alone, however. They are produced as both interviewer and interviewee work together to make sense of the occupational activity and life-task of *managing*. And it is central to the rationale of this book that to read and reflect on these sense-making processes is valuable and insightful to any reader who wants to further their own sense-making about managing.

There is a world which exists outside of our selves but it only becomes a 'reality' to which we can relate when we bring language to bear upon it. Rain does fall from the skies. Food grows or fails to grow in our fields. And there are buildings of wood, brick and metal in which people live and work. But all of these things are only realities, in the sense that we can connect them with our lives, when they have been 'socially constructed' by human interpretation through language. There have to be words and concepts which define what is rain and what is mist, what is weed and what is corn, what is a home and what is a workplace. This book is about the realities of people's lives as managers at work and as managers of personal and domestic existence. The only way we can 'touch' these realities is through talk. And there is no way we can avoid the implication of that very talk in the making of these realities. As researchers and writers we cannot be neutral observers or reporters unemotionally recording 'what is'. What we hope is that through our dialogues with managers and the negotiating of shared understandings with them we have produced stories about managing which the reader can put fruitfully alongside their own stories. We believe that it is through listening to and creating narratives – and especially through comparing the stories that we tell and hear – that we enhance our understanding of the world we live in.

Doing the study, making the story

Given everything we have said about 'emergence' and our concern with the way managers continuously engage in a process whereby the ways they understand and act in their role are changing, we have to recognise that as researchers and writers we are no different ourselves. And the same must surely apply to our readers. Each of you will make sense of what you read in the light of your own lives, your experience of management and managing and the pleasures and pains, beliefs and doubts you have experienced within that encounter. The same applies to us as researchers and research-based story-tellers. At the same time as engaging with the people we have met and talked to, we have been engaging with our own need for understanding about managerial work. We are, all of us, working with ideas about managerial work that have been influenced by our experiences of managing and being managed, and by the ideas we have read and otherwise learned about.

None of us comes to this research, then, as if we were approaching a blank page. But neither are we, as research writers, simply collecting 'facts' about people and dispassionately organising them into an objective analysis. We are working with accounts constructed in a particular situation, accounts that might well have been presented differently in another time and place. But we would not describe this book as a simple 'report' of a research project which straightforwardly represents these accounts. The book is a rhetorical construction, a crafted artefact (Atkinson 1990; Watson 1995b). Its writing inevitably involved enormous selectivity and shaping in the way it uses the words which people spoke into our tape recorders. We have drawn together our own theoretical reading from the social sciences, our personal experiences of the managerial and organisational world and our discussions with interviewees to *make* a book. No author, in any scientific writing, can do anything else.

In spite of our recognition of the artfulness of social science writing, we have striven to be as objective and truthful as we could be – following the conception of 'truthfulness' identified by philosophers in the pragmatist tradition (Urmson 1989; Watson 1997). This means that we have striven to ensure that the story we tell about managers' lives and work will be one which any individual involved in such matters will find as helpful as any other which we or anyone else could write in *informing their life practices*, as women and men, as managers and employees, as parents and spouses – and so on. Our study can no more than any other give direct guidance to people on how to manage a managerial career. But by exploring, along with ourselves and the people who contributed to the research, the experiences, tensions, frustrations and fulfilments of people entering managerial work, we believe that any reader will be better placed to come to terms with such matters than if they do not embark on such an exploration.

Although we came to this research with these kinds of issues in our minds, we were concerned that they should not constrain the kinds of accounts that people were able to give of their work and their lives. We tried to give them an opportunity to talk which would give space for their own issues to emerge, while, at the same time, prompting them to think about things that might not have been uppermost in their minds. This led us to a two-stage interview. The initial interview usually lasted about two hours. We presented it as an opportunity to talk, in a fairly open but not totally unstructured way, about the move into managerial work. Two broad areas were to be covered; how the person came to be a manager, and their movement into their current managerial post.

The second round of interviews took place roughly a year after the first meeting. They provided a chance to go over some of the areas we had felt emerged as important from the initial accounts. They also allowed us to hear about some of the ways that things had changed for individuals over that time. Some people had changed jobs yet again whilst others had come to feel differently about the posts they were in. It gave us an opportunity to tell people a little about the broad areas of concern that had come out of the first round of interviews. For example, we were struck in the first accounts by the complexity of the changes involved in 'becoming a manager'. It reinforced the idea that there are many ways in which people are 'managing' and that this is a move that reveals people 'managing' many different aspects of their experience. We used our awareness of these to organise and structure the second round of discussions – and indeed, this remains broadly the structure of this book. The main areas covered were: managing a change of job or task; managing changing relationships; managing in a wider context of continual change; managing oneself and identity; managing a career; managing work alongside the rest of life.

The cast

Who, then, are the people who participated in the research and helped us consider these issues? Most of the forty managers who appear in the book were formally interviewed in the way described above and their words tape-recorded and transcribed. Several were interviewed less closely but were included because they had something particularly relevant to say about their managerial lives. The story we have to tell is based on accounts given to us by these forty people, who saw themselves as having made a relatively recent move into managerial work.

Given the kinds of difficulties mentioned earlier in defining managerial work, and in locating a precise line that has to be crossed for someone to become a 'manager', we had to find a rationale for including people in our study. We were looking for people at a stage of change or movement in their working lives that they would themselves see as a significant step into a managerial career. We therefore sought people for whom a move would in some way be a 'critical' one in their career, one involving their going through an immediate and real process of coming to terms with and understanding a new role, new tasks, changes in relationships and a heightened awareness of themselves as 'managers'.

This helped to some extent but did not fully answer the question of when it is that one 'becomes a manager'. We chose to deal with this by explaining the broad aims of our project to people whom we saw as potential candidates for study or whom we felt would be likely to know such people, and we allowed likely candidates to decide for themselves whether they were appropriate. By some criteria, this might be seen as having produced a rather diverse group of people. For our purposes, however, this did not matter – they had identified themselves as people going through the process of making sense of and coming to terms with a transition into managerial work. Although they shared the uncertainty of where the boundaries might lie, the project clearly had resonance for them. They saw it as addressing issues that had meaning for them, and which they were eager, or at least willing, to talk about and explore with us.

The selection of individuals which emerged includes people taking their first steps on the managerial ladder, into jobs that some may define as supervisory rather than managerial. Most, however, were people who had reached a significant grade within their organisation or had been given the title 'manager' for the first time. This title and the formal status and power it carries in the organisation, may well mark a significant change in how people are seen, how others relate to them and what is expected of them. Some, like Colin Hawkins, Lucy Armstrong and Arthur Blakey, saw themselves taking significant steps in how they saw themselves, for example, coming to accept and see themselves primarily as 'managers', rather than engineers, teachers, or social workers. Nevertheless, as we recognised earlier, these people may have been 'managing' and doing elements of 'managerial work' for some time. And, for some, the latest move was clearly not their first managerial job. However, in some way they saw it marking an entry into a different kind of managerial work. Jean Holliday, for example, identified herself as having made a move from 'operational' into 'strategic' management. And Andrew Shepherd saw his position as branch manager in a bank as involving a significant shift in responsibility, autonomy and opportunity which he describes as if he were embarking on 'running his own business'. So, we accepted all these moves as significant steps into managerial work for those making them, and thus as important for our study.

The people who took part were usually approached directly as individuals and were found mainly though contacts and 'networking'. In the few cases in which people in senior positions approached individuals first, it complicated the situation in that we had to avoid the danger of their wanting to impress us, 'just in case anything should get back to the boss', as one person put it. Nevertheless, everyone seemed to share our feeling that there was a story worth telling about people like themselves. The only ones who declined an invitation to take part were the few people who decided they were not relevant because they felt they had not made a relatively recent job move.

It is frequently noted that studies of work organisations and of managers tend to over-concentrate on the industrial organisation and operate with the stock figure of a male manufacturing manager. We were very anxious to avoid this and sought a mixture of people from across a range of different kinds of employing organisation and from both genders. The way in which our selection was built up and its size, however, meant that we could not have total control to the extent which would ensure a comprehensive coverage of types of work or a full balance in terms of social category of subjects. Table 1.1 indicates the range and spread of our managers, however, and shows how far our sampling approach broadens the stock notion of 'a manager'.

In the same way that there is more than one type of manager, there is more than one main route into managerial work. As we built up our group of research subjects and began the process of interviewing, we began to see a pattern of three main routes into a managerial position. In practice, individuals may combine elements from more than one category and the boundaries between them are not sharp. However, as long as we are aware of the danger of over-simplification involved in using such a crude typology, this basic scheme can provide a useful starting point for any attempt to make sense of the complexities that apply to the specific experiences of any one individual. We can distinguish between the *career managers*, who early on identify a managerial

Table 1.1 Managers interviewed

PUBLIC SECTOR	PRIVATE SECTOR
Health	**Manufacturing, extraction, utilities**
Mary Rainey	Sally Vaughan
Nurse manager	*Marketing manager, pharmaceuticals*
Diane Washington	Shirley Stitt
Manager of a clinical specialism	*Health, safety and environment manager, chemicals*
Jean Holliday	Liz Carter
NHS business manager	*Personnel manager, food*
Betty Smith	Eddie Hayes
Practice manager, general practice	*Divisional training manager, construction*
	Harry Lyttleton
Education	*Production engineer, chemicals*
Marion Brown	Mark Taylor
Primary school head	*Project manager, engineering*
Will Evans	Arthur Blakey
Head of department, secondary school	*Operational team manager, engineering*
Lucy Armstrong	Mina Mangeshkar
Student services manager, further education	*Engineering manager, utility*
Carrie Bley	Kevin Berry
Finance director, further education	*Mining manager*
Jack Dodds	Dick Thompson
Acting university head of department	*Purchasing manager, packaging*
Welfare, social service, public administration	**Service, leisure, retail**
Colin Hawkins	Dan Tracey
Manager, residential social work	*Manager, logistics company*
Charles Parker	Julian Adderley
Housing manager with housing association, then student accommodation manager	*Manager, computer software*
Alicia Coltrane	Ted Ellington
Housing manager, housing association	*Quality manager, electrical retail*
Ron Scott	Lawrence Young
Prison wing manager	*Head office loans manager, banking*
Tom Smith	Andrew Shepherd
Deputy Clerk to the Justices	*Branch manager, banking*
Carol Laine	Ellen Fitzgerald
Executive officer, Civil Service agency	*Branch manager, building society*
Jenny Holly	Mike Davis
Social work area manager	*Bingo club manager*
Rick Prince	Stan Jordan
Local government manager	*Bingo club manager*
Alan Wilde	Kathy Westbrook
Development executive, local government	*Assistant manager, restaurant chain*
Jim Costello	Ken Pine
Executive officer, Civil Service	*Assistant manager, restaurant chain*
	Liza Potts
	Retail manager, supermarket chain

role as the key occupational activity in which they want to engage; the *movers-up*, for whom a managerial appointment is a rung on a career ladder within an organisation, and the *movers-in*, who make a career shift to become a manager. These career patterns will be a concern of the next chapter.

CHAPTER 2

APPROACHING AND ENTERING MANAGERIAL WORK

Children don't dream of being managers

Can you imagine your kid saying 'I want to be a manager when I grow up?' No! (Ellen Fitzgerald)

So, if you think back to being a child, and being asked what you want to do when you grow up – what did you say then?
Well, I certainly didn't say a personnel manager! (Liz Carter)

Would the idea of a manager have meant anything to you as a child?
No, I don't think it was even a word then, was it? It wasn't a concept in our house. You did jobs and that was it. (Lucy Armstrong)

I don't think kids say 'I want to be a manager'. I think they say, I want to work in this particular sector – I want to be a train driver, I want to be an aircraft pilot, I want to be a builder. People don't say 'I want to be a distribution manager', or 'I want to be a marketing manager, or a sales manager'. They just don't say that, I don't think. Do they? (Dan Tracey)

Looking at the people in this study, we can confidently answer Dan Tracey, saying 'No they don't'. They dream of being football players, dancers, actors, nurses, pilots, air stewardesses, teachers, vets, people who work with children or join the navy, bus conductors, mechanics who fix things, people who build things – but not managers. It may be that times are changing. As more is said about 'management' as a cause of and solution to problems in both the public and private sector, and as education is asked to become more 'vocationally relevant', maybe today's children are more aware of becoming a manager, as a career option. However, this was not so for those in our selection of managers, growing up and going through school in the 1950s, 60s, 70s or even the 80s.

The central issue for this chapter is about how people see themselves moving from children with little sense of 'managing' as an occupation, to people who are now 'managers'. As Kevin Berry shows in Chapter 1, the line between being a manager and not being a manager is by no means clear. The people in our study can see that they have crossed a social line, that they are now recognised by others as 'managers'. Things are different. However, they are still the same people they were before they were managers, there is no sudden transformation. They carry over experiences, ways of seeing the world, a sense of self that may fit more or less comfortably with the idea of 'being a manager'. Also, their upbringing and backgrounds differ. Their early lives have shaped them and led them in different directions. They therefore have different amounts and kinds of 'identity work' to do in coming to see themselves as 'managers'. So, they are in a process of 'becoming' managers. They are, as Chapter 1 put it, 'people continuously making sense of what they are doing and where they are going in the light of how they make sense of where they have been'.

In this chapter we look at how these people talk about 'where they have been'. However, we do this recognising that it is a story that can be told in more than one way. It can be constructed with a particular person or audience in mind and to convey (consciously or unconsciously) certain messages about the teller (Moir 1993; Potter and Wetherell 1987; Wooffitt 1992). Also, the telling itself is creative. In telling, people are actively 'making sense' of their pasts at a certain moment in the flow of their lives, with its particular questions and concerns in mind (Weick 1995). This process can generate new insights, new ways of seeing oneself and one's history, to which a person becomes attached and which may be used and developed in future tellings. For example, the coherence and persuasiveness constructed for the job application or CV (Metcalfe 1992), seeing things in new ways as one talks about one's family. The research interview itself is probably an unfamiliar event for most managers, where the constraints on what can be said are less clear than in the work environment. This is not to claim that they may feel able to be any more 'open' or 'honest', only that it may open up different possibilities for presenting themselves.

We bring together here two different aspects of the stories of how these people came to be managers – two rather different ways of reflecting on or charting their personal history. Our starting point is the way they present their entry into managerial work and the different routes by which they came to be in their present job. Alongside this, we listen to how they use the discourse of 'careers' in talking about their lives. The adverts for managerial posts in Chapter 1 invite people to frame their work history in terms of a 'career' – seeing and judging themselves and their past work through a particular frame of reference. However, most of these people did not set out with the intention of becoming managers, or with much idea of what managers do. Many present chance, luck and accident as important influences on the choices they have made and on the direction their work history has taken. These are stories of 'emergence' against which the notion of a 'career' may sit uneasily. The chapter, then, takes a retrospective look at these managers' lives. It sets the background for later chapters where we shall see how 'where they have been' colours what they bring to their work as managers.

How do people come to be managers? Routes into managerial work

At university you start looking through all kinds of jobs that are available for graduates ... The kind of areas I was looking for then were management or personnel and training. I knew personnel was very, very competitive ... they can choose really to pick people that have got more degree linked subjects ... So I sort of went for management because, you know, general degrees could go into that kind of area. (Kathy Westbrook, assistant manager, pizza restaurant)

It sort of evolved, really ... there wasn't a vision or a dream at all, it was just experiencing life, taking one step to the next. (Stan Jordan, bingo club manager)

I think if I look back over the last, probably ten years, I have a much closer sense of plotting the next step ... I think I spent the ten years before that not having any next step, just doing what I was doing. I was busy being a woman [*laughs*], busy being in love and all that business, and just really enjoying life and travelling and having the long holidays and being relatively well-off, I suppose. (Lucy Armstrong, student support manager, further education)

This was the next logical step up. I had two choices really – I either moved into a more senior housing management post, with some responsibility for some staffing – or I changed direction slightly, which is what I did, and moved into housing with care and support.

So it's a kind of specialism?
Yes, yes it is. There are less places to go from this post because there's less of this type of accommodation. But at the time, I would have gone either way to be honest. It was just whatever job came up at the time. (Alicia Coltrane, housing manager)

I have made a conscious decision ... I realised that to move up the engineering tree, you had to be exceptional and have a lot of experience with it. So, I would have had to be a good engineer, plus have about fifteen years behind me, before I made any in-roads ... it was at that point I decided, right, I'll move sideways and move around that way, so as to circumvent it. I would move into operations management, moving out of engineering. Really, the way of the management, or up the engineering tree is the way I've seen. And it's obviously worked for me. (Arthur Blakey, operations team manager, engineering)

The adverts in Chapter 1 appeal to managers as people who know what they want, where they are going – and who can show that 'where they've been' leads there. As these managers talk, we begin to see that they have reached their present jobs in quite different ways – that there are many paths that lead to 'becoming a manager'. Hill (1992) looks at one important route – the move from being a 'star performer' (the best insurance sales person) to a 'novice manager' (managing others doing the job they have just done so well). So, in her study, the organisation had set out a clear path these new managers had followed and a goal they could aim for. In our study, we have looked at people in many different kinds of work and different organisational settings. Not surprisingly, there is no single route that has brought them to where they are now. This diversity is echoed in a study by Storey et al., which found that people came into management at different ages and applied for jobs 'as and when they arose' (1997: 92). There are many routes into managerial work.

These routes bring people into 'management' at different stages in their lives. Kathy Westbrook has decided she wants to be a manager early in her career, as an initial career choice. Arthur Blakey sees management as a 'second career' or an alternative route to engineering. Stan Jordan seems to have just arrived there with little plan or intent. Some, like Lucy Armstrong, have moved into management much later in their working lives than Kathy. These people come with different kinds of skills, experiences and backgrounds that inevitably affect how they view the manager's role, and how others see them in it. So, Arthur Blakey is an engineer-turned-manager; Mary Rainey, now in a management post, still sees herself first and foremost as a nurse. Kathy Westbrook and Lucy Armstrong enter managerial jobs with very different life and work experience. Kathy is looking for work experiences that will enable her to learn and develop as a manager. Lucy brings a wealth of skills and experience and 'an ideological commitment to education'. She puts more emphasis on finding a job where she can use these to greater effect. Alicia Coltrane and Arthur Blakey identify alternative paths through their organisations – opportunities arise and they make choices. So, as we ask the question 'How did these people come to be managers?', complex clusters of work orientations, occupational identities, choices and judgements within a framework of organisational opportunities begin to emerge.

With all these issues in mind, we move on to look at how people present their paths into managerial work. We present three broad groups that seem, to us, to emerge from how people talk about their work histories. They are one way of making sense of the question 'How do people come to be managers?' However, these groups are by no means exclusive. Individuals may combine elements from more than one category and the boundaries between them are not sharp. This kind of messiness does not surprise us. Given our starting point that becoming a manager is a process of 'emergence', we are interested in the ways that individual, organisational and contextual influences come together to produce managers.

The people we met at the start of this section represent three different routes into managerial work. There are a small number, like Kathy Westbrook, who set out to become managers. We have called these the 'career managers'. Lucy Armstrong and Stan Jordan have arrived in managerial posts by 'moving up' within the organisations or fields they work in. Most of the people we talked to became managers by this route. Others, like Arthur Blakey, started out doing something rather different – they have become managers by *'moving in'*; they present themselves as consciously changing direction in some way. These are by no means clear-cut groups. The 'career managers' and 'movers in' may then begin a process of 'moving up'. The 'movers up' may reach a point where they have to make a choice about whether they want to 'move in' and accept that they are now managers rather than nurses, engineers or 'one of the girls'.

Career managers

As we saw, children do not dream of becoming managers. However, for some of the people we talked to, this emerged as a possibility through careers advice at university, or through weighing up the options open to them on graduation. These are people like Kathy Westbrook who have identified relatively early in their working lives with the idea of becoming a manager, people for whom it is an initial, or early, career choice. Not surprisingly, they are the younger ones in our sample. Most have entered organisations on graduate trainee schemes, often after elaborate selection procedures intended to assess their suitability and potential. An implicit (or explicit) contract or understanding is set up, reminiscent of the deals suggested by the adverts we looked at in Chapter 1. The graduate trainee will bring qualities such as energy and enthusiasm; willingness and an ability to learn quickly; a readiness to understand and engage with the organisational culture and goals; freshness and enthusiasm; hard work and a concern to produce results. In return, the organisation might be expected to provide training; opportunities to learn, to develop skills and abilities; appropriate challenges and experiences; good pay and conditions; status; recognition, progress and promotion; a bright future. This holds out an ideal where the needs of the organisation and employee are met in mutually beneficial and harmonious ways.

So, a clear path into management can be traced. However, within the group of young people we have called 'career managers', we can see important differences. Some have very clear ambitions. Others seem to set out with less definite ideas of where they are heading, or of how they will get there. They thus differ in how they present themselves 'managing' their own careers. Also, they join very different organisations and present very different experiences and expectations of how the organisation is managing their career. So, although the 'career managers' have all embraced the goal of 'becoming a manager' they do this with more or less clear aspirations and in very different organisational settings.

Moving up

People falling into this category are much more diverse than the 'career managers'. They have entered organisations at different levels, and with very different educational backgrounds. They are from a much wider age range. All have work histories which have involved 'moving around' within organisations. However, they have also 'moved up' hierarchically, they have become managers.

This pattern is part of commonsense thinking about 'careers' – starting out in a job with possibilities for growth and development, moving through the levels and ending up in more senior, managerial jobs. However, the widely used metaphor of 'moving up a ladder' has been questioned and criticised. The 'ladder' doesn't reflect the way routes change, get blocked or become hard to 'read' depending on changing circumstances, policies and strategies in organisations. Indeed, there may be more than one route; Gunz (1989) sees the 'ladder' more like a complex climbing frame that can be tackled in many different ways. Particularly with 'delayering' and flatter structures, many organisations offer employees increasingly limited opportunities for upward movement. Taylor and Lippitt (1983) see this reflected in the way international experience, secondments, project work and other ways of broadening experience come to take the place of upward moves, forming essential elements in management development programmes. Breadth of experience becomes a necessity for anyone aspiring to general management in a large organisation.

Metaphors of 'climbing' reflect assumptions that growth and progress involve vertical, or hierarchical, mobility that may also be challenged at the level of individuals' orientations and preferences (Bailyn 1989; Barley 1989). Bailyn (1989) and Schein (Schein 1978) emphasise the different patterns of people's lives, the variations in interest and energy they have for 'climbing', the ways their orientations to work change at different stages of their lives. 'Progress' sometimes leads people in directions they feel unsure they want to take. 'Moving up' also involves processes of personal change. People have to see themselves (and be seen by others) as able to do the job. Some have to come to see themselves and their working lives in a different way, to be able to step forwards.

Just over half our sample talk of their work history in terms of *'moving up'*, so this is clearly a significant route into management. However, for the kinds of reasons already touched on, they are by no means a homogeneous group. They seem to fall into two broad categories. There are those who left school and 'started at the bottom and worked their way up'. Amongst them are people entering organisations with very different 'opportunity structures' and with routes through them that are more or less clearly marked. They also entered with very different expectations of themselves and very different orientations to work.

The other broad category are those who have entered professional fields such as nursing, education, housing and engineering, as graduates or after professional training. Some reach a point where career paths force them to think of taking on greater managerial responsibility, thus raising questions of whether they come to see themselves as a 'manager', rather than a nurse, a teacher or an engineer. This raises important questions about the kind of work they want to be doing, the kinds of skills they want to use and develop and about their public and personal identity and credibility.

Moving in

These are people who do not present their route into managerial work as a logical outcome of 'moving up' in an organisation. Rather, they tend to recognise a more radical shift in their career than was the case in the previous category. It may be a shift linked to dissatisfaction and change in themselves, and what they want from work. It may be change in their organisations, where they have seen new kinds of roles emerge, and new career paths open up – or possibilities closing down. These changes have led them to see their careers taking off in new directions. Their initial job choice has not led to the place they are in now.

Many of the people who fall into this category are working in the public sector where 'management' has been expanding and new managerial jobs have been created. Some of the people we have interviewed see themselves having changed direction to take advantage of new opportunities, for example, to become a practice manager or a business manager in the NHS. Because these are new roles, and part of a new structure and ethos in the health service, they have been significant changes of direction for some of the people taking them on. These managers have the challenge of making new systems and new philosophies produce the outcomes they want to see achieved in the health service. They also live with constant expectation of further change and uncertainty about the form it might take. Other public sector employees, working in this changing environment, have also seen their jobs change and grow, in unforeseen ways.

A second group contains some of the people who have arguably had to do a great deal of 'identity work' to see themselves moving into management. Ron Scott and Harry Lyttleton, for example, started out as apprentices in skilled trades. They see critical moments, where they made conscious decisions to change direction, where they realised they didn't want to stay where they were for the rest of their working lives.

These were clearly major turning points, leaving the security and familiar culture of a trade to look for different kinds of rewards and opportunities. Ron joined the prison service and has since 'moved up' within it. Harry stayed with the same large company. He went to college and invested a lot of time and energy in studying. However, for Harry, the way he might go was by no means clear. He had a desire to move, to get on – but he could not have planned where it might take him, as that has emerged in a context of broader organisational change and development.

Becoming a manager: many paths, many experiences

We have found these three broad routes useful as they begin to identify some issues that are important for what follows in the rest of the book. We have seen that people enter managerial posts at different stages in their working lives and so bring with them different work histories and different kinds of work and life experience. The centrality of work in the overall balance of their lives varies. They bring different experiences of 'being managed' and watching others manage, which colour their ideas of the kind of manager they want to be. They work in different organisational settings. Sometimes the paths they are taking are fairly well-trodden. Some are entering new roles which are less clearly defined. Many people are shaping their careers in situations of rapid change. They have seen their careers move forward as a result of new developments and initiatives. They may have seen others made redundant or taking early retirement as part of the same developments. As they become managers, they may also, themselves, become responsible for bringing about further change in their organisations.

Having looked at different routes into managerial work, we now go on to look at how the people who have taken them talk about 'careers'.

Emergent careers: making sense of work histories

A career? What you're doing is worthwhile and interesting and stretching you . . . it's much more than just having a job. (Alicia Coltrane, housing manager)

It would only be a career to me . . . if it was some sort of professional role and if it was constantly progressing . . . you're very committed . . . you enjoy what you are doing. It's like your life, rather than you go to work 9–5 to get a pay packet at the end of the week. And it probably means that you've got a lot of potential and that things are going to progress. (Sally Vaughan, marketing manager)

[At first] a career was . . . a worthwhile, reasonably well paid job, which I would stay in . . . since then, I've watched other people in teaching, who've had much more of a plan in their mind of the path that career would follow. (Marion Brown, head teacher)

A combination of . . . something you wanted to do, something that paid and something that gave a certain stability. (Jack Dodds, head of university department)

My job in the motor trade wasn't a career . . . you got passed out, you were a skilled man. There were no avenues to improve yourself once you'd done that. (Ron Scott, prison wing manager)

I've had a career because I've always been in the Civil Service and I've worked my way through it . . . I did devote myself to it as well . . . I suppose you could say I did enjoy it. (Carol Laine, executive officer, Civil Service)

In the forces . . . it's all laid out, your trade career, and your promotion exams . . . it was definitely geared to a career pattern. (Colin Hawkins, manager, residential social work)

As these people talk about what 'a career' means to them, familiar ideas emerge. 'A career' is more than 'a job'. It offers prospects, progression, a sense of direction, a structure. It involves planning – on the part of the person and of the organisation they work for. There is personal engagement and reward, in terms of growth, development, commitment, fulfilment, enjoyment, a sense of achievement. It provides a certain level of material reward, security and status. This is a powerful cluster of ideas, which are part of how people write and talk about careers in commonsense understandings, in academic discourse and in the world of work. They appear as an 'ideal' against which these managers measure their own experience as they struggle with the question 'Do you have a career'? Their struggle is interesting, because they belong to a group of people whom common sense might tell us have careers – they have got on in the world. Having relatively recently moved into new jobs, it may seem obvious, they are 'moving forward', they have become managers. As the adverts in Chapter 1 suggest, these are people who may be expected to recognise and present themselves as having a 'career'.

So do you have a career?

Is career a word you'd use to describe your work history?

You mean lack of! And not planned from the company's point of view . . . I'm sure they're not planning my career. (Eddie Hayes, training manager)

I like the job [as a bingo manager] . . . it's enjoyable. I don't really view it as like it's my career, sort of like if I was working in a bank. (Mike Davis, bingo club manager)

Anybody that knows me would tell you that they think I'm very career minded. And I find that quite strange . . . it's by default really. It was never something I set out to achieve. (Ellen Fitzgerald, branch manager, building society)

With no intent at all, I've ended up with what people would perceive to be an absolutely fabulous job. (Carrie Bley, finance director, further education)

I tend to sort of informally review [my career] . . . I left my last job . . . I felt that part of the career had come to an end because I wasn't going to get on any further within that company. (Julian Adderley, manager, computing software)

They're no longer jobs for life. (Lawrence Young, loans manager, banking)

With cut backs . . . and them looking at slim-lining the management structure, I've become very despondent [takes a deep breath]. I know that I probably won't go any further now. Because the opportunities aren't going to be there . . . you've got to look at what is available . . . and manage that to start with . . . develop yourself and try and fine-tune. And if there is another door and opportunities open, make sure that you're well equipped to actually go into that. (Ron Scott, prison wing manager)

One simple answer to the question might be to argue that 'being a manager' is a career job. This approach works in other fields. Mary Rainey is clear she has a career – a career in nursing. Marion Brown and Lucy Armstrong both saw teaching as a career. 'That was almost a sort of end in itself – I don't think I saw it as going anywhere.' They could have remained classroom teachers for the rest of their lives and have 'had a career'. Carol Laine has no problem saying she has a career – working in the Civil Service. However, not even the career manager's immediate response is, 'I am a manager, therefore I have a career'. It seems that 'being a manager' can be a challenging and interesting job, a job with some status, an important step forward in someone's working life. However, for most of these new managers, there is not the immediate and straightforward recognition of having joined a profession, or embarked on 'a managerial career' that other well-established and socially recognised professions seem to give. This raises important questions about the nature of managerial work, its ambiguity and lack of social visibility, that are taken up in Chapter 3. So, how do these managers apply the idea of a career to their work history?

As people talk about their own careers, they are constantly making use of the cluster of ideas identified in the previous section. They are drawn into judging or evaluating their situations against this demanding list. Some are quite definite in their initial answer – usually, because they are able to focus on one aspect in this cluster of ideas that applies to them. So, Sally Vaughan has no doubt she has a career. She is committed to her work – 'It's my life' – and she can see clearly that she has made exceptional progress. Arthur Blakey feels he has a 'good career' because he has created a coherence and plan in his work history, 'I've moved about in a structured manner . . . it hasn't just happened to me . . . I do plan things quite a bit.'

Because 'the career' is such a multi-faceted notion, it is unlikely that all the criteria will be met. There is likely to be a 'but' – something missing or not quite right, some way in which a person's situation fails to match up to this exacting set of demands. Interestingly, most misgivings are about the extent to which their work history is the outcome of a plan, or 'strategy' and whether they have a goal or plan for the future. Unlike Arthur Blakey, many talk of ending up where they are 'by default', without planning it. By the time of the second interview, some people were feeling that possibilities were closing down, they could not plan ahead into the future. Carol Laine couldn't see much chance of going higher 'in the current climate'. Ron Scott could no longer see clear career paths ahead of him. At a personal level, he draws on the idea of broadening or deepening his experience and expertise, as a 'career strategy', 'fine-tuning' his skills and equipping himself in case a 'door should open'.

So, we see people drawing on the cluster of ideas evoked by discourses of 'career'. Despite, or perhaps because of, its vagueness as a concept, 'the career' is a powerful notion. As people use it to judge their own work histories, they may focus on a particular element to arrive at a strongly positive or negative evaluation. However, because it is multidimensional, there is usually something more to strive for, a more satisfying 'fit', a clearer plan for the future. As Grey (1994) shows, in his study of accountants, 'the career' connects with processes of self-surveillance, by which people come to accept organisational demands and 'shape' themselves to meet them. It is also important in legitimating differences and inequalities in success, power, status and rewards in organisations. However, some people are aware of and resistant to these processes:

I think career means . . . work history and future . . . people say 'I haven't got a career, I'm just working'. I mean, if you're working you've got a career. I wouldn't like to differentiate between the two . . . that really devalues a total section of society almost . . . It's one of those words that doesn't mean anything . . . it puts pressure on you, partly. 'Oh, where's your career going next Carrie?' I get a lot of that . . . Why does it have to go anywhere? I might be quite happy where I am. (Carrie Bley)

Career is perhaps a dated expression now, I think. Where people are brought up with some sort of destiny and channelled in a certain direction.

So it's not a word you'd actually apply to yourself?
I would, for the want of a better word – working life, career, adulthood – really, we are all getting older, so yes, we are pursuing our lives within that, and if it's a career that describes what you're doing, that's fine . . . But really, your life is your career, is it not? Wherever you choose, whatever direction. (Stan Jordan)

It is a hierarchical concept for lots of people . . . but you can move sideways or into different associated fields and feel that you are doing something different and productive, and changing yourself. (Lucy Armstrong)

Carrie Bley views 'career' in a very similar way to Arthur et al., as *'the evolving sequence of a person's work experiences over time* . . . Everyone who works has a career' (Arthur et al. 1989: 9). As she talks, Carrie resists the exclusivity of the concept and the way some fields of work and some work histories come to be judged as 'better' than others. She also shows some anger at the way it applies a kind of pressure – it is not enough to be in a 'career job', one also has to be striving for more. In a very personal way, she recognises that 'career' is a judgemental concept and that others around her collude in its use as a controlling discourse.

Stan Jordan questions the exclusivity of 'career' in an even broader way: why should it be limited to what we do at work? As he talks, he reflects the distinction between 'objective' and 'subjective' careers and the possibility of different ways of understanding and experiencing a particular life or work history (Collin 1986). His sense of 'career' echoes Goffman's; 'the term is coming to be used, however, in a broadened sense to refer to any social strand of any person's course through life' (Goffman 1961: 119). Lucy Armstrong, like Bailyn (1989) and Schein (1978), questions whether 'growth' and 'development' have to be associated with hierarchical progression.

Earlier, Ron Scott touched on another important issue. A 'career' is problematic not only because it is multi-dimensional, but because it is also dynamic. Any 'fit' is hard to sustain. The person changes and develops. They want new, or different things from their job. The situation in which they operate also changes. Doors can open, opportunities can also close down. If being able to plan, have goals, or a sense of 'strategy' is seen as an important part of a sense of 'having a career', this becomes complicated. It is to this we now turn.

Career plans and strategies

The career routes we have identified, and the importance of having a 'plan' in people's answers to the question of whether they have 'a career' leads us to look at how managers see their work histories having taken the shape they do. In this, an important concern is the relationship between 'strategy-making' and planning at the individual and organisational levels. The growth of the discourse of 'human resource management' and its alleged difference from personnel management (Legge 1995; Watson 1995a) emphasises the need for organisations to look at their 'human resources' strategically. This involves recognising employees' importance in the long-term survival and success of the organisation. A wide range of processes can then be identified which contribute to organisational strategies for monitoring and developing 'human resources', for example, through recruitment and selection procedures, succession planning, management development programmes, appraisal and so on. However, these 'human resources' are people who may have needs, wants or interests of their own, which do not necessarily coincide with those of corporate management. They can be seen as shaping their own lives, treating the organisation as a resource, in a sense, to help them manage their own existence. Thus, 'careers' or work histories can be seen as shaped, by how organisational and individual strategies interact.

In talking of 'strategy', we argue that it is more useful to conceptualise strategies as processes, rather than big plans. We see Mintzberg's notion of strategy as realised pattern as most useful in conceptualising both organisational and personal strategies (Watson and Harris 1996). This involves looking at whether the pattern that might be seen (if any!) was more or less intended or deliberate, or whether it is the product of many decisions and adjustments to changing circumstances. So, for example, the people we talked to have seen opportunities opening up and closing down in unforeseen ways as organisations react to the environment in which they operate. Their work histories have thus been shaped in a context of changing organisational policies or 'strategies'. If we then apply Mintzberg's (1987) approach to individuals' strategies, it suggests a view of employees as people who work out their identities and orientations over time, rather than as people who come with fixed plans and needs. People showed us how they could see themselves changing and how the things they wanted from their job had also changed.

So, following Mintzberg, we conceptualise strategies of employers and employees as *realised patterns* which emerge over time. This leaves open questions of how far rational planning, at an organisational or individual level, has played an important part in shaping patterns such as the routes into managerial work outlined earlier. As we look at how individuals actually talk about the way their careers have developed or emerged, we find these patterns are sometimes presented as more or less intended, planned, deliberate. More often, they are presented as 'emergent', the result of incremental moves and decisions, 'luck', unforeseen opportunities and circumstances. Also, work histories can be presented or constructed in different ways and given different kinds of logic and coherence (Metcalfe 1992; Moir 1993). Mary Rainey, a nurse manager, demonstrates this well. She talks, on the one hand, of how she seeks to be happy in what she is doing and how this would drive her to change jobs – 'you're too long on this world, and too long at work, to be miserable'. However, at the same time, she can also see a pattern in her work history that is similar to that described as 'spiralling' by Nicholson and West (1988). Sideways moves have broadened her knowledge in ways that have enabled her to also move upwards 'because very often, it's not that you've got the knowledge in that par- ticular field, but a broader base of knowledge to draw on, that gave you the edge over some of the other applicants'. She presents her 'strategy' in two very different ways. However, Mintzberg says, strategy, or pattern, involves '*consistency* of behaviour, *whether or not* intended' (1987: 11). Thus, a pattern may emerge unintentionally and be recog- nised retrospectively (Schein 1978; Weick 1995).

We now go on to look at how managers talk about their career strat- egies. Taking each entry route, we look at examples of individual strat- egy-making. They fall at various points along a continuum with 'more or less deliberate career strategies' being presented at one end, and completely 'emergent' ones being reported at the other.

Career managers: planning, learning, getting stuck

'I've very, very carefully managed my career'

Dan Tracey presents himself as a very active 'strategist' or planner. Dan originally chose a degree in business studies as a way of 'keeping my options open'. However, it was a 'personal disaster' when he failed an A level and had to take a year out. So, rather than drifting on to uni- versity, 'I really had to take stock and say right, I really need to focus here and get this A level, because that's what I want to do.'

Dan now says, 'I've very, very carefully managed my career.' He has a five-year plan: 'anybody who doesn't have a five-year plan is not managing their career, yea?' In ten years time, he sees himself as man- aging director of a small or medium sized company. Having imple- mented several successful distribution projects, he is looking to widen his business knowledge. 'So, I'm very, very careful in the decisions and the jobs that I take to build on that career.' Dan focuses on how his own decisions, skills and networks have shaped his career, rather than organisational planning or human resource management. He acknow- ledges there is some 'luck' involved, but the environment he works in is presented as a resource he uses, rather than a constraint, in shaping his career.

The way he talks about his work history can be seen as shaped by wider discourses of 'the successful manager'. He presents himself as having a big goal (to become a managing director), an awareness of the expectations of the job (a broad knowledge and understanding of business), a clear sense of the kinds of experience he needs to acquire to equip himself for this goal (at different points, he speaks of education, secondments, projects etc.). He presents himself as 'entrepreneurial'. Chances have to be seen, or created – and seized. He is aiming to reach a level that only a few achieve. However, achieving the exceptional means learning fast, producing results and moving quickly, 'having the bottle' to put yourself into new situations where you might fail. To 'achieve dramatically, quickly . . . it's all about risk'. Dan presents a strategy for a managerial career for those like him, who want to move far and fast.

'Thrown in at the deep end': planning and unexpected opportunities

Liz Carter has also actively planned her career. On graduating, she wanted to become a human resource manager, but soon realised she needed work experience to get a job in this competitive field. She did this by approaching companies, offering to work without pay. This paid off, she was then taken on as a graduate trainee. After a while, a senior post arose, as a Human Resource Manager, which she was asked to fill. It was a huge leap, for which she didn't feel quite ready – she had worked in some specialised areas of personnel, but lacked broader, more general experience. Liz accepted the challenge, but, like Dan Tracey, she felt she was taking a risk. However, Liz presents it more as 'being thrown in at the deep end' and as a risk that, in some ways, the company shared, by asking her to take on this job so early in her career.

I knew the other HR managers well, they would give me the support that I needed. And I thought, well, if they think I'm capable, then maybe I should think I'm capable, sort of thing . . . I mean, I'm definitely the most inexperienced human resource manager that they've ever put in straight at that role.

So, eighteen months later, she says, 'Gradually, I'm persuading myself that yea, OK, it was the right thing to do, because I seem to be managing OK.' A vacancy arose, Liz was identified as someone who could cope and she has done. However, her route into management doesn't fit with human resource management ideals such as succession planning, accumulating experience and incremental progression. The organisation could not synchronise its needs with her plan; Liz was 'thrown in at the deep end'.

'All I've ever done is try my best to work very hard and that's been recognised'

In saying this, **Sally Vaughan** suggests her experience as a graduate trainee has fulfilled the kind of 'implicit contract' we talked of earlier. Sally joined a large manufacturing and retail organisation as a graduate trainee in marketing and has progressed very quickly. She presents this as coming close to the ideal of a mutually beneficial 'fit' between company and employee.

I work hard to progress quickly. Not just to get paid, get my company car or what have you, but because I enjoy it as well . . . all I've ever done is try my best to work very hard and that's been recognised.

So, positive appraisals have led her through the various levels and into the managerial grades. So far, the company has been able to provide appropriate posts when Sally has felt ready to move on. So far, there has been a good fit between Sally's needs and the opportunities the company has been able to provide.

Learning how it really works

Lawrence Young was attracted to the bank by the promises made at the graduate recruitment fair. It seemed 'a safe option' and he had a large student overdraft to pay back! His first two years were marked by the failure of the graduate trainee scheme to live up to its promises. The personnel director made a speech pointing out that 'banking is no longer a job for life'. The level and breadth of experience provided was limited. The rate of progress failed to match his expectations. He sees this in part as his bad luck, to have been assigned to a branch where he felt he was seen as 'just an add on', a spare member of staff used to fill in, where he was not offered the range of experience and responsibilities he expected. However, with hindsight, he can also see, 'I was slightly slow on the uptake . . . if you let things wash over you and wait for things to happen, they won't.'

Lawrence has since moved forward and become a manager. Although still critical of the graduate trainee scheme, he feels he has learned important lessons about how to progress in his organisation.

The graduate entry scheme does not necessarily lay out a clear path. Graduate trainees will not necessarily be given the experience they need in a planned way. Promotion and advancement may not come automatically. He now believes he must take responsibility for 'driving his career forward', making his needs known within the organisation, recognising and seizing opportunities, making sure he is noticed and not overlooked or forgotten.

So, like the managers in Preston and Hart's (1996) study, he has had to let go of some of the messages given out when he was recruited and has had to look out for signs of how things 'really' work. This comes over as a very powerful process of frustration, disillusionment, adjusting expectations, pushing himself to take a more active role in defining and securing his own needs and goals. By watching the progress of himself and others around him, he has been able to judge where he has 'read' the situation correctly. Arguably, the learning is all the more powerful because the messages have not always been explicit – he has not been 'told' directly. It has been a more complex and difficult socialisation process. His view of the bank and how to 'act strategically' to progress has emerged through his own observations and experiences. He is still refining and testing it out, but he now sees that being a graduate trainee does not necessarily mean that there is a clear plan or path to follow.

Getting stuck: where do you go from here?

Kathy Westbrook and **Ken Pine** joined management trainee schemes in different restaurant chains. Both present this as a possibility that emerged, rather than something they actively chose to do. Kathy was working as a waitress, after graduating. She saw the management trainee scheme as an option, 'until I'd got my ideal job'. Ken explains his entry as the result of a chance meeting with a senior manager in the company. Initially impressed by the professionalism of the training programmes, and the frequent pay rises in the early stages, both then became dissatisfied with the lack of scope for initiative, the long, unsocial hours and the mundane nature of much of their day-to-day work.

At the time they were first interviewed, Kathy and Ken expressed mixed feelings about their jobs. On the one hand, they valued the training and managerial experience they had gained so far. Kathy gained valuable experience of induction and training of new staff, but learned that she only got this by pushing herself, telling senior people that she wanted to do it. They saw a wide range of opportunities that might be open to them, working in very large corporate organisations. As Kathy put it,

I was embarrassed to say that I worked at Big Pizza as a manager . . . Then I just sort of felt, why are you being so childish and ridiculous? At the end of the day . . . it's brilliant for me because I'm getting experience of every sort of management. Recruiting staff and training them, stock controlling, inventory, commercial business, advertising . . . I dabble in everything . . . I sort of woke up one day, and thought, no, I can make something out of this . . . I started taking it far more seriously . . . there is a long way you can go in the company, apart from running a restaurant.

However, for both, there were also nagging doubts about the company's interest in helping them to realise potential opportunities and a growing awareness that this might take a very long time. By the time of the second interview, Ken had left. Kathy was applying to other organisations. She was still an assistant manager and could see little immediate hope of getting her own restaurant, or 'moving into' other parts of the large conglomerate she worked for. She could see others in a similar situation to herself, a long queue of people she had to join.

Kathy suggests the company has moved towards graduate recruitment as a solution to its problem of high turn-over, as the graduates seem to learn and make progress quickly. Kathy and Ken had worked very hard and been noticed by their senior managers – they felt they had kept their side of the deal. They had been given first managerial posts, but were their companies looking any further ahead? The pace of progress is slow and the opportunities they can see in the large organisations they work for are elusive.

Moving up: following a path, finding a path, choosing a way

Starting at the bottom: a clear path, but how far do you go?

Some jobs are seen as 'good jobs' for school-leavers – for example, the Civil Service, local government, banks and building societies, large retail organisations such as the John Lewis Partnership or Marks and Spencer. Once in, they are seen as offering good 'opportunity structures', scope for training, for 'moving around' and 'moving up'. However individuals' plans for their lives may or may not involve taking advantage of these possibilities.

Andrew Shepherd entered the bank with A levels and great ambition. He would like to have gone to university, but ruled this out as he felt his parents 'couldn't really afford it, with other boys in the family to follow as well'. So, in his own mind, Andrew entered a race with those of his age who would start after him as graduates. He has been very successful, moving up the grading structure, broadening his experience by working at head office in different roles. When we met, he had recently become manager of his own branch, which he saw as a very significant move: 'it's more like running my own business'. It is a step in the direction of his goal of becoming a Regional Director.

Carol Laine and **Ellen Fitzgerald** joined the Civil Service and a major building society respectively shortly after leaving school. Initially, neither thought much about 'moving up'. Ellen Fitzgerald, as a young woman with a 'traditional upbringing', would 'get a good job, meet somebody, marry that somebody, have children, and that's it'. 'Moving up the ladder' as far as managerial work would take a considerable shift in Ellen's view of her world and of herself as a woman.

For Carol, becoming a single parent was the spur to move on. For Ellen, her divorce at 24 'shattered all of my illusions and caused me really to reassess exactly what I wanted'. Before then, it had been suggested she had the potential to go much further, but 'my attitude was, I'm not interested, thank you very much. I've got my husband, and I want my children, and that's all I want.'

Ellen is now extremely ambitious and determined to get on. She presents her work as her first priority and is a very successful manager. Carol Laine is still balancing work with being a lone parent. To advance further would mean moving towns, to work at head office, so she looks at progress in terms of her increasing responsibility and expertise within her current post.

Starting at the bottom, finding a path through

Tom Smith sees himself working in a field where the career paths are far from clear. He left school with two O levels, 'a clutch of CSEs' and a strong sense he wanted to get on, to do better, to move away from the council estate where he grew up. 'It didn't really matter what I did, I just didn't want to be there.' He got a job in the courts service, as a typist. However, he soon decided 'I've got to do something to be better, I can't be a £1000 a year typist for ever.' As Tom puts it, 'the question you're always conditioned to ask is "what do I need to do to become a boss" – that's how it's framed, one way or another, isn't it?'

Gradually, possibilities emerged: getting A level law; supervising a small section of three; doing the court clerk's diploma; qualifying as a barrister; moving on to become a Deputy Clerk to the Justices; studying for an MBA. However, the next step has never been obvious – there are different 'branches' and there are points at which people seem to stop and stay put. Tom takes some time to tell his story. It is a story of gradual change, people leaving and jobs becoming vacant; studying for qualifications; having a boss who encouraged him to take a leap and qualify as a barrister; jobs being advertised; watching others move on; coming to see things as possible. So, Tom moved forward, but with little sense of a long-term plan, or of where it might eventually lead: 'there is no structure in the magistrates court.'

Even now, he is not sure what his next steps will be. He sees the service restructuring and changing around him, with the likelihood of fewer layers and fewer posts at higher levels. At the same time, new career routes appear. He has an MBA and sees possibilities of new kinds of managerial posts emerging in response to pressures on public services to 'manage themselves better', to become more 'efficient and effective'. Tom has always had a goal 'to get on', but his plan or strategy for doing this has emerged gradually. He still has a strong sense of working out his career route, watching what others do, what opportunities are emerging: 'there's no real map in tablets of stone.'

Moving up in a profession: different jobs, different skills?

In our sample are a number of people who have set out in 'professional careers' – in nursing, education, engineering, housing, social work and accountancy. Opportunities to progress often lead into managerial work, rather than recognition and development as a practitioner. So, we have seen how Arthur Blakey came to recognise a choice between a career in engineering or in operational and general management. He made a decision to move into managerial work. **Mark Taylor**, who works in the same company, saw the same choice. He found operations management 'quite a different way of thinking . . . a shop floor mentality . . . there's not that much of a thread, between the actual work, what you do in the role'. Having tried it, he was pleased to return to a new project management post in engineering.

In other professions, similar choices emerge. Like Mark Taylor and Arthur Blakey, people react to this in different ways. Some seem to see their move into more managerial posts as 'moving up' within their profession. Others, like Arthur Blakey, present their current work more in terms of a 'move in' to management. However, this is not always a clear distinction.

Marion Brown talks of how she had always thought of teaching as a career in itself, 'something that you did until you had your family . . . I didn't make any plan for the path that career would follow . . . the idea of managing anything just wasn't an issue. Not even myself!' She progressed as a classroom teacher, but after seven or eight years of teaching, realised that if she wanted to go further, to become a head teacher, she needed to 'manage' or plan her career more carefully. However, she never saw this in terms of 'I want to go into a management position . . . I knew I wanted to be responsible for affecting what went on in a school.'

Lucy Armstrong taught in an FE college. She came to a point where she wanted to move on, to 'do something the same but different'. She was seconded to a project working with schools, which was 'rocket fuel' in the process. 'I was forced to identify skills which I had got, but I had not been conscious of using', interpersonal skills such as negotiation, team work, handling hostility and helping people manage change. Also, for the first time, her manager was a woman and 'an excellent role model'. Lucy sees these experiences as 'crucial' in enabling her to see herself as a manager. She sees, 'in retrospect . . . there is a strategy that paid off'. The secondment helped her recognise her skills, enhanced her credibility in the college and helped her to get promotion. Her particular skills and interests and her need to move on, happened to coincide with a growing emphasis in colleges on student support. She became manager of student services in her college, retaining a teaching and counselling role. The second time we met, she was beginning to think about her next move, possibly into a more managerial job or even outside education.

Diane Washington presents her promotion to manager of her section as accidental, unplanned, the outcome of 'fortuitous pregnancies'. It was 'a snowball', that grew as her former boss's role changed and developed, 'so mine carried on developing, until essentially, I was running the service here'. Diane is still reluctant to let go of her professional identity and practice as a physiotherapist. She negotiated a compromise whereby she manages her area, with some administrative support, retaining a reduced clinical workload. However, having gained this concession, it is a difficult juggling act she then has to manage herself. Nevertheless, she distinguishes between those who move into management from a clinical background and the growing breed of 'professional managers' in the health service, who she feels are less well received by 'clinical people'.

They haven't any experience of working in the health service, or they're less familiar with what patients are like, or the kinds of stresses and strains that are put on people who are working at ward level or in clinics, day in and day out.

Similar concerns are reflected in Lucy Armstrong's regrets at contemplating giving up her teaching role and in Mary Rainey's view that those who manage nurses need direct knowledge and understanding of what they do and how they see things. Mary still sees herself as 'first and foremost a nurse', just as Diane is still a physiotherapist.

So, we can see that 'moving up' in their professional careers has brought these people to a point where they may have to ask themselves difficult questions. There are questions about whether they see themselves as professionals or technical specialists or as managers. Where do they go if they don't take the managerial route? Is there scope to develop and move forward as a practitioner? Is it possible to combine professional practice with managerial work? Do the skills of a good nurse, classroom teacher or engineer make a good manager? These are not new questions. But as we listen to these people 'moving up' in their organisation, making decisions about their own careers, they have to deal with these questions at a very personal level. The answers that come from other fields seem to suggest they need to 'let go' of their previous expertise and knowledge – this is one of the lessons Hill's financial managers (1992) had to learn. The same message came across in a management course for health service workers that Diane Washington studied. However, here we see people raising serious questions about how this would affect their ability and credibility as managers of professional workers. As Diane puts it, 'I trained to work as a physiotherapist, I didn't train to be a manager . . . I think I have a lot to contribute, still, to that side of things and from my own point of view, it keeps my feet on the ground.' Here, she touches on a whole range of issues. There are questions about her identity and how she sees herself. Issues of where her expertise lies, how this experience is a resource that might be lost to patients. At the same time, she implies this makes her just the kind of person that should be managing other professionals. However, the people in our sample felt their organisations' 'strategies' didn't encourage or facilitate combining managerial work and professional practice.

Professionals turned managers

We have just heard people in professional jobs describe their moves into more managerial posts in ways that seem to see them as 'moving up'. Their professional identity remains central. Subjectively, their current post doesn't seem to represent a radical break with their professional career. Others do accept that they are now 'managers' and perhaps fit better in the next section, of people 'moving in' to managerial work. We have heard **Arthur Blakey** describe how he saw himself making a conscious and planned move from a career in engineering, where he saw limited scope for future progression, towards a career in general management. **Colin Hawkins** also accepts that he is now a manager, rather than a social worker. Colin entered social work relatively late, as a carefully planned exit from his previous military career. He worked with children and families, but 'realised quite quickly that I didn't have enough time to actually make any progression'. So, he 'swapped from being a worker to being a manager in residential social work' because he realised that he could make more rapid progression in that field.

Moving in: needing a change, new opportunities, new roles

Moving in: new roles, new possibilities

Betty Smith had always seen management as a possibility, as she 'moved up the ladder' in her previous field. She went to evening classes to study business and finance. However, she made a deliberate move into the NHS, which she felt offered possibilities for a more varied or higher-reaching managerial career. After a period working as a clerk and receptionist in a doctor's practice, she is now a practice manager. Her strategy involved stepping back to move forwards.

The business manager role has also offered a new career route, a new tier of senior management jobs for people working in the health service to consider. **Jean Holliday** took this path. She was a highly qualified accountant. However, returning to work after bringing up her children, she found it difficult to go back to the kind of work she had done previously. She took an MBA to 'prove my credibility'. She sees herself leaving accountancy to develop a career in 'strategic management'. Jean describes herself as 'a planner by nature'. Her work is important, but it is only one element in her bigger plan, her life-plan, the goal of which is to end life 'convinced that I've made as much of my life as I possibly could have'.

Carrie Bley left school after O levels, interested in 'earning some money and having a good time'. After a 'simple arithmetic test' she got a job with the county council and was 'totally amazed by the fact they were going to train me, I thought it was wonderful'. She did exams with the Association of Accounting Technicians, 'very practically accounting based'. There has been dramatic progress in her career in recent years. With incorporation and devolution of financial responsibility in FE, she has moved from working in county hall, advising schools and colleges on budgets and accounts to become a director in FE, initially in charge of finance but with an increasing involvement in general management. She seized the opportunity and took a great leap forward in her career – the first time we met, she spoke a lot of how she'd 'been lucky', 'in the right place at the right time'. However, the second time we met, she was more concerned about the future and the closure of opportunities. As the changes have consolidated, different kinds of experience and qualifications are now expected of people entering the kind of post she holds. The path she has taken would be much more difficult for someone starting out in her first job today. There is, then, both considerable personal benefit and risk in being there, to grab these opportunities. We see public sector employees 'moving in' – their backgrounds and experience have been seen as suitable for new posts at particular moments of considerable change – but what might become of these roles, and the career paths they are now embarked on, is uncertain.

'Moving in' from skilled trades

Ron Scott and **Harry Lyttleton** left secondary modern schools to take up what Ashton (1973) calls 'working class careers' in skilled trades. Ron worked in the motor trade, Harry as an electrician. Everyone advised Ron, 'Get yourself a trade, you'll never be out of work' or, as Harry puts it, 'once you were trained, nobody could take it away from you'. Ashton points out that such trades have a relatively short career ladder. Ron came to see he'd 'got to get out, otherwise I'd have been stagnant'. He talks of how he planned his move out. He looked at various possibilities, went to college to improve his written English, then joined the prison service, knowing his trade was always there 'as a safety net'. Ron had joined an organisation with a clear hierarchy and career structure, and he has 'moved up' within it.

Harry Lyttleton was working as an electrician in chemical production plants. He talks of a 'critical incident', a more sudden realisation that he had to change course. It happened the day his shop steward retired:

I know it sounds stupid . . . it was just this one thing in his retirement speech stopped me from wanting to be an electrician. He just said, 'I was really pleased to have been a fitter for 49 years'. And I suddenly had this dread . . . oh god, I've got another 38, 40 years of this. I couldn't face it.

Harry had a desire to move, to get on – but he could not have planned where it might take him, as that has been influenced by broader organisational change and development. He did courses on computing and European electrical regulations and 'before I knew where I was, I was the expert in our little patch'. Things moved on from there. In such a large organisation, 'jobs are there for you to apply for'. Also,

In certain instances, at lower levels anyway, jobs are provided for you if you do well . . . 'why don't you try doing this, we can't promise you anything, but it might turn into a job'. That's how you get jobs on the shop floor, because of circumstances, that's what happened to me.

So, he could not plan or manage his career, 'Someone else is doing it for you and more by luck than judgement.' At the same time, it is not just luck, 'You create a lot of your own luck mind – you've got to be there and you've got to be working hard . . . Right place, right time comes into it.'

Harry has progressed a long way. His company has been taken over, he has been involved in major changes in how production is organised in his plant – he has come to live with change and uncertainty and all its implications for his own life. Plans can't be made, both the person and the organisation are constantly changing, but 'you have got choices':

There's huge changes going off, there's redundancies. There's also huge opportunities. And career progressions can't be planned from one day to the next, you just can't ... The sort of 'greater good' of the company's being sought out at a higher level than I am. And what you've got to do is say that I want to improve, or I want to better myself, I want to stretch myself, before I get too comfortable in what I'm doing.

Emergent careers

These accounts show wide variation in the extent to which people see their work histories or career paths as 'planned' or the outcome of luck, chance, 'being in the right place at the right time'. Storey et al. raise the question of whether managerial careers are systematically planned, or are largely 'accidental' (1997: 66). They found differences between the Japanese companies they studied, which had 'very formal arrangements' for planning the careers of individual managers, and the British companies, where things were 'much more haphazard' (1997: 92). Most of the accounts of how people enter managerial work that we have gathered would be best described as 'incremental' rather than 'strategically planned'. People are shaping careers in uncertain and changing situations. They are also, themselves, changing in the process.

The organisations people work in are changing as they identify and attempt to respond to external influences or as they import new ideas and practices. Technology is changing. Julian Adderley is a manager in a computer software company. It wasn't a career he could have foreseen, when he was a student, 'it just hadn't really taken off'. He became interested after getting involved in the implementation of a computer system in the retail company he was working for. As Harry Lyttleton shows so clearly, individuals' lives are influenced by decisions made at different levels in an organisation – from major restructuring, down to a boss who 'puts in a good word' for one of his staff.

At the same time, people are changing and coming to see themselves differently. As Sally Vaughan looks into the future, to the most senior posts, it is 'scary'. However, she is aware that she has changed. When she was at school, she 'couldn't possibly have imagined myself doing this job'. So, looking further ahead, 'maybe things will change as I move on and I become more comfortable with that idea'. This is echoed by others, who talk of how, as they move through their organisations, the work of senior colleagues becomes 'demystified'. As one person put it, 'you see the chaos they work in . . . you look at some of the decisions they make . . . you think, what the hell are you doing? It's quite encouraging actually.' So, as people gain experience and move forward, or as their life situations change, their ideas of what is possible for them change.

To say that 'career strategies' are emergent is not to argue that 'planning' does not enter into it. Some people, like Dan Tracey or Andrew Shepherd, have clear goals they are striving to achieve. They have a broad idea of what is needed to reach them although they cannot plan exactly how or where they will fill the gaps in the outline they have sketched. Other people describe moments in their careers where they have to make significant choices or plan to change their situation. So, Marion Brown reached a point in her career where she realised that she wanted to go further, to become a head teacher. She then set about planning how to get the experience she needed. Lucy Armstrong and Harry Lyttleton talk of 'needing things to change', and taking steps to make this happen (Lucy takes a secondment, Harry goes on courses). Looking back, Lucy can see how her actions have contributed to realising a 'strategy' that has gained her progression and development within her organisation. The same is true for Harry. But this only becomes clear as it is 'constructed' retrospectively.

The examples we have looked at highlight issues about 'strategies' for individual careers and issues at the organisational level. Organisations cannot always match their needs with those of individuals. Liz Carter's big chance comes earlier than she would have planned. This has worked out well, so it is seen retrospectively as a 'wonderful opportunity'. But as Dan Tracey recognises, such leaps could also go badly wrong: 'You are only as good as your last success'. By the time of the second interview, a number of the managers were ready to move on, but could see nowhere to go. Ron Scott and Kathy Westbrook busy themselves extending their experience, but see themselves stuck in the same jobs for the foreseeable future.

Although 'planning' may be a problem, there seem to be significant differences in how organisations deal with their employees' concerns for development. There are also differences in what individuals expect of the organisation and the extent to which they feel 'implicit contracts' about this are met. So, Sally Vaughan presents a positive picture of dialogue between herself and her manager, which recognises her achievements and, so far, has produced timely moves and fresh challenges. Others, like Lawrence Young and Kathy Westbrook, have changed their expectations, they have learned that they need to be more pro-active if they want to be noticed and to be given chances to develop. They may, then, feel the 'contract' has not been kept if they are not given opportunities to move forward. Dan Tracey presents yet another, more active, entrepreneurial model, whereby he expects little, in terms of planning his career, from 'the organisation'. He has 'a very clear idea' where he wants to be. He 'manages his abilities', 'ticking it off' as he collects the skills and experience he needs to reach his goal. To Dan, 'the organisation' is a collection of individuals with whom he must actively network and form relationships to 'create' chances for himself. He has to 'manage the perceptions' of people in positions to make decisions that affect his career, that way 'you can speed your rise up the manage-ment ladder'. Dan emphasises ways in which he is 'managing' his career as he pursues his plans.

Here, we see people presenting their part in shaping and planning their careers in different ways. Some see themselves as active, 'entre-preneurial'. Others could be seen as having a more 'responsive' orien-tation, explaining their work histories more in terms of spotting and reacting to changes they saw going on around them or taking advan-tage of new situations and opportunities. Some present themselves as passive, emphasising the role of luck and chance and almost arbitrary decisions in bringing them to where they are now. There are also ques-tions about ways in which moving into managerial work have involved battles about their sense of identity and how they see themselves. For some, this takes the form of a struggle between seeing themselves as professionals rather than managers. For others, it involves recognising ways in which they have changed and a sense that they could not have done this job as they saw themselves at some previous time. Others point to discrepancies between the demands of the role of manager, the expectations this places on them and some sense of their 'real' self, the 'kind of person that I am'. These are matters taken up in more detail in Chapter 5.

Growing up to be a manager

Looking back over your life and your background, do you find it surprising that you are where you are now?
No, not at all. Having successful managerial parents has always made me aspire to be in a chal-lenging position, the same as them. I've had an honest, open, adult relationship with my family, in general. We have managed problems, we have managed issues at home. Also, I have always been encouraged to manage my time myself. The independence I was brought up with made me into a manager before I left home. (Liza Potts)

Oh yes, incredibly so. I still do. And I marvel at it! *[laughter]* I mean my sister still calls me a snob and has done for many years. But no, no, I'm very comfortable with the background from which I originate . . . I don't feel I have to be dutifully bound to it and call myself working class for ever.

Good heavens, no. I wouldn't categorise myself at all really any more. But to answer your question, I'm staggered that I have become what I have become. (Jack Dodds)

Although 'management' may not have been a childhood dream for the people we talked to, some are more surprised than others at the jobs they have ended up in. Given the importance of goals, planning, strategy and a strong sense of purpose in managerial discourse, it is interesting to note that 'drifting', indecision, ill-informed and arbitrary choices and keeping options open are recurring themes in how they talk of their pre-work lives. They present themselves as participating in a process that shaped them in certain ways and pushed them in particular directions, during which they made significant choices and decisions but, in most cases, without any strong sense of purpose or direction, and sometimes with little realisation of the significance of the decision for their future. However, looking back, many people make connections between the background they came from and the paths their lives have taken. Thus they identify continuities, ways in which they see their backgrounds and upbringing fitting with where they are now. At the same time, they also highlight discontinuities, ways in which they have moved away from the world they grew up in or have come to question some of its taken-for-granted ideas. So, for some, like Liza Potts, this is very much a story of 'taking their place in the world'. For others, their story is more one of 'changing their place in the world'.

It was a very natural progression to go on to university, at the school I was in. I felt there was a lot of pressure there, and I was actually not sure whether that was right for me ... [I took a year out] By the end of my year out, I was absolutely adamant that I did want to go on, not just because I felt pressure ... for me, it was definitely the right thing to do. (Liz Carter)

I was in the top stream of the secondary modern ... they were going to be the electricians or the skilled trades. And it was just expected that's what we would do. As you go further down the streaming process, the lower down the pecking order you would get, you ended up stacking shelves at Sainsburys, or something like that. (Harry Lyttleton)

These extracts show how Liz Carter and Harry Lyttleton went through schools that had very different aspirations and expectations for their students. In part, these reflect collective stories of how social patterns are reproduced through individual lives. For example, almost all of those who see themselves coming from middle class and professional backgrounds went from school to higher education. This was a step they grew up knowing they would probably take. As they look back, people see their lives patterned by social constraints, expectations and opportunities. Yet, at the same time, their lives are also unique configurations of events, influences and group memberships. They are also very much individual stories, in which the actors see themselves having made choices and decisions along the way, sometimes arbitrary and ill-informed, sometimes conscious and deliberate. As Plummer (1983) points out, biographies reveal pattern – and chaos. Individuals' choices may have little impact on broader social patterns. In these terms, it matters little whether the son of a joiner goes on to be a bricklayer or an electrician, or the daughter of a teacher becomes a nurse or a social worker. However, at the individual level, these may be decisions of considerable significance which influence the particular path of that person's life in important ways. These collective stories thus embrace a variety of individual experiences and outcomes. They contribute to reproducing, or changing, social patterns and structures but are lived out at a different level of personal significance and meaning.

As they talk, people touch on the social patterns of which they are part. So, people identify themselves as having 'working class' or 'middle class' backgrounds, as 'from a benefit family, a council estate boy', or 'coming from a comfortable background'. For some, like Liz Carter, it was taken for granted that they would go to university, others, like Jack Dodds, come from families where no one had ever done that. A large proportion had mothers who worked, but usually in ways that fitted around family life. Carrie Bley's mother worked in the evening, as a telephonist, others worked part-time or returned to work as their children grew older. In some families, home and work were intertwined. Lucy Armstrong's mother worked alongside her father in their own business, Betty Smith's parents kept a post office. These women grew up with different 'models' of how work might fit with being a wife and mother. However, these broader social processes are acknowledged only in the process of telling more complex stories, of lives where, looking back, they see conflicting and competing influences, challenges and rebellions, arbitrary decisions, moments of choice where they imagine their lives might have taken off in quite different directions.

From these accounts, other themes emerge, which link with these broader patterns. People grew up in particular 'family cultures' which shaped their expectations of the place of work in their life and the kind of work they might go into. Most talk of growing up in homes with strong work ethics. There are also issues of 'cultural capital', different kinds of knowledge of the education system, of the labour market and the realities of work. Inevitably, education is seen as important, reinforcing or changing expectations learned from parents. So, many people commented on their parents' emphasis on the importance of education and their support for it, but there are also significant differences in how they present this. For some people, particularly those with professional or 'middle class' parents, home and school reinforced assumptions that they would go to university and would enter jobs that would be rewarding, both financially and personally. Others talk of parents who gave their support and wanted them to continue their education as far as possible. However, they were looking for signals from the school that their child had the ability and application to continue, to do better than they had done. All parents want 'the best' for their children, and want them to have 'good jobs'. For some, this meant the security of a trade. For Carol Laine's mother, it was the Civil Service. Carol started sixth form college but wanted to leave. Her mother got her the forms to apply, 'I filled them in thinking 'Oh, what do civil servants do anyway?' I was so naive.' For other parents, a 'good job' meant going to university, having a 'career' or a 'profession'.

In telling their stories, people are making sense of the courses their lives have taken, trying to trace their 'trajectory of self' (Giddens 1991; Harré 1983). These accounts have to recognise and explain continuities and discontinuities. They have to take account of external events and influences and the person living through them, reacting and changing in the course of their lives. Later chapters explore some of the ways this is reflected in individual understandings and experience of managerial work, and in the sorts of difficulties that people experience in adjusting to managerial roles and in the different amounts and kinds of 'identity work' involved in making that transition.

CHAPTER 3

MANAGING TO MANAGE

We have now seen the various ways in which our managers talk about how they have emerged from their childhoods, their education and their previous work experiences to take on the managerial posts they are now in. Throughout the last chapter we saw people learning about themselves and learning about the world. It might seem that the obvious thing to do next would be to look at how our emergent managers have learned to carry out the responsibilities associated with these posts. However, we are not going to focus upon such matters until the next chapter. We first need, ourselves, to learn something of how they make sense of their managerial work – what conception they have of what they are there to do. In particular we need to appreciate how they make sense of the challenges which they feel they face in their jobs. Only when we have a clearer picture of this can we get a realistic appreciation of how they have learned – and are still learning – to handle the tasks, responsibilities and challenges inherent in their work. In the present chapter therefore we will build up a picture of the work in which our managers are involved by listening to what they say about the managerial tasks they are currently engaged in and the occupational challenges which face them. Our interest is in how they make sense of the managerial work they do – a key aspect of how they manage to manage.

Being a manager and not being a manager

What we *do* in our work as well as in our lives more broadly cannot be separated from what we *are*, or rather what we are continually *becoming* as persons. How we know and understand ourselves and how we get others to know and understand us inevitably requires us to manage both our ever-emergent self-identities and our occupational or social identities. The challenge of doing this takes a particular form for people engaged in managerial work because of significant ambiguities about the occupation and because of its social status connotations. Some of this is apparent in the following conversation with Alan Wilde.

If people ask me what I do for a living, sometimes I say I am a manager and sometimes I just say I work in local government. I suppose that if I want to impress I say I am a manager. It sounds important. And, indeed, my job is that of a manager.

Which is what?
My job title says I am a manager.
But what is it about the job – as opposed to the title – that makes you a manager?
I don't really know. Well, I suppose I do but I have to say that I find it very hard to put it into words. That is why I often avoid the issue and call myself a local government officer.
But not always?
No, because I want people to know that I carry quite a high level of responsibility and that I am involved with really quite major budgets. But you see I don't actually have a direct responsibility for any staff. I don't manage people. And I don't want to confuse the issue. I am not really a boss.
And people think managers are bosses?
I suppose . . . well, hang on. I suppose I am seen as one of the bosses in the building where I am based.
So, do you think of yourself as a manager?
Yes and no.

Alan Wilde works at a senior level in a local authority and explains his work as involving 'the planning of managerial activities and devising better ways in which fellow managers can run their departments'. At first sight there is little ambiguity about whether or not he is 'a manager'. Yet he is equivocal about his position. To the question of whether he thinks of himself as a manager he answers 'Yes and no'. This is something we see in a number of the people in our study. They tend not to question the appropriateness of their inclusion in a study of 'managers' (and note that, early on, Alan says 'my job is that of a manager', as well as revealing that he has a managerial job title). But they do seem to have doubts about how far they have 'emerged' as a manager, in this case both socially and in task terms. The task-related issue about the managerial nature of one's work (turning in particular on whether or not one directly 'manages people') is something we will return to later. For the moment, let us consider the social or occupational aspect of 'being a manager'.

The social opaqueness of management

In our consideration of Kevin Berry's managerial 'emergence' early in Chapter 1 we noted references to both a *task* element in the way he spoke about his work (applying special knowledge and skills to 'managing change' for example) and a *social* element which involved his becoming part of 'the management' and being called 'Mr Berry' by those who previously addressed him by his first name. The social dimension of engagement in managerial work was clearly an issue for Kevin and it appears to be one for Alan Wilde too. Part of the problem for Alan appears to be the social opaqueness of management jobs. He speaks of finding it difficult to 'put into words' what the work is and therefore finds himself telling people simply that he works in local government.

It would seem that there is no clear public knowledge of what the occupation of management entails (Watson 1994a: 29–31). An occupation where there is little social opaqueness would be one which a child might name when asked what sort of work they want to do when they grow up. In the last chapter, however, we saw Dan Tracey recognising this when he pointed out that children tend not to say that they want to be managers. He thought it more likely that they would speak of being train drivers, pilots or builders. And indeed, we saw that the occupations named by our future managers were those with unambiguous public images and relatively high levels of public visibility-footballers, dancers, nurses, vets and so on. The relative lack of public visibility of a single type of work which could be called that of a manager potentially, then, creates a problem for the manager in managing their social *presentation of self* (Goffman 1958). But this is further compounded by the status aspect of holding a managerial position. Alan Wilde recognises this when he tells us that he tends to refer to himself as a manager when he wants to 'impress people'. He appears anxious to stress that there is nothing dishonest in this by quickly moving on to remind us that indeed his job and his job title are those of a manager (this in spite of his later equivocation). We can thus infer that the social aspects of managing to *be* a manager – playing the social role of a manager and handling the associated occupational identity – is made difficult both by the lack of occupational clarity of the work at a public level and by its association with people's social status.

To throw light on issues of this kind we asked our managers to reflect back on what they knew of managerial work earlier in their lives – long before they became associated with it. This helps us understand further aspects of where – as we put it in Chapter 2 – our managerial interviewees had 'come from' in their lives and work careers prior to their taking up the occupation and having to 'manage management'. But it can also give us valuable insights into how people generally conceive of the work of 'the manager'. We might well expect the people we are studying, as individuals currently involved in different ways with managerial work, to have been relatively well informed about the nature of management work. But if these, of all people, appear to have had little knowledge or understanding of it prior to their subsequent management careers, then we can reasonably infer that managerial work is not widely understood in the non-managerial population at large. This, indeed, is what transpires.

In our research, most people were emphatic about how little they knew earlier in their lives about managerial work. Ron Scott, for example, said that a manager for him 'Would have probably been a bank manager, or a manager of a supermarket, or . . . somebody in a suit, yea, a tie and a suit.' He was reflecting on the sort of person he saw around him as a child who was referred to as 'the manager', it would seem. He went on, 'Yea, you stereotype people into that sort of role, don't you?' before adding (not untypically for male interviewees), 'or it could be a football manager of course'. As Diane Washington observed, one sees managers in places like shops but learns little of the detail of their work; 'You could look at what a manager of a supermarket might do, and have a rough idea of what is involved in doing that but you wouldn't know what their day-to-day life would be like, would you?'.

For some individuals, insights into managerial work came from jobs which they had done earlier in their careers, but we have no evidence of this inspiring people towards their own managerial career. Charles Parker, for example, spoke about the manager of the bacon counter he encountered when working as a shop assistant. He didn't like him, and thought that he was 'so protective of his little empire', which was 'really quite pathetic at the end of the day, because his empire was a twenty foot long counter of bacon'. This meant that such a job 'was not going to be my career'. He 'wasn't impressed at all': 'If that's what it's all about, then I wasn't bothered.' Similarly, Alicia Coltrane, working in a pharmacist's shop earlier in her working life, saw at different times both a pharmacist-manager and a store manager being in charge and she thought it was 'a nightmare of a job, because of all the hassle with his staff'. Although there was some appeal to the work – particularly when computer systems were introduced to the shop – Alicia decided that 'I wouldn't want to be in that position'.

'There were tram drivers, there was a coal man, there was a dustman'

Negative views like that expressed by Alicia Coltrane were based on some direct observation of people engaged in managerial work, but others emphasised how their social contexts as children precluded their knowing anything of such work. Harry Lyttleton spoke of his 'naiveté' about such matters because one saw nothing of managers in the 'council estate world' in which he lived. Colin Hawkins spoke similarly of the limited occupational knowledge one would have coming from 'a working class background, where the people that I knew were workers like my dad'. 'There were tram drivers, and there was a coal man, there was a dustman, there were people who worked down the pits . . . Those were the types of jobs that I equated with.' Mike Davis spoke of how a background like this meant that a managerial job would not have occurred to him 'in his wildest dreams' – these were jobs for people with a 'public school level of education'. For Tom Smith, who also spoke of his 'council estate upbringing', managerial work could be seen as a highly questionable undertaking;

I think back in what, the late sixties, early seventies, manager was almost a dirty word. Do you know what I mean? And I can remember saying to one of my brothers, I said, 'Oh yea, I fancy being a manager'. 'Oh bloody managers,' he says. They were almost the other side.

A quite different social background to this could also lead to a negative evaluation of managerial work. Ellen Fitzgerald explained that she did not come across people in managerial positions. Most of her parents' friends had their own businesses. Her father associated managers with 'men in clerical positions' and he had 'a very low opinion of managerial and clerical people'.

'My father was a manager – or I think he was'

It might be thought that individuals whose own parents had been managers would have been better informed about the work. And it might possibly mean that they would have a more positive view of the work. Neither of these appears to be the case, however. Ted Ellington was early on interested in being a dentist. His father was a manager but Ted says he took little interest in what he did and felt that the most significant aspect of his father's work to him was 'the freebies he used to bring home because of his position'. People spoke to us of their 'naiveté' about their parents' managerial work – Eddie Hayes going as far as saying that he only *thought* his father was a manager. We asked Carrie Bley,

Would the idea of being a manager have meant anything to you at the time when you were first thinking about jobs?
No. No, I'm sure it didn't. No, I wouldn't have had a clue.
Even though your dad was one?
Well yes – but I did not have a real concept of it. OK, I mean, I knew he supervised people. He got other people doing different things. There was just this office with people doing things. And OK, he was checking what they were doing. That's as far as it went. Very, very naive.
It wasn't something that you had a notion of doing?
No, crikey, no. I never thought 'I'm going to be a manager'.

Most people who had managerial parents spoke in ways not unlike Carrie.

Something vaguely senior

An alternative pattern to be found among our accounts about early ideas of managerial work was one where people tended to speak of a rather remotely conceived of occupation which was, as one person put it, 'in some vague sense, senior'. There were references to 'people wearing the suits', to 'middle aged blokes who are, you know, in charge, senior' and to 'some sort of boss-type man'. Here there is more emphasis on the social aspects of managerial work, as opposed to the task element. And this was important in a proportion of such accounts in which there was a more positive evaluation of management as something that one might 'end up doing because it was a job at the sort of level I felt I should eventually be at', as it was put in one such account. Will Evans, for example, connected his own emerging notion of a future work career when identifying managers as those who 'do the bossing' as opposed to 'being bossed'. This he could identify with. Ken Pine, in a similar vein, said that 'I always thought I would end up being in some sort of management – because I was always in the top band at school.' Everyone told Ken that he 'would do well'. He had no concept of what field he would do management in – it would simply be a matter of 'being at that level, with that sort of income'. This is a view of managerial work which envisages it simply as something of a relatively high social status – something of a broadly 'professional standing'. Kathy Westbrook speaks in this way and explains that she only began to think of it as 'at a professional level' when she was at university and began to see a career in something like personnel management as appropriate for a person of graduate level standing.

The social baggage of management work

We may be helped in making sense of all of this by returning to Alan Wilde's equivocality about being a manager. 'To move in managerial circles', he argues, 'means carrying a lot of baggage which you have to handle.' This, it would appear, is the 'social baggage' which goes with involvement in management, as opposed to a task-related burden. It is to do with the social opaqueness and status ambiguity or discomfort of the occupational role. This is implied in his claim that one cannot 'just get on with the job' because 'you are always conscious that people, inside and outside of work don't really understand what you do'. Also, 'you are conscious that your position well up the pecking order' is sometimes 'a help in getting things done – or being well regarded by others inside and outside of work – and sometimes a hindrance or something which makes people not want to know you'. His equivocation about whether he is a manager or a local government officer can be seen as one of the ways in which he discursively handles this aspect of managing to manage.

The managerial nature of management

Alan Wilde tells us that he finds it difficult to put into words what it is about his job that makes it 'managerial'. In spite of a degree of discomfort, he appears to accept that *socially* he can be defined as a manager: through his job title, and through being seen as 'one of the bosses' in the building where he works. When it comes to the *task* element of his job he points to his high level of responsibility and the size of the budget with which he is involved. All of this makes his work managerial – yet he feels that this is undermined by the fact that he doesn't directly 'manage people'. But does it really matter whether Alan Wilde, or anyone else, sees his work as managerial or not? One can argue that some greater clarity about the nature of managerial work is an important social and economic issue relevant to the welfare of every member of an industrialised society. Without a degree of clarity, focus and definition, processes of recruitment into managerial work, processes of management education and management development are inevitably compromised. Wilde himself expressed concern about his own unsureness when he commented that 'There is a problem here: if I am not clear about what a manager is, how do I know how to judge my own managerial performance or how to improve it, let alone know who to appoint or promote in the organisation?'

The people we are looking at in this study have all been appointed to management posts, in some sense of the term; they all face issues of their own training and development, and all can expect to have their managerial performances judged by others in their organisations. So how do they conceive of the managerial task they are engaged in? The conception they have of managerial work is important because it is likely in various ways to 'frame' the way they handle their work tasks. In the research, however, we chose not to ask directly what they believe 'management' to be. We wanted to avoid vague generalizations which were not rooted in their personal experiences and specific organisational or sectoral location. We therefore asked them to tell us what it is about their own job that 'makes it managerial'. We have already seen that this can lead to a degree of equivocation, if not confusion. So be it. There does not appear to be a clear and widely shared notion of just what management is and it is valuable to look at how people engaged in the activity make sense of whatever ambiguities they might feel face them in managing to manage.

In Chapter 1, a theoretically derived and research-informed conception of management and managerial activity was set out and this can provide a set of bench marks or a frame of reference which we can bring to the accounts and reflections which our respondents have given us in the interviews. In the earlier chapter it was argued that the most useful way to think about *management* is as a functional element of a work organisation – the element of the organisational practices and arrangements which is concerned with the directing or steering of the enterprise as whole so that it is able to continue to exist within its environment. Management is an outcome, in effect. And it comes about as a result of the *managing* which occurs in the organisation. This, it was recognised with reference to the body of existing research on managerial behaviour, is a messy, confusing and highly varied set of activities. People employed to contribute to the overall 'steering' task ('managers') will vary in the extent to which they can be seen directly 'commanding' people, planning the work tasks of others, or whatever. So whether, for example, Alan Wilde directly 'manages people' or not is beside the point. He is clearly and centrally involved in management. In our terms he is a manager. He is engaged in activities the key logic of which is to steer and direct his local authority as an organisational entity. But he does not have anything like as clear a notion of his work as this. What about the range of other people we have studied?

'We have no uniformal concept'

When people spoke to us about the ways in which their job was or was not 'managerial', it was quite normal for them to express difficulty with the question. As Jean Holliday commented, in reflecting on how the business manager's job in the National Health Service compared to other managerial jobs, 'We've got no uniformal (sic), universal concept of what management is, have we? And if we've got no uniformal, universal concept, then we can't really compare.' Implicit in Jean's discussion of management in hospitals, which included reference to American as well as British practices, was a recognition of the value of there being some definition of managerial work which everyone could use – not least in identifying 'managerial costs' within health service provision. But she had little idea of what this would look like. However, respondents would often express difficulty with the question at the same time as throwing out a whole series of answers. In part, these appear to derive from a mental checklist of the tasks of 'management' which are found in standard management discourse. Note how Dan

Tracey engages in a dialogue with himself, drawing on various standard managerial discursive resources (budgets, resources, people, planning etc.) as he switches about from 'knowing' and 'not knowing' what is managerial about his work:

What's managerial about it? I suppose you could probably say that, well, you know, I am responsible for a 13 million pound budget. Right? OK. So I guess there's something managerial about that. Something! [*laughs*] What's managerial about it? I don't know. I mean, I'm managing resources, yea? I manage – I manage people who are in the organisation, to achieve what I want to try and achieve, yea? I carry out – I do a lot of planning, which is management, I guess. Yea? I – I'm sometimes exposed, yea? The job I do is quite risky to me personally, yea? Managers aren't – managers don't always have easy jobs – some managers do, some managers don't, yea? I guess I'm paid quite well [*laughs*]. I don't know, I mean, what's management? I don't know.

At the end of this displayed internal dialogue the question has switched from one of what is managerial about his work to one of what management 'is' again. And the answer is, Dan doesn't know. At the same time he does know. There is no final concept of managerial work which he is able to *arrive at*, but there is an *emergent* notion of what it is all about within all the equivocation. And it is one which relates to the social element of the managerial occupation which we considered earlier as well as recognising the task element. In addition to the budgeting, planning and resource references he makes, he alludes to his being well paid, and to his risky and exposed involvement in this 'difficult' job.

'You become an M4 and then you're a manager, OK?'

Dan Tracey is by no means alone in drawing on these 'social' discursive resources. Various people, for example, recognise that they are managerial because they are located in a particular social way within their organisation. One – only half jokingly – said that they were a manager because 'I am one of those who goes to meetings', whilst another pointed to the significance of his chairing meetings of the university department of which he was head. In other cases, people referred to being in a position where they were 'looked up to' or where they were 'always expected to know what is what'.

Another approach is taken by Liz Carter who, having reflected on the variety of different jobs done by people called managers in her food company, becomes almost impatient with her own attempts to identify what makes a job managerial, 'I mean, I think you can get hung up with this, whether you're a manager or you're not a manager. It's not something that's particularly important.' She then turns to formal bureaucratic definitions:

I mean, it's very clear in a lot of companies, I would have thought. They have what we have – a management grading structure. So, as soon as you become an M4, which is the entry level of manager, then you're a manager. OK? You are a manager by definition. But there's so many diverse roles in the organisation that come under M4, M5 and so on, that it's very difficult to actually sort of pin-point, well, why because you're an M4 does that make you a manager?

Liz nevertheless attempts to find something task-related to point to before taking the concluding way out of claimed ignorance.

I suppose, really, at the end of the day, it's having clear defined responsibilities, objectives, you need to work together and achieve. And if you don't, then, you know, you're not doing your job effectively. And that's the only way I can really – really define it. I don't know.

She finally asks, 'Am I making sense?' and one could respond to this by observing that this is exactly what she is doing. She is revealing in her contribution to the interview a process of ongoing sense-making. Although she has no final definition of what makes certain work managerial, there are significant, if vaguely articulated, emergent notions of performance criteria which she would apply in practice when judging what made a manager 'effective'.

Managing people, managing systems

Part of Liz Carter's reflection on managerial work was a debate with herself about whether 'managing people' was significant or not in making one a manager. We saw this earlier in Alan Wilde's reflections. And it arises time and time again in the words of our respondents. It seems to be a starting point in the standard discursive framework within which we all locate management to take a manager to be someone who is in charge of other people and who directs them to run a shop or win football matches. This may go back to people's childhood and non-work experiences of seeing particular people identified as 'the manager'. But, frequently, people move on from reference to the stereotypical people-manager to say things like, 'But I think that it is managing resources which is the issue, and people may or may not be one of these resources for a particular manager', or 'It is getting the results by whatever means, whether people directly come into it or not' or 'You may not actually direct any staff of your own, but if you are a manager you will be affecting or influencing what happens to people somewhere in the business if not across the whole piece.'

Mary Rainey tries to bring clarity to these issues by developing a notion of a 'proper manager'. She recognises that she was doing managerial tasks as a senior nurse but now in her job as 'the manager of six surgical wards and the outpatients' she is a 'proper manager'. Whereas she was 'at the top level in the ward environment', she is now 'sort of like bottom rung on the management level' and 'it's more ... well, instead of working with people, it's working with systems, making sure that they're all in place and that things move properly'. Others spoke similarly of 'identifying priorities for others', 'setting targets and monitoring performances' and 'facilitating the work of those managers who do directly manage people'.

Operational and functional, operational and strategic

One discursive resource which some people used to help with these matters was that of a distinction between 'levels' or 'types' of managerial post. Dan Tracey makes a distinction within his logistics company where 'we have two very distinct types of manager. We have what we call *operational* managers, yea, and then we have like *functional* managers.' He explains,

What I mean by an operational manager is effectively a manager that manages an operation – a particular service, yes? He's responsible to the customer for the levels of service and the cost of manning that service. He's responsible for managing the people, yea? And managing the aspirations and the motivation of those people. Very much man management. But very much – and very much – service management. It's operational, day-to-day, get in there, do the job, yea?

Dan explains that he did such a job but has now moved into 'the second stream, which is more like functional management, yea?' He explains that

I'm in a business development role at this moment in time. I'm responsible for getting new business into here – getting new business from the customer for my company Topclass Logistics. So, I'm going out meeting customers, putting together solutions for them, tendering for business and doing presentations. Now I don't actually – at the moment now – I don't have anybody directly responsible to me. I had 90 people working for me before, but that's now gone, and it's a different – completely different process.

We can note that Dan is using the word 'functional' in a way about which he is not entirely sure. He is not using the word in the conventional way, to distinguish a 'non-line' job like that of a personnel or accounting manager from that of a 'line' manager, although his particular personal usage is close to this. He is in no doubt that he is a manager in the business and this would fit our own conception of how 'management' is most usefully to be conceptualised – as dealing with the broad direction of the organisation as a whole. A discursive resource he might have used here would be that of working 'strategically' within management. Such a notion is utilised by Jean Holliday who explains that her 'definition of management falls into two main categories'. There is *strategic* or 'long term management' and *operational* management which is 'day-to-day'. The first of these, she says, primarily involves *planning* whilst the second involves *implementation.* The 'bit' she was recently doing, she explains, was 'operational' whilst 'the bit that I've got buttoned on to now is strategic'. Like Dan Tracey, Jean is involved with the strategic direction of her organisation through dealing with 'the contracting process of basically saying how many patients we can envisage we're going to treat, and then making sure we've got contracts that bring money in to treat that number of patients'.

Framing management responsibilities: sectional and corporate

Both Tracey and Holliday make their dual distinctions about managerial jobs in the process of identifying the way their own managerial career has emerged. They are conscious that the responsibility they currently have is different from a previous one. But the broad type of distinction they are developing to help make sense of their own experiences can be helpful when looking for patterns in the diverse accounts we have heard across our range of emergent managers. Beneath all the ambiguity and confusion there appear to be two underlying notions which are used when talking about what makes the managerial role 'managerial'. The first of these is to locate the main responsibility of the manager as being for the 'performance' or 'output' of a specific unit, department, branch or team within an organisation. This is a discursive strategy of 'framing' the job in terms of a *sectional responsibility* within the employing organisation. The second approach to discursively framing the role involves a rhetoric of *corporate responsibility.*

A sectional focus

The notion of sectional responsibility has a clear logic which appears to fit well with the circumstances of many of those who speak along such lines. Mark Taylor, for example, had a clear and specific 'territory' within the engineering company when he worked as an 'operations team manager'. This job title is interesting, because it covers the dual aspect of his work: that of heading a 'team' of people and that of fulfilling certain 'operations' through that team. As in many of these accounts it is the people or 'team' side that is referred to first:

You're managing a team – a number of operators – of, say, 60; you have a team leader – a supervisor; you have material people – that's people who get the parts from the other stores and get them there on time. You have engineers, who are the guys who solve the problems, supposedly. In your cell, you've also got your quality people.

He then moves on to the tasks that are performed through the orchestration of all these players:

So, you're basically trying to run all these various different functions. You are trying to get the job out as efficiently as you can; at as low a cost as possible, at the best quality possible, and to a schedule that everybody's agreed on. You are basically managing a lot of people to try and get these activities out, within set measures that you are measured against.

We see a similar pattern where Charles Parker, who is in his 'first step up', 'first line' management post in a housing association, initially talks about the 'team' he is responsible for before going on to more substantive aspects of his 'territory':

I've got line management responsibility for a team of four people.
It's having a team that makes the job managerial?
Yeah. It's a small team and they carry out all the administration of the office. I have direct line of responsibility for them. It's everything – appointments, appraisals, disciplinaries, leave entitlements, supervision. Anything, you name it, we've got it.
So you're in charge of a group of people?
Yeah.
But aren't you also in charge of an area of housing?
Yeah, I'm the manager of a small patch which is in Old Fairport, of about 60 houses. And in addition to those two things, I've got management responsibility for the system of allocating rented houses.

In this case the link between the 'people managing' role and other responsibilities is nothing like as close as that of Mark Taylor. But, without prompting, Charles Parker might well not even have mentioned his not inconsiderable non-people-supervisory responsibilities. Once again we can infer the influence of the discursively central notion or stereotype of the manager as someone in charge of people.

A popular discursive device which often plays its part in the rhetoric of sectional responsibility is that of 'the buck stops here'. Notice how it is used in Ron Scott's account of his job and his comparing of his prison wing managerial responsibilities with those of an industrial manager:

I look after the everyday running of the wing and deal with any problems that crop up on that side of it. Ordering stationery, you know, making sure that – well any problems that crop up during the whole day, really. You're responsible for about a hundred and six inmates and five members of staff. You can put that in perspective [by comparing] it to a shop floor manager. It's quite something to be responsible for so many people – you're managing people, whether they be prisoners, or whether they be staff. They're still people. So, yes, I sometimes, think to myself, 'Crikey, you know, I'm the only person here. The buck stops with me really'.

This being the 'only one there' is also referred to by Ellen Fitzgerald in talking about her building society branch manager job:

It's managerial because of the responsibility for people in a location that is off-site. It is a branch of the Society. There's nobody else there. The buck stops with me. If there are any decisions to be taken, it's me that has the final say on whether those decisions go ahead or not. So I have the responsibility and the accountability for the whole managerial operation of that branch. It's within given targets and objectives, you know, that are set higher up within the central organisation. But that's what makes it managerial. And as I've already said, it's the responsibility for a team of staff.

It is interesting that, once again, an account of a manager's range and variety of responsibilities is framed (opened and closed in this case) with reference to the team of people. We have suggested that this can be understood as a reflection of the way in which managerial work is conventionally framed discursively as 'people management'. And it can also be seen as reflecting the ultimate inseparability of the social and task elements of management work – with the task or technical element always having to be humanised through the prioritising of the 'people aspect' of the job. This is something done in a distinctive way by one of the youngest managers, Liza Potts. People are prioritised by Liza through her aspiration, in principle at least, to manage herself out of her own job. She refers first to the tasks to be done and especially to 'prioritising – asking for things to be done and ensuring that things that are done routinely are being done to a standard'. But, introducing her principle of managerial self abolition, she turns to the social dimension of her work and 'at the same time as all of this, building the team and keeping the team together – getting people to work with each other'. She explains that her 'total aim is for the department to manage itself. It means giving people the power to manage themselves.' Management is managed here by setting out to manage oneself out of having to manage.

A corporate focus

Liza Potts is focusing here on her department but there is a move from a *sectional responsibility* style of discourse towards a *corporate responsibility* one when she explains her notion of 'prioritising' by referring to the 'quality of service to customers' which 'the business is going to be dependent on if it is going to cope with the competition which we face from the other big stores'. Her ideal is to get the members of her team to think in this way – to see that 'they have a part to play in the business and not just a blinkered job to do'. Stanley Jordan, who is also concerned about the 'service to the public' provided by the bingo hall he manages, speaks similarly. Note how initially in the interview he has to deal with the 'people management' convention:

So in what ways is yours a managerial job?
You mean is it about managing people?
Well, whatever.
No, I feel . . . No, I say no. Why do I say no?
No to what?
'No' to the idea that I am managerial because I manage people. Managing people is not something you're ever completely good at. I think it's an on-going experience, because you're indeed managing your own ability to mix with people. And you can never be completely – I don't think you can ever be completely in control of it, totally, all the time.
So it's what?
You are there to drive a business forward. That's the purpose of all of you being there, it's a common denominator.

Stan suggests that his relationship to the people working in his bingo hall is one in which he strives to get everybody working towards a common purpose. 'Having accepted your salary, your terms and conditions of employment and ending up doing a job of work – whether you're pitching tents, or working in a factory, or a pub, or in a solicitor's office, in a court of law, what have you – then basically you all accept that you're there for a common purpose.' And what is this purpose? 'The agenda', Stan says, 'is what the business dictates.'

The words used by Julian Adderley are slightly different but suggest a similar discursive move when he explains that 'our philosophy within the business is that we don't really want managers sort of *per se*, really, who are there just to manage'. He suggests that such managers are not really 'generating revenue' and what the 'business wants' is to have 'as many people as possible generate revenue'. When describing his work in the software company he says that

It's project management, it's consultancy, it's meeting the customers, it's systems analysis work, that sort of thing. I'm doing a fair amount of that. And generally, there's dealing with the people here. And this entails getting people to 'understand' that what we do is not just as a department but as a company. We're a service industry, and we have to provide service to customers. If we don't provide a service, this is what the customer says to us, we all get hassle, we all get problems. You get the chairman shouting at you, or me shouting at you.

Andrew Shepherd, in a similar vein, talks about the 'excellent people' he has working in his branch of the bank but talks of how he is beginning to demand 'more of them' in terms of a more corporate focus. He wants them to be guided in their action by 'thinking about the bank like I think about the bank'. He has an 'admin manager' who is 'functionally superb' but only thinks at the level of administration and he has a deputy manager who 'concentrates on his customers' rather than how they fit into the 'broader picture'. Andrew sees his own role as 'more global' and more 'strategic' in how he relates his branch to the bank as a whole. He worries that other managers have a 'narrower view than this of what their job entails' and would like to get them sharing what he calls, 'if I can put it politely, this enlightened vision'.

Much of this corporate responsibility rhetoric uses as a key discursive resource the notion of 'the business'. Different words are used by those public sector managers who speak of their job in corporate rather than sectional terms, however. Carrie Bley describes her further education college finance director job as 'managerial in almost every aspect'. She talks about 'still doing some tasks' – such as 'doing the budget' and 'administering the governing body' yet identifies her 'ultimate role' as 'to try and ensure the survival of the organisation'. Lucy Armstrong also works in a further education college as the student services manager and describes detailed tasks like 'doing the budget for my area'. But she is anxious to distinguish between what she calls the 'fine detail' and the 'broad sweep'. Getting the budget to balance is a matter of 'fine detail' but this has always to be seen within the 'broad sweep' of how the college is 'performing in its environment'. She relates this to the 'new type of management culture' which has evolved in further education – a 'culture of accountability'. Survival of the college in a 'very difficult environment' makes the role of the manager in further education much more like that of a manager in the business world, Lucy suggests.

Survival of his organisation, as such, is not referred to by Tom Smith, but having explained the detailed court procedures for which he is responsible, he talks of the 'ultimate thing'. 'Our overall priority', he says, 'is to make sure you can keep the court running, if you see what I mean. Come hell or high water – if you've organised a court to go ahead, there will be someone there to take it, I mean, that's the ultimate thing.' Tom continues, however, by moving from this very corporate-sounding talk of the 'ultimate thing' to mention very specific and detailed tasks which he might carry out. To keep the court running he might, for example, have to take on the role of an absent staff member and, for example, 'go in and be a technical clerk'.

Keeping in touch with the real action

In making this shift from references to 'overview' aspects of the management role – corporate or sectional – to carrying out very 'hands on' functions, Tom is following a pattern seen in many of our managers' accounts of their work. It seems important for them to stress that managerial work is not a matter of 'hovering at a very great height above the real action ' as one manager put it. Kathy Westbrook is currently the assistant manager of a restaurant and she feels that she is 'at the stage where I could run my own restaurant'. She has the whole overview of the task, including an understanding of 'the profit aspect'. In spite of the fact that 'each manager in the company runs his restaurant like it's his own business', Kathy recognises that

You've got to be very flexible in a job like this, and so adaptable. You've just got to be wherever you're needed, basically. You could spend a day just sorting out paper work, and things, you know – and not even necessarily being in the restaurant, but being in the office, sorting out business, or training or whatever. Other days, you've got to be very hands on, and running around and – like today – I've spent the whole day just clearing and setting tables and it's really got me mad . . . You see all the waitresses, like, running about and earning their tips, and I'm just clearing up after them. But you have to be prepared to do that.

This is a matter more of necessity than choice, it would seem. Liza Potts, on the other hand, chooses to work on the checkout tills in her supermarket from time to time. She points out that 'this can be to fill a gap' but that 'it also shows the staff that I am not above doing an ordinary job'. However, she adds that 'it is invaluable to me managerially' because 'you can judge a great deal about what is going on in the store, and how well your own staff are performing, from what you see at the checkout'. For Diane Washington, on the other hand, it is central to her personal career strategy and to her notion of professional credibility that in spite of being the manager of her specialism she maintains a direct 'clinical input'. She has actually developed an office manager's post to take on 'a lot of the administrative tasks so that I can say I am still a physiotherapist'. And, as Jean Holliday observes, it can be very difficult in health service management to 'split out what's management from what's clinical'. She illustrates this:

It might be a justifiable clinical decision that this patient wants a bandage on each leg. However, if you've only got three bandages to last you the week, you prioritise that patient's needs against the other patients'. You are always having to balance the clinical and the managerial, the strategic and the operational.

Managing the challenge

Jean Holliday describes the need constantly to 'balance' these various aspects of her jobs as 'a key challenge'. In Chapter 1, we observed that the notion of *challenge* is often a central one in the way managerial work is framed in job advertisements. Jenny Holly spoke of the advertisement for her own job and how it involved, in her reading, an invitation to 'rise to a challenge' (p. 5). But the challenge she sees in the advertisement's discursive framing of the post is a double one and it incorporates the two types of discursive framing of responsibilities which we have noted in the present chapter – a sectional framing and a corporate one. There was both the sectional challenge of turning the 'bunch of people' Jean managed into a 'dedicated team' and the more corporate challenge of working 'strategically' to 'take the service forward into the next century'. Jenny was conscious of a degree of 'hype' here, but nevertheless appears to take seriously this rather grandiose challenge as well as the more immediate – but perhaps no less grandiose in practice – one of building a 'team' within her section of the larger corporate entity. But these are ways of talking about managerial work we tend to hear when the speaker is standing well back from the everyday realities of actually *doing management*. What we want to focus on here are the more mundane 'challenges' which our managers identify when they look at their ongoing work activities. What do they find they are 'up against', what do they find most difficult to cope with, what do they find challenges them most when it comes to handling the managerial tasks which they have taken on?

It is almost a cliché of everyday managerial discourse that the greatest challenge, headache, frustration, or 'pain' of managing is 'people'. Cleverley tells the story of an observant and self-confident executive at a corporate dinner who was bold enough to ask the company chairman why it was that whenever he used the word 'people' in his after-dinner speech he did so 'through clenched teeth' (1971). And in her study of nineteen new American managers, Hill (1992) notes how 'unequivocally' they spoke of the 'people challenge' as the biggest issue in their first year in the managerial post. In our own conversations with managers we found variations of a standard joke which is frequently found in occupations which deal with people: 'It would be easy to manage the factory if it wasn't for the workers,' 'The school would be straightforward to manage if it wasn't for the pupils, the teachers, the head, the parents . . . ,' 'Without the colleagues this place would be a doddle to run' and 'Sometimes you say at the end of a hard day, wouldn't this job be great if there were no patients, no consultants, no nurses to deal with.' As we shall see, the 'people challenge', in various forms, was a major one for our managers and this could be seen as inevitable given that managerial work by its very nature is a social activity – a 'people' thing. However, we can helpfully continue here to use the distinction we made earlier in this chapter between the *social* aspects of managerial work and the *task* aspects. Therefore, before we examine the various different ways in which we heard managers speak of the 'people challenge' of their work, we will look at a number of respects in which they pointed to what might be identified as task aspects of what they are 'up against' in their work.

Keeping on top of it all

It was quite clear to us that none of the managers with whom we spent time had an easy or a quiet life at work and a key challenge for many was simply that of 'keeping on top of it all', to quote a phrase heard more than once. It was far from uncommon for the manager simply to point straightforwardly to the scale of the job. Ted Ellington, for example, said of his work as a quality manager, 'The challenges, the tasks are just immense, you know; they really are absolutely phenomenal', illustrating this with the observation that 'sometimes it requires working all day and night'. Such comments were typically framed in the language of 'challenge', as in this case, rather than in terms of strain or stress. However, Sally Vaughan after speaking of the 'hard work' and the 'high level of pressure' in her marketing management job recognises that this is 'good while you are young and you've got the ideas and the energy and stuff'. But she worries about when she is older and 'getting to middle-age and, like, really sort of cracking under the strain of it all'. She can cope with the load now but does not know whether she will be doing such a job in fifteen years 'because I think it's the sort of job that you can burn out in'.

It was most obviously in the public sector that the shortage of resources was spoken of as the most challenging aspect of the job. Lucy Armstrong spoke of the situation in further education 'getting out of hand'. She spoke of it 'getting really difficult to deliver' the student services for which she is responsible. Her staff are simply 'up to here' which means that she has to take on more student counselling work herself than she ought to. Consequently she feels, 'I'm being squeezed I suppose. I'm kind of trying to take some of the pressure off the people that I line manage, but I've got no leeway any other way, if you see what I mean.' Health service managers similarly identified resource constraints as key issues in their jobs and Jean Holliday, from her perspective as a business manager in a hospital, spoke of such 'issues' as 'totally out of our control' – the problem in her view being the very fundamental one that the National Health Service will simply not be able to 'continue in existence' because 'as I see it . . . the problem is that our economy can't afford the health service.'

Crises and loss of control

Where Jean Holliday identifies these large-scale structural issues reducing her ability to 'achieve control' in her health service business planning, Diane Washington instead illustrates the more operational ways in which the health service manager can 'feel . . . out of control of what is going on'. She says that the 'hardest thing to handle is balancing the clinical work with the managerial work' and the feeling of loss of control comes from constantly having one's plan for the working day disturbed:

Well, you would think that if you are a manager, you could set your day out, and say 'I've got that meeting to go to at that time, and I'll do paper work between here and here, and I've got to get this report out, so I'll do it there'. I do this. And then I get a phone call from the ward saying there'll be four new patients coming in. Then orthopaedics give me a ring, and there'll be two patients that need seeing there. All your planning's gone. You set your time aside to do whatever, but your door's open and somebody'll come and say, 'I've got this problem with such and such, can you help me with this?'. Then somebody else'll get on the phone about something else. And I think that sometimes it's just . . . I suppose you feel that you're out of control.

Managers in various sectors spoke in similar terms about 'fire-fighting' or 'crisis management' as something which particularly challenged them because they felt that their job should involve more than simply reacting to immediate pressures. Colin Hawkins spoke in very similar terms to Diane Washington about frequently having to abandon his 'plan for the day' – worked out during his forty-five minute drive to work. Because of what he describes as the 'the never ending crisis or chaos' which he experiences in residential social work management he feels that he too often 'gets involved in things that I don't feel that I should be involved in at all'. Eddie Hayes brings together the particular pressures of a training manager's job with the 'contract driven nature' of the construction company he works in. He gives a good insight into the work he does as he illustrates the problems which arise for him:

I mean, I had a classic this morning. I came in and found this envelope on my desk. I opened it. So what's inside? It's joining instructions for a course for one of our commercial graduates. It starts tomorrow – but she's gone to Scotland for a week. And over the weekend she's realised that she's going on this course tomorrow and forgotten all about it, you know, and she's gone up to Scotland for a week. So she's not going on the course. So I'm left now with a spare place on a two-day course that I'll have to pay for. But that quite often happens. We'll get a problem on site and the engineer has to be there, or there's an engineer who's got a particular skill, and there's a problem on another site so he gets shipped across there. That happens on a regular basis. I would probably say that – I don't know, every third or fourth course that I book gets cancelled or gets re-arranged. Thirty, forty percent of my nominations for courses either never get to the course – probably even higher if I worked it out. It's a real juggling act. So actually planning coherent programmes and training becomes exceedingly difficult.

Eddie sees it as important to his role as a training manager to have planned and coherent programmes. But the crises that arise on construction sites in this contract-driven business which has to prioritise on-site problem-solving fundamentally challenge his ability to do this.

Time sheets, meetings and nitty gritty paperwork

In contrast to those managers who stressed having to cope with challenges to control, to routine and to a planned day, others spoke of aspects of their job which were much more routine but which similarly, in their view, distracted them from the work they should be doing. Some people simply talked of coping with boredom, as Harry Lyttleton did when he told us how he 'gets bored with doing time sheets and gets bored with checking people's work sheets'. He strove to get this out of the way in 'a couple of hours first thing in the factory on a Monday'. However, Will Evans talked of his overall efficiency, both as a teacher and as a manager, being undermined by the pressure of 'so many meetings and things'.

Complaints about paperwork and meetings are common in all bureaucratised work settings but we often see managers quite seriously challenged by the pressures these create – pressures which can go well beyond having to do tasks to which one does not feel temperamentally suited. Sally Vaughan is clearly not fond of administration and says that 'anything to do with number crunching drives me up the wall'. She admits she does not like doing such work but suggests that there is more of a problem than simply one of personal preference. She says that 'the really boring things like sales forecasting, just like all the nitty-gritty sort of paperwork, are the bane of my life'. She explains that she has to 'manage the promotional money that I spend on the product' but that she has to contend with 'this awful purchasing system where you have to raise requisitions and have them signed and then you've got to match them back to your order and your invoice'. Such 'really tedious book-keeping and things', she says, 'drive me insane'. This is to do with her conception of her marketing management job, she suggests, and not just to do with her personal tastes; 'I sit there doing it for hours on end thinking, you know, that I could be doing something so much more productive which would be doing some good for the product and for the company.' But instead she is 'sitting here doing these stupid invoices'. She admits that 'it is not interesting and not exciting' but claims that it really has her 'bashing my head against the wall' because she should really be doing something 'much more productive'.

'It's woolly, very very woolly'

Where some managers speak as if they have a clear idea of what they should be doing in their jobs, others feel that they are left too vague as to what is expected of them. In some cases this is a problem relating to a specific set of organisational circumstances – such as the 'contract-driven' nature of Eddie Hayes' company, which created particular problems for him. Liza Potts suggests, for example, that the greatest challenge facing the shopfloor retail manager day-to-day is being left 'to plan or structure my own time'. She specifically relates this to the weekly nature of the deadline which a departmental manager in a supermarket has to meet. She explains that 'You are aware that this or that has to be done at some point in the week – as long as it is in the in-tray by Monday. So how do you prioritise? There is no one checking up on you, there is no-one motivating you, or looking for standards in the job.' Dan Tracey speaks similarly about a personal preference for having something 'clearly defined for me before I set to try to achieve it' but argues that his senior management fail him in this respect, frequently leaving him with 'ambiguous tasks and objectives'. He personally dislikes this and sees it as counter-productive in task terms:

I find it quite disturbing, because at the end of the day, you can spend time – you spend a lot of time wasting your time, if you see what I mean. I like things quite clearly defined. You're mobilising a lot of resources, spending a lot of money, and you're trying to stimulate people and motivate people to achieve a particular goal, yea, and it wasn't what we were trying to achieve in the first place. And the last thing I want is to have to keep going back and saying, 'Well OK, sorry, we've got it wrong, we – you know – we weren't communicating it properly and we're going to have to start all over again.' That demotivates people. You don't get the best out of people that way.

Where Dan blames his senior management in general terms for this state of affairs, Tom Smith points specifically to the individual to whom he is deputy and suggests that he 'never makes it clear what it is he wants me to do'. Tom's role, he says, is not clearly defined and he moves between what we might call a personal and a structural explanation. The structural explanation relates to the tension in any court between 'the quality of justice and the need to be efficient'. Within this, however, there is 'my boss's failure to be a manager'. This is in part because he is primarily a lawyer but it is 'also because we've got these characters on the magistrates courts committee, who are his direct bosses and they don't know what they want him to do either'. This leaves Tom 'trying to sort of make some clear definitions from below'. Doing this, however 'is fraught . . . the whole thing is woolly, very very woolly'.

The people challenge: difficult cases, awkward sods and 'bloody human nature'

So far we having been stressing the task-related challenges which managers suggest they face in their day-to-day work. We must not go too far, however, in separating these from issues of human relationships – as the accounts given by both Tracey and Smith should make us aware. Other managers spoke of problems created for them by the senior managers with whom they work, as did these two men. Mary Rainey, for example, has particular problems managing her job as the result of a bad relationship with her immediate hierarchical superior as we shall see later when we look at the broad 'human relationship' issue of organisational or managerial politics. For the present, however, we consider what our managers have to tell us about the 'people challenge' in the way which Hill (1992) used it – to refer to problems of managing 'subordinates'. Insofar as one can create a pattern from the myriad of accounts which we have collected on this issue, we would suggest that people talk in three broad ways about the challenge of what is sometimes called 'managing people': difficult cases, awkward sods and people in general ('bloody human nature').

The first – the *difficult cases* – way in which managers spoke of problems as a 'manager of people' was to point to the particular challenge they felt when having either to discipline an employee or to remove them from their job in one way or another. Shirley Stitt speaks of the 'nightmare' of 'having to do a disciplinary'. She 'had to do a formal disciplinary within two or three months of being in the job' which entailed 'giving a formal warning to a man who was sexually harassing one of the women'. Others, in speaking of the most challenging things they have had to do, talk of 'asking someone to retire through ill health'; 'telling people that their job no longer exists'; 'warning people about their poor attendance'; 'handling difficult or distressing cases like getting rid of people or having to cut people's hours'. Why are these things picked out as especially difficult? When asked this we would be told such things as 'if anybody tells you they enjoy getting rid of people, they are a bloody liar or they are a sadist'. Ellen Fitzgerald, however, went further than most people who were especially concerned about this aspect of their jobs by explaining that a mixture of factors are at work. First she speaks of a fear of not being liked or trusted. Then there is a 'moral worry' about denying somebody a job and an income that they and their family need ('however inadequate they have been in their job'). On a more task-related level there is the fear of creating 'an un-settled atmosphere within the team' whilst at a very personal level there is the 'little nagging sensation that you are just not personally comfort-able with what you are doing – you are just not naturally this hard'.

In this 'difficult cases' category, the managers are talking about a particular type of task which typically involves giving bad news to an individual employee. The challenge for the manager is one of handling the specific task rather than one of dealing with an especially difficult individual. This takes us to the second – *the awkward sods* – type of 'people problem', a category of challenge which was indeed referred to on one occasion as the 'the awkward sod problem', on another occasion as 'the difficult character situation' and another time as 'the non-per-formance or chronically under-performing issue'. There was also a reference to 'dealing with bolshy bastards'. More specifically, Mary Rainey spoke of two nurses whom she believed were 'working the system' by taking the maximum sick leave that was possible under their contracts of employment, and Charles Parker referred to an 'extremely difficult member of staff who got pretty close to running rings round me'. Two factory managers, Mark Taylor and Arthur Blakey, referred, respectively, to 'rabble raisers' within work groups and to 'all sorts of shites' that you can find within a work team, whilst Ted Ellington spoke of 'those people who are very verbose and need controlling' – either through being 'spoken to diplomatically' or through the manager 'finding a way to embarrass them or something'.

We were told by one of the managers that he had seen courses adver-tised for managers who find that the 'stroppy-customer type of employee is a big thing for them in their job'. The existence of such a course was taken by this commentator to be an indicator of just how significant 'this type of bugbear is' for many managers. Indeed we found that our managers tended more frequently to point to the chal-lenge of handling specific difficult employees than to employees in general. Nevertheless, there were significant examples of managers saying that the key issue for them, in the people sphere, was the general one of our third category, which we name after the colourful phrase used (but immediately and, with embarrassment, apologised for) by the manager who said that the biggest challenge for him in his job was coming to terms with 'bloody human nature'.

The *bloody human nature* type of 'people challenge' is often dealt with in the 'if only it wasn't for the workers' humourous manner referred to earlier. Alicia Coltrane, for example, tells us

When I was a housing assistant I used to joke that this job would be all right if it wasn't for the tenants. Now I think the tenants are lovely [*laughing*] and I would much rather get rid of the staff.
Seriously though?
No, but for some staff, whatever you do is never good enough. I am doing my best but a lot is beyond my control. I should not take this personally, but I do take it personally when people are still dissatisfied with terms and conditions or feel they have been hard done to.
Why do they?
They think there is a hidden agenda when there isn't.

Alicia takes us back here to the problem of finding there are things she cannot control and for her the 'people challenge' is one which leads to her feeling hurt because of the suspicions and dissatisfactions which staff continually express – whatever she does. Colin Hawkins similarly speaks of his frustrations and his striving to overcome the 'bickering, in-fighting and talking behind people's back' which he had to confront in the residential social work setting. Others spoke in similar terms and would tend to shrug and make a comment like 'Well, it's just people, isn't it.' Some managers, however, were more specific and spoke about the major people challenge in terms similar to what old-fashioned industrial sociologists sometimes called 'resistance to change'. This one-time popular discursive resource was not used by any of our managers. Instead, the tendency was to talk in terms such as 'the length of time it takes to get people to understand things'. Liz Carter, for example, spoke about her task as a personnel manager of 'getting these performance management systems into place'. This was something that each employee could benefit from. It was 'something actually specifically for the individual, an individual development plan that they could then work towards'. In spite of this she struggled to 'make headway' in 'putting it in place'. This was 'very frustrating'. Ted Ellington spoke in a similar way about his frustrations in getting employees to understand the principles or 'concepts' behind the quality management practices he was responsible for developing and implementing:

It's the time things take. People don't understand. People in the organisation are very 'tasky'. To get them to think of these things – these sort of conceptual-type things – and then convert them into the real world, it's very difficult for them. And you have to be ever so careful. If they don't understand it, then they'll kick against it, and it creates problems. So, you have to ensure that you assist the capability of the rate of the drip feed. You know, otherwise, you create problems. Because if they see too – if they see it too fuzzy, too conceptual, then they don't see the benefit, and then they start talking about it and they get negative about it, and you've got a problem.

The politics of management and the management of politics

The 'people challenges' we have been looking at so far are generally ones relating to influencing and shaping the behaviour of people subordinate to the manager in the hierarchical structure. However, these issues have to be seen in the context of the wider institutional pattern of power relationships in the organisation. The way in which work organisations are structured – and especially the way they encourage managers themselves to become rivals with each other for scarce and valued resources and rivals for career advancement – is widely seen by social scientists as making 'micropolitics' or *managerial politics* inevitable and endemic in bureaucratised enterprises (Burns 1961; Jackall 1988; Pettigrew 1973; Watson 1977; Watson 1995c). The political dimension of managerial life was something spoken of in one way or another by all of our managers. It was frequently seen as a challenge for the individual but, however regrettable its pervasiveness might be, it was often recognised as inevitable or, as several people put it, 'It comes with the territory.'

Ego, domination and back-stabbing

Some managers made sense of what we are calling the political dimension of management by viewing it in a way similar to the 'human nature' category considered above. Stan Jordan, for example, spoke about 'mankind's need to acquire, dominate, control power'. He saw this as a factor both in the way businesses relate to each other ('I'm sure Napoleon was the same [as business leaders] in always wanting to get another country and loot some more wealth from it') and in the way managers within organisations operate. Mina Mangeshkar used psychological discursive resources to account for political behaviour saying that 'It's back to ego – all that rubbish. It's self gratification. Everything is for self.' However, she felt that the circumstances of her own organisation – the approach of the senior managers in particular – meant that this general human tendency operated destructively rather than being 'channelled' as she felt it could be with the development of a culture in which there was 'give' as well as 'take'. Instead of people setting out 'to get the job done' there was a shocking degree of 'pettiness, nastiness and back-stabbing'.

Interests and hidden agendas

One discursive resource whose use rivals that of the notion of politics itself in our managers' accounts is that of the *hidden agenda*. We have already come across this when it was used by Alicia Coltrane with reference to her staff. Jack Dodds, however, used the term in a broader way and spoke about the challenge of 'seeing through the smokescreens' set up by senior managers in his university and of generally working out the 'hidden agendas' of the various individuals and constituencies he dealt with. This was a commonly discussed way of speaking about politics and Ted Ellington was not unusual in denying that he was a political operator himself whilst, at the same time, making it clear that this was precisely what he needed to be:

I'm not a political animal at all, but other people are. And as long as you're aware of what their hidden agendas are, you can use that to your advantage. The skill is knowing the difference between what they say, and what they really intend, you know. They all have different agendas, they all want different things, and it's just being shrewd enough to identify what direction they're going in, if at times it's different to their sort of published agenda. If you know what people's interests are, and where they want things to go, and you're doing something in that area, they're far more useful than somebody that isn't. I mean, there's no point in having people that are opposed to what you want to do.

This type of account sees 'interests' as central to political intrigue but doesn't focus on any particular type of interest. Others, however, tend to stress one of two broad types of interest: 'territorial' interests or career advancement interests.

Territorial rivalries and whipping boys

Mary Rainey explains that in the hospital 'you have to ring-fence, defend, be very protective of your territory' and illustrates this by pointing to the way she has to cope with the decisions made by a 'particular person' within the management who has 'no particular loyalty to any specialty or anything' but has to 'make sure that beds, nursing, doctors and everything will be available for the patients of whatever specialty when they arrive'. This can mean that Mary has to face the possibility that this other manager may 'take one of my nurses' to another part of the hospital to help out or say that 'you will accept some transfers of medical patients – without it having been agreed by you'. Colin Hawkins speaks in similar terms of having to deal with being 'manipulated by other managers' and illustrates the problem with a story about a difficult young social work client who ended up – in Colin's view inappropriately – in prison as a result of wrangles which had occurred within social services, especially between 'adult services and children's services'. A clash between territories led to a potentially disastrous outcome.

Harry Lyttleton suggests that it is quite normal to see political disputes in manufacturing between production and engineering. The engineer, he says, often finds himself the 'whipping boy for production':

You'll find that with every engineer. If something's gone wrong, it's engineering's fault. That means it's your fault and you have to deal with it – even if it's them that's done the problem. Yea, I've had what we call dummy damage – which is where equipment has gone wrong and failed because the operator has failed to recognise a problem. You know, it's gone out of spec, and before you know it, bang, it's gone down. And then all hell's broke out because you've got to get this piece of equipment going again, because you've got forty, fifty people in the production area doing nothing. And all the pressures are on you then to get that machine going again, and it's the engineer's fault because the machine's down.

Harry says that he finds 'that type of thing very frustrating', but, not at all untypically adds, 'but that comes with the territory, that does'.

Clambering over each other to get on

The bureaucratic control structures which create the organisational territories within work organisations function, at the same time, as career ladders for the managers who rule these territories, as Burns (1961) pointed out in his classic writing on 'micropolitics'. This aspect of political activity was often noted by our managers and references were made, for example, to colleagues 'doing you down, even in front of your staff' or to people 'slagging you off behind your back', something which Shirley Stitt puts down to people trying to prove that they, rather than you, are the 'top dog' and have 'the upper hand'. She sees this especially prevalent among 'young production managers' who are 'clambering over each other to get on'. She gets 'caught up in all that from time to time' but struggles to 'keep out of the cross-fire' – a claim which is reminiscent of Carrie Bley's talk of her striving to 'stay out of the game' as individuals from different 'power bases in the college' fight one another.

Most managers did not, however, expect to stay above or out of organisational politics and career competitiveness. Career rivalry and the unpleasantness which often goes with it, whilst typically regretted, were again spoken of as 'something which goes with the territory' (this meaning 'goes with the managerial job' in general terms as opposed to going with a sectional interest). Kathy Westbrook spoke with particular eloquence of career politics in the restaurant business she was in:

If you want to get on in this business it's all down to politics. If you want to get on you've got to creep to the right people. It's horrible and I hate it. I mean you can see people that are getting on because they've crept to the area manager who has to have his little favourite person in the area. This character does his tricks and everything and he gets on. I mean it's not all – it's not down to politics. I mean, yeah, he had to have a certain talent in the first place to get known . . . But from then on in, you know, he did a bit of bum-licking and was seen in the right places and he's away.

Kathy gives a further illustration of what she saw with this particular 'classic bum-licker' by referring back to a job she had had in a previous restaurant where

There was another girl there who was in the same situation as me. She was also a classic case of playing politics. She had been trained in a certain way which was very standards orientated. I'd been trained in a way that was more relaxed and more, like, people-development orientated. So, yeah, I might have put slices in the wrong place or not got the cake out or something – you know not particularly difficult things. But she'd be like, 'Kathy hasn't done that and Kathy hasn't done this'. She would always be, like, looking to put – not just necessarily myself but other people – down. She would say 'I've had to do this to rectify it' and make herself look better.

This woman has apparently 'played it quite well', because 'she's got on really well'. However, Kathy goes on to suggest that the woman has done no better than herself in career terms and that, as the area manager is 'beginning to notice her tricks', she is finding her tactics 'backfiring on her'. This fear of one's career-political stratagems backfiring on one is a danger that others noted and can be seen as especially important in what one manager referred to as 'the challenge of being political whilst not being too political' and another as 'the subtle skill of advancing your career without being too obvious about it'.

These subtleties of managing to do a managerial job and of managing the politics of both territoriality and career are ones which our managers had learned about and were continuing to learn. In the next chapter our focus turns to the learning process itself.

CHAPTER 4

LEARNING TO MANAGE AND MANAGING TO LEARN

The picture that emerges from the previous chapters is of managerial work as a rather vaguely defined, and often poorly understood, occupation which is made sense of by those who do it in a variety of different ways. People enter managerial work, too, in various different ways and each individual works out for themselves how to come to terms with the quite considerable challenges which such employment entails. We have seen something in the earlier chapters of how individuals, in the process of talking about their work, make sense of what they do and how they come to be where they are. We ourselves have tried to make sense of what they have to say by presenting their words within patterns which we have created in the hope of bringing out common themes and concerns. Central to this endeavour has been our idea of the emergent manager. There is no point at which the manager suddenly becomes, for once and for all, a fully fledged manager, any more than there is a point in their life when any human being finally settles into being what they will always and unalterably be. The human individual is best understood as continually 'becoming' in the way we outlined in Chapter 1. But this process of 'becoming' is not some simple matter of an embryonic being developing along fixed genetic guidelines inside a shell, protected from the world. The human being – the manager no more nor less than any other – is in a constant state of becoming as they actively come to terms with the circumstances in which they find themselves.

The process of emergence for the human being is first and foremost a matter of learning. The process of first becoming and then continuing to 'become' a manager is, by the same token, primarily a process of learning. This is our way of making sense of what goes on over time in a manager's life. But we haven't invented it without reference to the ways in which our managers themselves make sense of their own development. The whole point of our approach to research is one of doing our own sense-making in the light of what we understand about the sense-making of the people we are studying. We are putting shape on what they say to a large extent. That is our role. But it is something that parallels what some managers themselves do – especially when their circumstances have required them to step back and reflect on processes of management learning. This was the case with Dick Thompson, a purchasing manager in a packaging company. Some months prior to the following conversation he had taken on the task of acting as mentor to two young managers. He was in his late twenties and he was asked to help and guide a young man and a young woman who were only about five years younger than himself.

What you learn, how you learn it and who you are

I was both thrilled and terrified when the personnel woman asked me if I would take on these two young people, as their mentor.

You sound like an old man, saying 'these young people'.

Well, exactly. I'm not am I? I said this to Sally, that I was a new manager myself and was hardly in a position to guide anybody. She said this was exactly her point. She said that I was learning very fast myself and was therefore in an ideal position to show them how to learn.

Does it mean that you are teaching them to learn rather than teaching them to manage.

Nicely put, my man. But I'm not so sure about 'teach'. I can't do that. But you are right, I've got to ... No, I suppose that the best I can do is to show them how I have been learning myself so that they can take from me what is most useful to them.

You say 'how' you have learned.

Yes, that's right. One of the first things I did was to sit down and try to write out what I had learned since I came into this manager role I am now in. I thought – in this systematic way I have of looking at everything – that I could then go on and write in another column, how I had learned each of these things. I found this a useless exercise. I would put things in the 'what' column like 'company invoice procedure' and then in the 'how' column, say, 'look up in procedure manual FS2'. Two problems. I am not sure whether this is management as such. And, second, such things are far less important than things that I have learned like how to watch your back when dealing with the bastard accountants upstairs. That really is management. I think it is, or perhaps not. You could call it the rough side of the people thing – as opposed to the smooth side, the motivating, delegating and all that. Anyway, the problem was, what do you put in the 'how' column for things like that?

What did you put?

Well, I dropped the exercise. How could I put down things like 'burned my effing fingers too many times'?

Why couldn't you? That makes a lot of sense to me.

Yes, yes. But this is where I hit the rails. I realised that what works for me might not work for somebody else. You see, I can cope with finding out the hard way about the people I deal with. Others are not happy with this – they like to 'research it', if you know what I mean. They get 'briefed'. You know, they go around all the people they know saying 'Tell me about so and so.'

So there's more than one way to learn?

Yes and the point is that the way we learn best is a matter of what sort of chap you are. It's down to personality, chum.

So you have got three columns now: what you learn, how you learn and who you are.

Well perhaps I'll try again. But how do you relate the three? Perhaps I'll forget about it. Change the subject.

Dick Thompson has very neatly brought out three aspects of the management learning process which we can make use of in making sense of the sense-making talk of the rest of our managers. There is clearly some content in the learning process – 'what' it is one learns. There is then the process of learning – the 'how'. And then there is the 'who' to go into the equation. In our interviewing we directly raised the first two of these three aspects of learning. We asked people to identify for us the skills and knowledge which they had needed to acquire to do their managerial job. And on the 'how' issue, we asked a range of questions ranging from ones about their past to ones about their current situation. As we shall see, in talking about both the 'what' and 'how' aspects of learning, the issue of the uniqueness of each emergent manager – 'who' it is doing the learning – is continually present. We will now turn to what our managers had to say about the skills and knowledge they have had to acquire.

The skills and knowledge of managing

By directly asking about 'skills and knowledge' we fully expected to find a mixture of references both to technical/task aspects of managers' jobs and to social aspects. This expectation was fulfilled but, to a very significant degree, the social or relational dominated the more specific or detailed skills or techniques associated with people's work. But what did they say about these latter requirements?

How to budget and do this and that

If we were to go to the management shelves of a business school library or look at the curriculum of a management qualification course we would see a great deal of material on such matters as finance, decision-making, information technology or strategic analysis. Few would question the importance of skills and knowledge in these areas. And most of us would expect significant reference to be made to these by people working in and learning managerial roles. However, only a small proportion of the managers we asked about 'skills and knowledge' necessary for their managerial work made reference to these and, with only a handful of exceptions, they quickly moved on to stress the more relational requirements of the job.

Among the limited references made to technical aspects of managerial work, that of finance, or budgeting was the most common. Mary Rainey spoke of having to acquire an 'awful lot of skills and knowledge' as a nurse manager, not least because she had previously had 'no idea about finance and budgeting'. She compared the skills needed here to technical ones relating to people – writing job descriptions, short-listing job applicants, interviewing and selecting – but these were a matter of building on things she had already experienced. Budgeting was a much bigger challenge. Marion Brown spoke in very similar terms. Having been a teacher, the curriculum development skills needed were not too problematic, 'I'm not suggesting they come naturally to me, but they come much more naturally because I've had more experience of doing them.' But being a head teacher means 'managing the massive budget'. She refers to this as 'a whole new side', in spite of the fact that she had been 'shown the ropes before'. She explains that 'It didn't matter how much the head at my last school tried to involve me in it. Until you're doing it, until you're out of the classroom and actually doing it, you have no idea.' She therefore puts this area of skill and knowledge 'first, because for me at the moment it is the biggest challenge. Because it is completely new.' More typical than either of these two accounts, however, is that of Sally Vaughan who simply mentions what she calls 'the work related skills' she has had to acquire in her development as a marketing manager. She is almost desultory in her reference to 'how to budget and how to do this and how to do that and how to read market research and you know, things like that' before moving on to what she sees as much more important skills in the political sphere of managing – as we shall see later.

Another category of skills mentioned are those of 'decision-making' and 'objective-setting'. Colin Hawkins sees the skill he has developed in decision-making as the most important one he has acquired. But when he is asked to explain this skill, it does not appear to be anything of a particularly technical nature. He simply talks about having learned to 'think things out more clearly'. He gives an example of a decision to give a resident of his social services home a sum of money for a patio he had built onto the home. The 'skill' appears to be one of having learned always to have a 'reason' for whatever action is taken – something necessary to 'make one comfortable'. Ron Scott's reference to 'decision-making skills' similarly does not appear to be of the type to be found in business school textbooks but to be a straightforward matter of planning how to deal with prison inmates. He refers especially to 'sentence planning', an activity carried out in a committee which decides the pattern to be followed in each inmate's sentence – including such matters as home leave. Again, little of the business school curriculum appears to be utilised here, one of the rare references to any technique likely to be found there being Alicia Coltrane's brief mention of her occasional use of 'SWOT' analysis – the listing of the strengths, weaknesses, opportunities and threats associated with 'potential actions' in the housing management sphere. Ellen Fitzgerald suggested that 'action planning and objective setting' were the 'two key skills' she had developed as a building society manager but, again, these seemed to be relatively commonsensical approaches, matters of 'organising oneself sensibly'.

When a manager is asked in the middle of a long interview to say what skill or knowledge they have had to acquire, we cannot reasonably expect them to report accurately every detail of the 'content' of managerial learning that they have confronted – or anything like it. The specific or technical skills which are most likely to come to mind are either going to be things about which they were particularly worried or things which are especially significant in their specific context. This was the case with those accounts which mentioned finance and budgeting, and the same pattern is there with mention of information technology. Lucy Armstrong tells us that she 'has to develop more IT skills', something which she 'resisted for a long time' and has now had to 'embrace', not least because in her student services management work she has had to 'actually make decisions about a whole computer system for something we do'. She reveals her anxieties and, in doing this we are reminded of Dick Thompson's points about the importance of the 'sort of chap you are' in learning processes:

You are talking to a complete computer illiterate. I'm still having problems switching them on, you know. I'm that sort of person. And – but, you know, I just – well, I've got to do it, you know. Nobody said to me 'You've got to do it', but I could see that we were going to have to do it because there was no way we could manage this system without it. So I just thought, 'Don't panic. You know, it's like having a new kitchen in – you don't have to do it yourself, you might be able to choose the units, but you don't have to actually wrench the pipes through the wall.' I just talked myself down and into it that way. I thought, 'Well, I'll go and look at a few and get other people to demonstrate them and see if they do what I want them to do, and then, you know, get somebody else to order it' [*laughter*]. I mean, it's worked and it's taken me into building good links with the IT Support people and gradually building my own literacy and skills into it. They're not much good, I mean, actually I am a bit more competent now than I was. I twiddle about with the network and find what I want. But I couldn't do that two years ago even when I was trying. But I just had to in the end.

This little case study in how skills acquisition relates to personal characteristics can also be read as illustrating how issues of technical skill also relate to social aspects of learning: it was only through recognising dependency on others and having to make working links with specialists that it became possible for Lucy to develop her 'own literacy and skills'. Something similar is suggested by Harry Lyttleton when he reviews the skills that he brought into his current managerial job – skills in electrical engineering, in computing and in pipe-fitting. The management skill he has had to acquire is different. He has got to pull together the skills of all those who are interdependent within the manufacturing factory to make the system as a whole operate: 'Increasingly, you are becoming a facilitator for something to happen, rather than being the technocrat, expert, which is what you used to be.'

Knowing the organisation, knowing the faces

Part of the knowledge that Harry Lyttleton needed to do this more managerial job, in addition to the obvious social skill of doing the facilitation, is a detailed knowledge of how the factory worked. The importance of this kind of knowledge was stressed by a number of managers, and we should note the point they are making, not least to counter the more simplistic versions of the notion that there are to be found such people as 'generic managers' who can turn their hand to managerial work regardless of the type of business they are located in. There is no necessary problem with the idea that there are generic managerial skills which could be applied anywhere, but as Kotter (1982), among others, has shown, effective management requires a high level of organisation or industry-specific knowledge too. Dan Tracey speaks about how he felt it necessary for his job to 'learn about the company from top to bottom, from invoices to strategy'. Especially important was getting to know the 'nuances of the personalities of everybody in the place'. You have to 'know the company and know the faces'.

Betty Smith – the only one of the managers in the National Health Service who had moved into the health service from another sector – stressed just how vital it was for anyone to 'get to know all the quirks and complexities of the NHS' to be able to manage. Betty is more likely to mention this kind of knowledge than the other NHS managers, who might well have taken such a thing for granted. However, it may be that someone with a reasonable knowledge of their organisation nevertheless finds themselves needing to know more when they move in a managerial direction. Such a point is made by Mark Taylor. He explains that 'coming from a technical background' he knew a great deal about the engineering company he had worked in for many years. But, in spite of this, he says:

I didn't really know about the functionality of production in engineering. Outside production, basically all the different departments come together to make the product happen on time – at the right cost and quality. So I had to learn the sort of structure of who did what, where and when. And that's the sort of – the knowledge side of it. And then, based on that, I can make decisions as to how to improve it within my cell. What the inputs and outputs were to and from it – yes, I had to learn that up.

'The smooth side of the people thing'

Mark Taylor followed up the above analysis of the importance of knowing your organisation's operating structures by talking about what Dick Thompson referred to earlier as the 'smooth side of the people thing' – the 'motivating, delegating and all that'. Mark focuses here on his learning about the importance of 'controlling a supervisor, you know, managing a supervisor'. He had never had one 'under me before, and he's the guy who essentially makes the cell tick, if he's a good supervisor'. The key skill is one of pointing this individual who is 'at the interface' in the 'right direction'. That gets 'nine tenths of the managerial job done'. The subtleties of this (the 'smoothness' in Thompson's terms, perhaps) are suggested in the way Mark corrects himself: 'So, it's very important to learn about teaching him – no, not teaching, no, sorry – understanding what makes him tick, and getting him both motivated, and able to understand what your needs are.' He adds, 'And it's a difficult one, you know.'

A popular discursive resource with our managers when talking about their skills with people was this one which Mark used here of learning about 'what makes people tick'. It is frequently connected with a skill of making two-way relationships and building trust. Charles Parker illustrates this way of talking, again using the notion of 'how people tick':

If I set aside developing the basic skills of the job that I had before when I did the bog-standard housing officer's job, it's the inter-personal skills that I've needed to develop. You've got to try to motivate people – people you've never had to deal with before. You have to learn to get their trust, communicate with them, and to motivate them. It's really finding out what makes them tick. I've found that if you know a little bit about them, what makes them laugh, what makes them fed up, what sort of people they like, then you will know a little bit about how they're going to respond in certain situations, stressful situations say. If you don't know a bit about your staff, you're not going to get the best out of them. So, getting round those sort of issues, and then, you know, making people feel that they're valued. It might mean sending them on courses that you perhaps wouldn't normally be able to send them on, but swinging it with somebody so that they get onto other areas that might interest them, and keep them interested in their job, which might not be all that demanding. There's always a little bit of leeway there. A member of staff can see I'm trying to do something for her, you know, it's not all one way. I think, I believe very strongly, that there should be a two way thing. It shouldn't be just me getting something out of them. It's not the right thing to be doing. So, I would think that's where I've had to learn. And that's really getting right down to the nitty gritty of how do you get the best out of people, because I think that's what it's all about. There's fancy definitions of that.

Just what is meant here by 'fancy definitions' is unclear but the 'lay theorising' which is going on here combined with the moral injunction about 'the wrong thing to do' can be paralleled with various attempts in the academic literature to show the importance of trust and reciprocity in managerial work (Watson 1996). Such matters, expressed in various ways, are indeed often said to be close to what management 'is all about'. Julian Adderley uses the quite common language of 'communication skills' to argue that 'the essence of management really, is good communications' which is why he has learned to 'sit down with people on a very regular basis, just to get a feel for what's going on'. Dan Tracey puts it another way by claiming that 'At the end of the day, industry's all about people. It's all about people, yea? And it's the way that you deal with people. You know, if you're not – if you can't be trustworthy, or whatever, then you're not going to form relationships.'

Throughout the accounts which our managers give about the management skills and knowledge they have acquired are terms like 'diplomacy', 'tact', 'listening rather than telling', 'delegating'. All of this might seem a little obvious or even banal. But what we need to recognise is that these managers are telling us that they *have had to learn these things*, obvious as they might seem to us as we read them here on the page in front of us. Carol Laine, for example, tells us that the 'biggest thing I have had to learn' is the art of delegating and, as she puts it, 'being creepy' (shades of Dick Thompson's 'smoothness' again):

I'm a bit sort of creepy, you know. I try to please people – you know, I'm all the time thinking, 'Oh don't upset them, don't upset them, be nice about it.' I think about how I'd rather be asked to do something than told, you know, when I was a clerical officer – and asked nicely, 'Would you mind doing this please?'

Beneath seemingly innocent words like these there may well be a subtext of managerial manipulation. There is roughness below the smoothness. But what about when the roughness is nearer the surface?

'The rough side of the people thing'

In the previous chapter we heard from our managers about the challenge of handling managerial politics – of recognising and handling, for example, 'hidden agendas' at whatever level these might arise. We heard about people having to defend their territories and needing to cope with the career rivalries which arise between managers. Given the extent of this kind of challenge we should not be surprised to see the skills of handling such matters being spoken of when we raise questions about the management learning process. Although, as we also observed in the last chapter, the popular discursive framing of the work managers do identifies it as centrally involved with gaining the compliance of the manager's subordinates, it quickly becomes obvious as soon as one gets involved in managerial work itself, or researches it, that relationships with people other than 'subordinates' engage the manager just as much, if not more. Indeed we found that our managers spoke of learning about Dick Thompson's 'rough side of the people thing' at least as often as they spoke of the 'smooth side'.

We saw Mary Rainey explain, in the previous chapter, the complex politics of managing in a hospital and, in the present chapter, we see her point to her need to overcome her ignorance of finance and budgeting. She talks about her previous experience of the 'people side' but says the difference now is that this is on a 'grand scale'. What changes the 'scale' of the relational content of her work is the political complexity and the intra-managerial conflicts. The variety of values and what she calls 'different attitudes' towards NHS general practice are stressed by Betty Smith, who says that there is no such thing as a 'born practice manager' – not least because you have to learn from experience how to handle the various attitudes one comes across, 'I mean, some people are totally against fund holding and they will never become a fund holding practice'. On the other hand, 'Some people see fund holding as the way forward to making the changes that the non-fund holders want.' A particular problem here for the practice manager is that the doctors often 'don't want to be committed to actually making the decisions'. Betty has thus had to learn a great deal about fund-holding and develop skills of handling the complexities of general practitioners' and others' varying positions on this 'new concept'.

These two health service managers tended to stress what we might call 'structural' factors behind the clashes and tensions that occur at the interpersonal level within management. Within this, there is still the need, they suggest, to understand the different 'personalities' of the people they deal with. Most managers talking about the 'rough side' of relationships, however, simply talk about the skill they have had to develop to deal with particular 'personalities'. Ted Ellington is quite typical of this when he talks about having to learn how to 'resist certain personalities' by which he means learning how to see when certain people are having more influence over what you are doing than you at first realise. One has to overcome one's naiveté in this respect and learn to 'protect your back'. Sally Vaughan speaks of learning how to avoid being pushed into the background by other people in the marketing field in which she works where there are 'lots of quite aggressive and lots of sort of big personalities'. Kathy Westbrook argues that in the restaurant business the most important skill she has had to learn is what she calls 'the knack, you know, of the politics thing'. What this entails, above all, is learning 'how to talk to the right people' so that you can compete effectively with what she calls the 'bum-licker types':

There is a knack of talking to the right people without sucking up to them, and I think I've just about started to learn how to do it. It's basically just letting them know that, like, I've done lots of things, and achieved quite a lot of things. Before, I didn't let people know about it. But now I'm more in touch with my area manager. I've said, 'Oh I've been doing this, and I'm doing that now', just so that they're aware.

Kathy gives an illustration of this:

Like I'm training up a supervisor at the moment, just to sort of try and promote my training. And I know he's impressed. Well, he'd know that we were promoting a supervisor, but he might not realise that it was me who was the person that was taking charge of the training. It's stuff like that.

She reiterates that it's 'just the knack of it' and she explains that 'it bothers me that I did actually need to learn to do things like that'. Again, here are things that might seem obvious to the distant observer of managerial life which are nevertheless 'facts of managerial life' (as one manager called them) which have to be learned about – and can only be learned about through experiencing them. But in learning about these things, Kathy points out, you are making decisions about yourself as an individual.

Learning about the job, learning about yourself

Kathy Westbrook's learning about these particular political skills has occurred in the process of comparing herself to what she calls the 'bumlicker types'. She saw such people getting ahead of her, as we saw in the last chapter, but she then began to recognise that 'they're not as well respected', and that 'other people will get there as well'. Recognition of this showed her, she says, that you have to 'value yourself', and consider 'how much you want to be a yes-person and how much you want to be your own person'. This kind of thing was spoken about frequently by our managers – when asked about learning skills and acquiring knowledge they would more often talk about learning 'how they should be' or 'how they would need to be' as a person to be able to manage successfully in their organisation. Sally Vaughan, for example, when explaining how she had to learn how to relate to the 'big and aggressive personalities' she meets in her marketing function goes on to explain how she has learned to be 'a lot more sort of confident than I was, you know, when I started'. Her learning, she tells us, has not just been about 'doing the job well' but 'in the more sort of personal area as well'.

We are here very much in the 'who' area of management learning identified in the discussion with Dick Thompson and it again reminds us how much the 'emergent manager' is also an 'emergent person' or, as it was put to us on one occasion, 'It's as much learning about your-self as it is learning about the job'. Throughout our managers' accounts of their learning they tended quickly to shift from the notion of skills or knowledge to their own emergent personal characteristics. We hear for example that,

The important thing has been developing my personal credibility through showing that I can get things done.

Learning about management has really been learning about myself – what I can do and what I can't do – and then working within what I am able to do, or develop myself to do.

I've learned to be more assertive than I used to be.

Resilience and tolerance have been the most important things for me, rather than what I specific-ally know or can do.

I've had to develop a lot more confidence than I had when I started, which obviously comes with experience anyway. But I've sort of had to consciously make the effort to speak up and have my voice heard and so on. And having sort of made myself do those things when I was perhaps, you know, a bit shy and wanted to sort of sit and say nothing. I have sort of made myself at certain stages, you know, be an active member of groups and meetings and so on. I think, you know, I've really benefited from that. And, you know, this has actually helped my progression.

I've had to become a much more pro-active person.

It's just developing the ability to sort of stay fairly calm, you know, when you're juggling all these priorities.

Skills and knowledge? Well it's really awareness, determination, tact, diplomacy. It's 'Don't go in there like a raging bull'. I did at the beginning and I got my face smacked because I was not looking at the whole picture.

I have managed to adapt my personal qualities to the job I am doing. I am good at building relation-ships with customers. I can manage relationships well. And a lot of this is to do with your basic honesty and integrity.

A number of managers were led from making observations of this type to reflecting on the extent to which, in a phrase used two or three times, you 'either have it or you don't'. There is clearly a widely shared view that a manager does need to change, and can change, in terms of personal characteristics as they adapt to the pressures and challenges which they meet. However, it was suggested, especially by Arthur

Blakey, that there were certain people who were incapable of learning to be managers – or to be 'good managers' at least. He gives an example:

Well, oh, we can take another team leader, who went through all the management development. He went through a lot of education – they see management development for the role taking about two years. And he hasn't learned that [*snaps fingers*]. And it's – he never will learn, obviously. He wants to be a dictator: 'You do things my way, and that's that.' So, he can't learn to be a good manager.

Arthur generalises from this:

There have to be some things intrinsic in your – your make-up, or something, I think. There has to be a certain base-line of – of authority. It's not that a manager's got to be any great shakes or anything, but there has to be something to allow you to do that. It seems there has to be some sort of base-line to form a good athlete, and to make a good athlete. I think there has to be some good material there to work with. Then you can build on it, I believe.

He has developed himself – built on what he was:

And obviously, personally, I've developed a lot over two years, so yes, there are building blocks to add on. But without a certain amount of base material, some people just aren't cut out for it. No matter how many courses you send them away on, no matter how much you try to get them to see it. There's some people don't seem to be able to make the transition. And I think it's just in their – their internal make-up. No matter how much you teach certain people, you just will never, ever, ever be able to do it.

Doing it is more than techniques or skills:

Getting on with people, they just never, ever will be able to do it, no matter how many techniques or skills they've been told in the teaching.

Common sense, street knowledge, part of life

It was argued in Chapter 1 that although managers have to become accomplished and sophisticated performers in their work, their organisational managing is not essentially different from the 'managing' that one does in the rest of one's life. Although management is undoubtedly a challenging sort of activity, it is nevertheless a relatively mundane activity, as opposed to a science-based or professional specialism. Similar arguments were put forward by a number of our managers. Eddie Hayes was keen, in this spirit, to demystify managerial work in the construction industry and point to its commonsensical nature.

This industry is all about applying a lot of common sense. It's not a high tech industry. It all revolves round getting men and materials in the right place at the right time. That's our main thing. Getting men and materials in the right place at the right time. If that doesn't happen it costs a fortune. And it's making sure, from a design point of view, that we don't put too much concrete in a foundation, because that can cost us a lot of money as well. So you know, there's a little bit more to it than that but it comes down to making sure that we don't have labour standing round doing nothing, because labour costs us an absolute arm and a leg and to not putting too much concrete in a foundation, because concrete costs us money.

Eddie is aware that he is exaggerating here but he seems to feel strongly that management should not be mystified or fetishised. Stan Jordan seems to be doing something similar with his concept of 'street knowledge'. In the leisure industry, he points out, 'we're all basically unskilled'. Employees in places like bingo halls 'don't have a professional skill or a taught skill, it's a street knowledge'. This applies to managers as much as to other employees and managers in service industries have to carefully develop this knowledge so that people's 'street skills are polished up in a customer facing role'. The simple lesson that has been made by some of the 'very formidable managers of people' in major retail and service companies is that ordinary street-wise people 'control the destiny of large organisations'.

The overall thrust of what we have been told is that learning to be a manager is not so much a matter of learning a series of skills or absorbing a body of knowledge as, in Carrie Bley's words, 'just life-learning really'. Sally Vaughan speaks similarly. She has 'learned a lot about relationships with people and how to sort of persuade and influence people and build relationships with people at work'. At the personal level she has learned to 'be more resilient and not take things personally'. All of this, however, is 'really just part of life'. Nevertheless, 'it's the sort of thing that I've had to learn in my job'. Yet again, we can say that it is most helpful to see the emergent manager primarily as an 'emergent person' in a broad sense. To become a skilled manager basically involves becoming a skilled human being, albeit one with a degree of technical management skill and, equally if not more importantly, one with a close and detailed knowledge of the business and the organisation one is in and of the specific individuals and groups to whom one has to relate.

Early learning

It would appear, then, that many of the qualities which are needed by the manager are rather general and basic 'life skills'. Nevertheless, quite of a lot of our managers, as we have seen, talk about still having to learn a lot about these when they enter managerial work. Inevitably, each of these individuals will have brought a reasonable understanding of these matters into their work from their earlier life experiences. But they become much more conscious of and feel much more challenged about their abilities when they face the everyday realities of a managerial existence. In noting this way of speaking about what has to be learned, however, we must not play down the extent to which earlier 'life learning' is positively talked about by managers when they speak about their managerial work in the context of their lives as a whole. We deliberately asked each person about the ways in which they see their past lives as having had any kind of influence on their current managerial situation. They tended to deal with this issue in three broad ways.

Determination and driving forces

The first way in which people spoke of the influence of their past on their current occupational life was to look back to their parents and their upbringing and say how it influenced them in some broad way as an individual (Dick Thompson's 'who' issue again). Mina Mangeshkar sees her own 'drive and determination to do what is right' as central to her managerial work and relates this back to her parents' influence. She says that 'both are real fighters' who 'came from a very very different culture when they were very young, with no support'. But they 'did what they felt was right' and 'pursued what they believed in'. Mina feels that she is 'carrying on what they were doing in effect'. Her 'determination' has also been developed in the light of her own ethnicity and gender, as she has striven 'to overcome the obstacles of my sex and my colour'. This has required a level of 'patience and tolerance and a real drive to fulfil what I feel is right in my heart', which she believes is a vital part of her concept of herself as a manager.

Where Mina Mangeshkar points to the parental influence on her life learning in the context of race and gender issues, others tend to talk of their parental and class background. Ron Scott speaks in terms we heard from managers from a variety of class backgrounds when he talks about learning that 'if you wanted anything in life, you went out and worked for it' but he emphasises what he calls his 'working background' and how what his 'dad used to say to me was, if I don't buck my ideas up, I'd end up down the pit'. This experience 'sort of installed in my brain' ideas that are 'still important in what I do'. Andrew Shepherd talks in similar terms of something that has been 'a driving force all the way through' – a 'desire to do better for my parents because they'd take a great deal of pride in what I'd achieved'.

Managing in the family

The second way in which managers spoke about early influences was one where there was a more direct linking of the family background to managerial work itself. The above type of account could have been given by people in a range of other types of occupation – in spite of the fact that these factors do appear to be important to the individuals themselves in making sense of their current managerial situation. Lucy Armstrong connects what she calls her 'sense of building, you know, creating and making things come together in an intricate kind of way' to what she does as a manager. And she relates this back to her parents' occupational activities. She explains that her father was 'an engineer and a designer of precision equipment for the aerospace and car industry'. And 'my mum's skills were there too'. Lucy's mother 'has always worked in engineering, in terms of reading drawings, ordering materials, planning jobs all of that kind of thing'. This is reported as an important shaping influence in Lucy's 'emergence':

I always admired what they did, you know, and I had admiration for the ability to turn ideas and lumps of things into something, and to bring it together as a process. Even when I was in my early teens I used to, in the holidays, go along and help out. I don't know how much help it was, but I did things like checking material prices or filing and stuff like that. I always enjoyed it – as I do now. Does that make sense?

Here is sense-making in practice – an individual creating a continuity not only between her parental experiences and her present life but between activities she carried out as a child and activities she carries out now. Lucy asks if it helps our sense-making. It certainly does if we view the 'emergent manager' as an 'emergent person' shaping their biography as a whole. And Betty Smith's account of the continuities in her life makes unusually direct links between past and present in this spirit:

There was always the intention that I wanted to coordinate and organise things. I was always very good at sort of, you know, coordinating my brothers to make sure they were where they were supposed to be and they didn't forget Mother's birthday and things like that.
Your parents . . . ?
They owned the local Post Office. So there was always a work environment and from an early age it was never, 'Oh here's your pocket money'. It was always, 'You earned your pocket money.'
How did you do that?
Home, in effect, was a shop as well. We sold greeting cards and stationery. It was always my responsibility to make sure that the floors were swept at night for the start of the next day and that the card racks were filled and all the stationery was filled, for me to earn the pocket money. It was never given to me, it was always – I was paid monthly even then.

And this is relevant to your work now?
Yes, oh yes. Very much so, very much so. It taught me to manage my finances from an early age because I was paid monthly for pocket money.
Oh right, that's unusual.
Yes. I had to work for a month and then I would receive the pocket money at the end of the month and I had to manage it then to last me the following month until I got paid. So, yes, it taught me to organise my finances and to recognise that you don't get anything in life for free. Yes, it – yeah – I learnt a lot from my childhood and my parents.

Yet again we see learning, about things as obviously 'managerial' as coordinating, organising and 'managing finances', related to an individual's personal values and their sense of where they have come from in their lives. Jean Holliday looks to her more recent family life and to her experiences as a mother when she left accountancy for a full-time family role before returning to work as a business manager in the health service. She draws on this experience to stress that 'what matters' in management learning is 'experience of living, rather than training'. She believes that her ten years as a 'full-time mother' taught her far more than her previous accounting experience: 'It's the prioritisation of all the issues you have to deal with, that makes you a better resource manager.' What she learned most of all, she says, is that 'there's no such thing as black and white'. Although it may look 'ridiculous, absolutely ridiculous', it was 'life experience' as a mother that 'corrected' her accounting training and has thus made her a 'better manager than I would have been without my ten years away from work'.

Learning in schools, clubs and sports teams

Shaping influences on the 'manager-to-be', according to our managers, are not only to be found in the family but in individuals' experiences in educational and recreational activities. This gives us our third way in which managers spoke of early learning relevant to managing. Sometimes managers talk about how they think back to what they observed of human behaviour in the organisational context of the school or college. Ron Scott, in the course of arguing that management learning is a continuous process, refers back to observing teachers at school (this, however, building on 'watching parents' at home):

You learn all the time to be a manager. It's something that you're picking up right from being at school. You watch how teachers deal with situations and watch how the headmaster deals with the teachers, you know. And you watch how teachers deal with parents and so on. So, I think it's something that you're watching all the time. And this probably goes back further than that to how your parents deal with you, deal with a situation, deal with a problem that crops up. I think, again, it's something that's ongoing.

Kathy Westbrook looks back to her experience of observing the lives of fellow students at university and tells us that this is very helpful in understanding the pressures on many of the young people she currently employs. Whilst Liza Potts traces her learning from observing fellow pupils and students all the way through her educational career:

Right from being at school (senior school and probably even back to infant school), I watched how girls and – especially – boys interact. I noticed, for example, how the relationship with the first teacher you have affects things in your life. It goes right through to meeting different people at every stage. At every stage in my education I met different people. Each has a different role to play and different strength of character within different groups. I watched all this and learned from it. It is immensely useful now in managing human relationships.

In contrast to these accounts of learning through watching, others talk about experiences in their years of growing up when they became directly involved in activities which they now see as broadly 'managerial'. Julian Adderley claims that the British private education system attempts quite deliberately to provide such experiences for its pupils, starting in his case with 'the responsibilities I was given right back at prep school'. Early on he had 'house-prefecty sorts of responsibilities' and later 'school prefect' ones. And, he says,

This really is a managerial sort of role, you know. You are looking after people, and you are telling them what they should be doing, what they shouldn't be doing, and so on. And you have to make decisions on whether indiscretions should be punished or not. And the people are there twenty-four hours a day, for the whole term, and obviously they have to delegate – the staff there have to delegate. So there is – looking at it in business terms – a management structure there, a very clearly defined management structure. It doesn't stop at the teachers, it goes on way down the – below that. And I think it is good experience for people, very good experience for people. It does give them that opportunity, the experience at a very young age of having to sort of manage and look after people.

Lawrence Young speaks in a similar way about being the captain of a cricket team – his first 'leadership role' which he took on when he was 'about fifteen'. He claims that he 'learned a huge amount' from this, especially 'handling a team, giving direction and encouragement and all that'. This claim is not one that has recently occurred to him, however. He tells us how he 'emphasised it' in his original application to the bank. Andrew Shepherd also lays heavy emphasis on the relevance to his current managerial work in a bank of such experiences. In his case it was involvement in a boys' club which, 'from a very early age really opened my eyes'. He became 'a junior leader, a committee member, a youth leader, an organiser of a canoe camp' and in this he was doing things that were later to give him 'a great advantage' in his career competition with others in the bank: 'I was far more streetwise and aware of what was going on – I wasn't a youngster like the others.' But Andrew is anxious to generalise beyond his own experience on this matter. He talks about working on a human resourcing project in the bank where there was an attempt to identify what it was that distinguished 'the young people in the bank that we thought most highly of'. The conclusion was that 'one of the common links between them was team involvement at an early age – whether it was in a church group, a football team, a committee, or a youth club'. Once again, however, this was not simply a matter of skills or knowledge acquired. The personal characteristics of the potential manager are again emphasised. 'All of those people', claims Andrew, 'had that inner confidence as well as the team skills that maybe people who weren't exposed in those areas who maybe played individual type games or sports, or read a lot, might not have.'

Occupational learning

It is becoming increasingly evident that we might have to abandon the notion of management learning to talk instead about 'life learning relevant to management'. But, so far, we have only considered learning which has occurred prior to the individual even starting full-time employment. From everything that we have seen so far we would expect managerially relevant learning to occur in work experiences which are not, in any formal sense, managerial ones. So what do our managers say about what we might call 'work learning relevant to management'?

Learning for management in non-managerial work

For managers who are 'moving up' within their own organisation, there is often emphasis on how important their previous jobs in the organisation were in helping them know about and understand the details of the organisation or the business they were in – echoing what we saw earlier in this chapter (p. 91) about the importance of specific organisational knowledge. Diane Washington, for example, says that although she did not pick up managerial skills as such, her previous work as a physiotherapist in the hospital meant that she had developed an invaluable 'knowledge of the hospital, the way the department runs, the culture of the department and the vision of where we're trying to go'. And Ted Ellington talks about the value of his having gained a deep understanding of the 'brown goods business ... whether it be at the repairing end, the materials end, or whether it's the quality systems'. He learned to understand 'technical issues, and supply issues', but was less sure about 'management issues'. However, what he did learn that helps with this is the human network he operates within; 'I know everybody in the business', he says. He could not 'do what I do managerially without that'.

Two of the managers who recognised that their previous jobs had contained significant managerial elements stressed that the learning they did here was only a partial preparation for a more fully managerial position. Colin Hawkins talked about his role as a non-commissioned officer in the forces where 'there were some processes of management that I carried out, in terms of monitoring, supervising, evaluating, organising shifts, organising the daily routines'. But he learned little of the 'higher level managerial issues' which were solely the concern of the officer 'up the hierarchy'. And Mark Taylor talks of a partial managerial learning in his earlier engineering role in the factory. He had easily learned about budgeting ('I've always loved that') and found a small group of people 'easy to manage, because it was face-to-face stuff'. What he did not learn was 'just how different it is when you move up to being in charge of fifty, sixty or seventy people'. For him 'that was the shock I wasn't prepared for'.

Probably the most common type of response made to questions about what the individual had learned from earlier work experiences that was relevant to their subsequent managerial career was about how their job as a physiotherapist, photographer, engineer, social worker, shop assistant or whatever had taught them about

the importance of interpersonal relations in all business matters,

the need always to be liaising and persuading if you want anything to get done,

the importance of communications and having to build up contacts with all the agencies you have to deal with,

how you have to listen and always see things from the operator's point of view before you make a decision,

establishing networks and constantly liaising,

building up trusting relations with the people whose help you need in getting your job done.

It appears, then, that the relational aspect of management is the most strongly emphasised when people talk about what they 'picked up' from earlier jobs to bring into their subsequent managerial position. But some of our managers also point to ways in which they almost 'slipped into' managerial work in previous occupations.

Learning to manage in non-managerial work: management avant la lettre

A number of our managers look back and talk about earlier occupational experiences in terms of learning which they were later to *bring forward* into a subsequent managerial appointment. And others refer to experiences in which they felt an urge to act – or actually did act – in a quasi-managerial way in a non-managerial job. Betty Smith talks of often finding herself working out 'better ways of doing things' in the medical practice when she was a receptionist. In this she was, in some ways, anticipating her later work as a practice manager. This is a very specific kind of what has been noted before as *anticipatory socialisation* in the context of managerial careers (Pahl and Pahl 1972: 20–2). Mina Mangeshkar talks in similar terms when explaining how as a young graduate engineer she was always asking managers, 'Why do you always do it that way?' These are the sorts of questions a good manager should constantly be asking of themselves, Mina argues. Carrie Bley, on the other hand, simply talks about how she often found herself 'taking over' in certain situations. She was always seen as being 'very good at organising things, very good at meeting deadlines, making sure things are getting done, that type of thing'. This meant that in her pre-managerial career she would often 'end up as the chief organiser, chief Christmas organiser, "lets go out and have a drink" organiser, social organiser – "Oh Carrie'll do it" '.

Ellen Fitzgerald further illustrates this theme with a story of how, when she was 'working in a solicitor's office', she found herself 'almost being given the responsibility of running the office'. She remembers how this started:

One of the part-time ladies, who was in her fifties, had made a real mess of some legal contracts. And I was listening to an audio tape one day, when Richard, the senior partner, said, 'Oh Ellen, can you go and get Barbara and show her how to do these contracts properly, because you'll see in the pile, that they're a real mess. Can you just talk her through it, and train her to do them properly?' So I then went and got Barbara, and tried my hardest to say in a nice way, 'Oh you've done these wrong, Barbara, this is what you could do.' She took great exception to this 18-year-old, who didn't know anything, – 'How dare she?' That was very, very difficult. But he then took on another part-time lady, who was in her forties, and said to this lady, 'Ellen is going to train you, is that OK?' And she and I had a very, very good relationship. I learned to nurture and coach and train her. So, probably at that point, I started to almost manage, if you like.

Ellen sees a strong continuity between this experience and her current work as a building society manager. It is not anticipatory socialisation in the sense that she was anticipating becoming a financial services manager at that age. But the way the story plays a part in her current notion of who she is and where she has come from can be seen almost as a kind of *retrospective* anticipatory socialisation. Liza Potts, however, tells a story which perhaps has a more directly 'anticipatory' dimension to it – given that, as we saw in Chapter 2, she had every expectation of a managerial career even earlier than at eighteen. In a way which reminds us of Lawrence Young telling his bank's recruiters about his having been a cricket captain, Liza used the following story when the graduate recruiters in her retail company asked her for examples of 'managerial things' she had done.

Most people of that age would not have had managerial experience. But the example I remember giving at my interview goes back to having to clear the tables at the university hall where I was waitressing. I just took a step back from the task and realised that, to save time, you could do things in a different and more logical order. This sped the process up and made it more efficient. But you could also see the morale of people lifting as the job got done more efficiently and faster. They were much more motivated than before, not least because the new approach meant that they were getting away from work more quickly – for the same pay.

Liza relates this to principles of teamworking and says that these people 'had never worked as a team before – the pot washers had never worked with the waitresses to see that we could make their job easier and they could make our job easier'. But being a manager is more than just having a 'bright idea'. You also have to 'implement it' and, to do this,

You had to use tact and diplomacy and be sensitive and work with people and empathise with them as well. This is what being a manager is about, isn't it?

This story is being told with hindsight of course. It is the hindsight of someone who, within only a year of this vacation work experience, was in charge of a team of thirty shop staff in a company whose formal socialisation processes place great emphasis on notions of teamworking. Liza is using discursive resources from her formal management socialisation to frame a story from her pre-managerial socialisation. In her self-understanding, it would seem, the management learning process is a seamless one. The process of emergence is a remarkably smooth and rationally controlled one.

Sinking and swimming: watching yourself and watching others

Whether their emergence as managers sounds smooth and controlled or bumpy and random, our managers – across the variety of modes of entry into the work – almost all speak in a similar way about *how* they learn once they are in a management post. The theme which sounds loud and clear throughout their accounts is one of learning through jumping or being thrown into the 'deep end' of a swimming pool and then discovering which actions and styles help one float and which lead one to sink. This learning is done with reference both to one's own actions and by the action of other managers. We repeatedly hear statements like the following:

There is simply no alternative to learning by doing.

There is no way you could learn it from a book or a course and then go and do it.

Whether you jump in or are thrown in – it is then that you learn to swim.

You have to do it hands on, the hard way – always keeping your eye on others' performances.

Management is a practice and practising is the only way you pick it up.

You learn a lot more from your mistakes – and other people's mistakes – than you can learn from paper.

It's a mixture of role models and what you find works for you and doesn't work for you.

You are constantly learning lessons by watching what you get right and you get wrong and by observing what other managers get right and get wrong.

It's the sort of thing where you have to have an apprenticeship model – even if, in practice, you are nearly always an apprentice without a master.

All you really do is learn from each other.

It's a school of hard knocks. It's just like a baby: 'This hurts – this doesn't hurt.'

The theme of learning from experience – with that experience being both your own and that of observable managers around you – is typically connected with the notion of a fairly slow, often painful, cumulative process:

It's a snowball process, you pick things up as you roll from one thing to another.

It's a sort of built-up common sense. You are acquiring it as your successes please you and your failures hurt you.

It happens in stages; you build it up by trial and error and by pumping others.

It's a gradual snowball sort of building up. You learn to ride the bike with the stabilisers on and later you ride without them.

Learning just sort of develops; it happens by default and it's feeling the impact of others.

It's a slow apprenticeship-like thing – you know, takes years.

It's mistakes and mistakes and it's time.

After an instant baptism of fire, it's a matter of picking things up. It's slowly chipping away.

It's feedback, feedback, feedback – constantly learning from the loads of situations that nobody can train you for.

You're constantly sucking in information, picking things up every day.

You pick up tools of how to manage like you used to pick up tools as an engineer; it happens as you go along.

Throughout all of this we are reminded of Carrie Bley's observation that management learning is just 'life learning' really. But perhaps the most useful single statement we can pick out from the above selection is the one to the effect that management is a *practice* and that it is only through actually practising that one becomes accomplished at it. The fact that the most frequently used metaphor is one which compares management to swimming suggests that the managers are generally conscious of what some pointed directly at: the impossibility of treating management as a 'science' or a classroom or textbook based thing. Nobody ever learned to swim without entering the water. And the new swimmer, just like the new manager, not only learns by a process of trial and error but also by observing what other swimmers do. You have to find what breathing techniques, arm movements and leg movements suit you best as an individual but you may well improve your performance more quickly if you note what styles and techniques are adopted by other swimmers who, in your eyes, are good at it. By the same token you will note which actions bring other swimmers to grief.

What about books, courses and management theory?

The swimming metaphor, and the other popular one – the snowball metaphor – are clearly very helpful to managers when they are making sense of their learning processes. And they are helpful to those of us standing back and trying to get some insight into management learning. The fact that manager after manager launches straight into the 'sink or swim' type of account when asked about how they learn to manage does suggest that we perhaps ought to see 'learning through experience' as at the core of the management learning process. But it is not wise to view it as the whole of the process. Even if we stay with the manager–swimmer analogy, we might quite reasonably ask whether people might not be helped in the processes of learning to swim by such additional and supportive things as reading books about swimming, attending classes, being coached, consciously reflecting on personal progress, comparing one's experiences with those of others – and even studying some theories from physics and biology which might inform their practice. As learning theorists themselves have persuasively argued, learning occurs more effectively when 'practical' learning is incorporated in a fuller learning cycle which includes processes of reflection upon experience and a process of articulating what it is that has been learned (Kolb 1984).

Waving but not drowning?

Whilst our managers almost universally stress that learning by experience is the major way in which they acquire their skills and knowledge, they also recognise the need for other 'inputs'. Most typically this is talked about only when they are directly asked about courses, books, theory or about how they might have been better helped to learn by others. But the need for some guidance beyond the simple 'sink or swim approach' is sometimes spoken about in the context of the distress which the individual experienced when learning. They may not have drowned whilst learning to swim, but they would have liked to have been able to wave to the shore for some help. Mary Rainey, when reflecting on problems in her own initial management learning, makes the generalisation that, whilst you do indeed learn mainly from experience, you should nevertheless 'actually be supervised when you're learning through experience'. She believes that learning from experience 'has got to be done properly for it to be beneficial'. One would be guided by a person who not only was experienced in management work but would know 'what they ought to be teaching you about – they would have a list of things'. Mary illustrates her argument with her own experience of having 'acted up' – deputising for her own manager:

So you would have liked a mentor who would reflect on how they themselves learned?
Yes it would make you feel more confident. It would not necessarily mean that you make fewer cock-ups. But I would have been able to function at a higher level, more efficiently, a lot quicker, if I'd have had a more structured training programme of deputising.
It would have taken away some of the anxiety?
It would have taken away a lot of it. I mean, the thing is, I'd no idea of all the personnel procedures and things, you know. And some of it's really quite simple. I wanted to order a piece of equip-ment out of trust funds, for example. It took me five weeks because I was going to all the wrong places, and filling in all the wrong forms.
And nobody told you?
Well, nobody actually sort of said, to order something out of trust funds there's this, this, this and this.
But when you took it to the wrong person, nobody said?
Oh, it all seems to come backwards and forwards, and you get notes from them – instead of somebody just saying to you, you know, do it like this. I think half of it is though, they don't like you to know how much money's in your trust fund. I don't think it's done with any malicious intent, but I was surprised – there are things that I could desperately have done with, like, for example, textbooks about developments in nursing. I found out once I got up there, there was £2000 in my trust fund, and I could have spent £30–£40 and had some text books, and I don't think that would have been wasted money. Daft things like that.

Mary is looking for fairly straightforward information and guidance from her desired 'mentor' or swimming instructor. But she expresses a need to be given confidence by such a coach. She seems fairly tolerant, however, of those who failed to coach her or denied her information which she needed. She sees no 'malicious intent' behind the political manipulation which, in part, she was experiencing. Shirley Stitt, however, is much more critical of her employer. She says that she feels 'bitter that I've just been flung in the deep end'. Yet each time she refers to her bitterness she admits that, for example, she 'can understand that approach, because it's the only way you learn sometimes'. If she were to go through the process again,

I think I would ask for more support in the managerial side, instead of just thinking, right, I've got to do this, I've got to figure how to do it. I'd ask them, say, are there courses I can go on to help me develop in this way or develop in that way, rather than just looking to other people and asking them what should I do with this, what should I do with that. And probably be a bit stronger in that sense and say, right, I think I need this, this and this. You know, how can we go ahead and do it, sort of thing. Because I feel quite bitter that I've had fourteen staff to deal with, I've had a huge budget to deal with and I've also had to learn to manage or liaise with managers at a higher level, which is quite different to what I did before really. They see you in a different way when you're on their scales, management. So I think those sort of things I would try and get them to help me with next time round. Yea, very much – I feel quite bitter if I'm totally honest with you, that I was dumped in it and left. But as I say, that's the way you learn sometimes.

When Shirley is pressed to be more precise about what help she might have been given, it turns out that she was indeed offered courses to go on and was given advice on various matters by the personnel department. But, she feels, it was left 'too much to me' to say which courses to go on. And the personnel department 'kept changing – there was no continuity'. Shirley seems less than fully confident that she could actually have been helped more, in fact. She recognises that it would not have been a simple matter for someone else to say which courses she might have gone on.

The vagueness of Shirley Stitt's notion of what is required, in addition to learning by trial and error, is echoed in other managers' accounts of inputs other than simple sink-or-swim learning. Sally Vaughan, for example, talked about 'the academic side' of her learning. But she is extremely difficult to pin down on how her formal study of marketing – which has happened at various stages in her career – has related to her practical learning. She says in one breath that she needs 'marketing theory and stuff like that' because her job involves much more than 'just sort of life experience or what have you'. Yet in the next breath she is saying that learning is a matter of 'just putting a lot of hours in and, you know, enjoying it, and just being involved in everything and sort of taking all the opportunities to be involved in projects, and things like that'. This, she claims, 'is the only way you learn – it's virtually all on the job training'. But, barely taking another breath, she continues, 'As I say, I have studied marketing as well. I mean, I went to night-school last year and I did my Marketing Diploma.' This she says 'is very useful as well'. Finding out about her understanding of exactly in what ways this is 'useful' was more than we could achieve, other than her explaining that a key thing for her, something she 'found hard at the beginning', was that 'marketing isn't a science'. And this learning – which perhaps provides the context for her academic study – was initiated by one of her early 'bosses':

He said 'If you really want to work in marketing you've got to get rid of that attitude [that marketing is like engineering], because it's not science and he said to me, 'Go off and do this' and I said, 'I don't know how to do it because I don't know how many retail outlets there are'. It was something about forecasting some sales. He said, 'Well make an estimation' and I said, 'But it's not going to be accurate because I don't know exactly how many there are' and he said, 'But there are sort of somewhere between ten and fifteen thousand, so you'll just have to guess'. And I was like, 'Oh no! I just – no, no! I'm not comfortable with that at all'. [*laughter*] But then you learn that it is all about approximations and forecasting and basing things on assumptions and, you know, putting in sensitivities and that kind of thing. So I'm comfortable with it now.

It is almost as if a process of negotiation has occurred in Sally's head over her years of management education and practical experience, with a compromise having eventually been achieved between formal knowledge, technique and measurement, on the one hand, and the contingencies and ambiguities of day-to-day managing on the other. A similar interplay is often suggested by the way managers talk about their 'reading'. They rarely specify what books or journals they have looked at ('I just sort of pick things up as I go along') but explain that their reading helped them be sure they were 'on the right lines' or that their approach to an issue was taking them 'in the right direction'.

Putting on the fat and developing common sense

Sense might be made of this common vagueness about the nature of the interplay between formal and informal learning in managers' experience by comments made by some individuals to the effect that the learning process is, as Diana Washington put it, 'not a conscious thing'. Jean Holliday explains this in a particularly graphic way. She tells us that she is trained and educated 'up to the eyeballs'. She 'can't take in any more' and her 'memory is completely shattered now'. Jean feels that she has 'soaked in what I am capable of soaking in'. This 'soaking in process' is then explained with a biological metaphor comparing what she has absorbed to the creation of 'body fat'. She applies this notion both to her earlier accountancy training and to her more recent MBA studies:

To some extent at least, you're carried forward on the fat that you've laid down in earlier years. Accountancy, for instance, . . . if you were to ask me to do an exam paper on accountancy, I would not have a clue. But there are some things – like driving or pedalling a bike – that you do automatically, even though you can't describe how you do it, or why you do it. Accountancy is part of my very being. Accountancy is not just about number crunching, proper accountancy is about resource management – i.e. management. So there's a lot that I do without thinking. I couldn't describe why I do it, and I certainly couldn't quantify it or write a paper on it. It's just there. And it's the same thing with the MBA. The MBA is now incorporated into my fat.

Jean is nevertheless able to articulate something of her understanding of how formal management education can help the manager. She talks about how she has learned both to 'look upwards' in the hospital to see strategic issues at the same time as 'looking downward' at operational matters.

I look up with an ability to also look down. What the MBA gave me was an ability to formalise the way that I'm looking up. It gave me the ability to think about the power structures, the need for cultural change, how it's possible to effect cultural change, given the power structures we've got. It's given me a format, a formal structure. As I said to a young manager I was speaking to earlier today who is finding the health service too complicated to understand, he has a problem of not seeing the wood for the trees. The MBA's given me the ability to see the wood for the trees.

What we might understand here as an inter-meshing of theory and practice that goes on in our managers' overall learning is often expressed by them in terms of their studies having simply made them more conscious of, or, as Marion Brown puts it, 'more able to verbalise so that you can more consciously analyse' things that they knew about anyway. 'Theory' is most commonly identified by our managers with 'common sense'. Harry Lyttleton finds that the theories he has formally learned about are 'what I knew about anyway – without being able to name the theory or the theorist'. For him even the 'strategy stuff' is 'commonsensical'. And Arthur Blakey tells us that 'Quite a lot of the management ideas [which one studies] fit closely with my own ideas.'

Theory and practice – in practice

Managers were typically vague about the shorter courses they have attended but where they spoke in detail it tended again to be in terms of their consolidating or extending what they either 'knew anyway' or were 'learning on the job at the time'. Lucy Armstrong, for example, talks about attending a 'Women into Management' programme. She says she was, at the time, doing a lot of what was in the modules in her job. This meant that 'the two things were sort of coming together'. She doesn't think that she 'actually kind of learned much new'. But what the course did was to help her focus better 'on things like time management, handling conflicts, dealing with teams'. Lawrence Young talks with immense enthusiasm about an 'outdoor training' course he went on and he talks of its powerful effects again in terms of 'things coming together', in this case quite explicitly 'theory and practice'. But it was 'what worked in practice' that had the edge over the formal theories it would seem:

I just learned a hell of a lot about leadership and teams and communications and – just from the practical application, or the practical application of theory.
You studied theory on the course?
Oh yes, we studied a lot of management theory as well as rock climbing and stuff. You'd learn about how what 'so and so' had to say about how teams work, and then you'd go out and do an exercise, and then come back and say, 'Well, was that how he said a team would work?'. And

we'd decide, 'No, it wasn't the least bit how a team worked'. So, we learned a lot about theory, and the practical application of it.

And do you think it's influencing how you operate now?

Yea, undoubtedly. They said when we started the course that we would remember this course for the rest of our lives. You can read all the books until you're blue in the face and you can work in every possible office or team situation but you'll never forget the things that you learned when you were half way up a rock, or down a cave. And they're quite right. Yea, I think about it all the time.

Short courses, books, theories and university masters programmes were generally treated with caution by our managers. With the exception of occasional references to courses which gave one 'space to stand back and reflect on your practice' or 'to sit down and compare notes with managers from other organisations', it was only where managers could identify a reasonably explicit link between 'theory and practice' that they spoke positively of these formal inputs to 'practical' management learning. And we can see no general difference in the way the younger or more educated managers we studied spoke about these matters and the accounts given by older or less educated individuals. This is most strikingly apparent in the case of university business school provision – something we might expect the more highly educated individuals to be more enthusiastic about than those who dismiss such provision with little direct experience of universities. Eddie Hayes (a training manager we should remember) not only spoke rather reservedly about his own MSc studies, as we saw earlier, but spoke disparagingly of the 'thick graduates' he had seen training as managers in his previous company. And if we listen to our two youngest managers, we hear Liza Potts – recognised as an 'academic high-flyer' by her employer – speaking scathingly of people she has met who 'have done an MBA and have learned nothing'. And Mina Mangeshkar dismisses the bulk of her fellow students on the MBA she is studying as 'people who are only interested in getting a qualification, and want to do this without having to think at all'.

Serious questions are raised for management development practices in British organisations by these stated reservations about courses generally and management education provision specifically. Does learning to manage have to be simply a matter of being left to sink or swim or is there something more formal or systematic which can be done by way of management development? This is a question to which we return in the final chapter.

CHAPTER 5

MANAGING THE SELF AND FITTING THE PART

You manage yourself every day don't you? I think it's just a natural thing that you do, you know, yea.

Ron Scott takes us back to Chapter 1, where it was proposed that 'managing', in its broadest sense, is an activity of everyday life. Our everyday 'managing' requires us to manage tasks – organising our time to fit in all we want and have to do. It has social elements – presenting ourselves in all the different situations and to all the different people we may encounter in the course of a day. We 'manage others' as we try to persuade them to our way of thinking, or try to smooth relationships in the family or amongst friends. We make endless decisions as we manage what to say, when to reveal our feelings and when to hide them. The focus of this chapter is how people talk about 'managing themselves' in their lives at work, and more particularly, in their continuous emergence as managerial workers.

In looking at people's experiences of 'becoming managers', earlier chapters have considered their accounts of how they work to make sense of what is expected of them as 'managers' and how they learn to cope with this role and all its demands. Throughout, there is a sense of people's emergence involving them in coming to terms with and dealing with their understanding of external demands of them as 'managers'. For example, in Chapter 1, we saw how job adverts and job descriptions carry powerful representations of the kind of person the organisation is looking for, the organisational style and culture that people have to fit into and work within and 'discourses' or ideas of how 'management' is accomplished. The person contemplating taking on this job has to be able to make sense of these demands, to come to a positive understanding of what might be involved, and to recognise themselves as someone who can cope with what is entailed. Having got the job, they have to adjust and develop these understandings as they are presented with new ideas, for example through staff development and training, and as they encounter the reality of actually doing the job. So, in Chapters 3 and 4, we have seen how their understanding of what it means to 'be a manager' is constantly developing and changing – it is 'emergent'.

At the same time as this is occurring, as Ron Scott puts it, 'you manage yourself, don't you?' It may involve coming to see or to present oneself differently. People may feel they need to change themselves in certain ways to be successful, or even survive, in their new post. There may be aspects of the work that they feel more or less comfortable with. In other words, there are questions of how they view the 'fit' between themselves as a person and the job that they do. There are questions about the extent to which they experience a continuity of self, as they carry over experiences and feelings from past work, or have a sense of themselves as a person moving through all the different situations they face every day. At the same time, there are possibilities of discontinuities. So, as Kevin Berry pointed out in Chapter 1, it's about being 'the same but different'. These discontinuities may be experienced as exciting, moving forward, a sense of personal growth and development. However, they can also be disconcerting, raising uncomfortable questions about whether the new work situation suits them, whether it fits with the way the person sees themselves and their 'other selves' and 'other lives' outside work lives.

These are challenging and potentially difficult personal matters, through which people are working out their sense of themselves as 'managers' and as 'people'. As they do this, they are engaging in what Harré terms 'identity projects', working to reconcile a 'social self', the self as presented in the social position of 'manager' with a 'personal self', the self experienced as a unique individual with feelings, values and a particular history (1983). Taking up the social position of manager may leave people with feelings of ambivalence and discomfort about things they have to do and how they feel they are expected to present themselves. Höpfl argues that such discomfort, or 'dis-ease' is often concealed in organisational life and that it is unlikely to be addressed explicitly in programmes of staff development or in relationships at work (1994). Yet, as Fineman (1993a) reminds us, feelings and emotions are an important part of organisational life. In the transition to managerial work, some of these feelings and emotions are positive, some are part of the 'dis-ease' or discomfort that people have to deal with.

We are all involved in 'identity projects', working on presenting and securing our identities, whether as managers, parents, friends – and these identities are always open to change or threat from new ideas, challenges, from negative or unexpected reactions from others. These 'identity projects' are 'reflexive' projects, requiring continual re-working to integrate new experiences and changing situations (Giddens 1991). Our view of ourselves is constantly subject to question, to re-affirmation, negotiation and change in the light of how we see ourselves dealing with situations in our everyday life and how others view us and respond to us. The workplace is thus an important forum in which we work out our identity and our sense of 'who we are' as we deal with the opportunities and situations we encounter there. 'Becoming a manager' is a process which has social meaning, which affects how others see a person, what they expect them to be like, how they relate to them and deal with them. It is also a change of considerable personal significance, affecting how that person sees and feels about themselves, and one which changes their perspective on the world they work in and those with whom they work.

'Becoming a manager' involves absorbing new aspects of identity and incorporating them into their sense of 'who they are'. In this chapter, we look at the way people view the 'fit' between themselves and the role of manager. Of course, in their job different 'selves' may come to the fore in different situations – meeting and entertaining clients, talking to senior managers, having a heart to heart with a colleague in the pub, disciplining an employee, empathising with an employee's problems outside work. Also, people recognise there are choices in managerial styles and approaches. People do the job in many different ways, there is no one way to 'be a manager' and organisations are, within limits, able to contain this diversity. Thus, the identity of 'manager' is complex and negotiable, there are continual decisions and choices about how to present oneself and how to manage oneself.

In all of this, the manager is engaged in a process of 'dual control' (Watson 1994b). They are responsible for managing relationships, for achieving the cooperation or compliance by which people work together to fulfil organisational ends, whether it be health provision, the education of children, the production of chemicals or the sales of computer systems and software. As they do this, they also have to 'manage themselves', working out how best they can get others to work, dealing with their feelings and those of others around them, motivating themselves, constructing and developing their understanding of the situations they are in and so on. Their understandings and actions are part of the process Giddens calls 'structuration', whereby the structures and relationships within which they work are reproduced and reinforced, or challenged and changed (1984). This is also reflected at the personal level; they are being shaped and changed by working as a manager. They are also, to different degrees, complying with or changing expectations of managers in the places where they work: 'The person is shaping the work and the work is shaping the person' (D.H. Watson 1996: 241).

Fitting and not fitting: managing a new aspect of identity

'Becoming a manager' places a person in a new position, a different social category, which requires them to incorporate new aspects of identity into their sense of who they are. However, they are 'still the same person', even if it is 'the same but different' as Kevin Berry puts it in

Chapter 1. For new managers, there are tasks of establishing their 'right' to this social identity, demonstrating that they have the appropriate attributes, skills and experience to take on this role and to appear 'credible' as managers. They have to show that they are suitable people to 'take up the challenge', in whatever way that is defined and presented in their particular organisation. Thus, there are both local and more widely available ideas or discourses of what it means to be 'a manager' and of the kind of person that is suited to this role.

How, then, do emergent managers see the 'fit' between their 'social identity' as managers and their 'personal identity' as people with particular histories or biographies and with their own reflections and feelings about their work? In talking about how they see themselves as managers, they have to reconcile a 'social self', addressing public, collective, external, social notions of being a manager and a 'personal self', an internal, private sense of themselves as unique individuals, with their own way of seeing the world, their own feelings and reactions to it. They are thus actively involved in social and personal identity projects, bringing these different aspects of themselves more closely into line, or reconciling themselves with and coming to terms with any discrepancies (Harré 1983). The 'social self' is, to some extent, negotiable. There are discourses of management and ideas of the 'manager' to draw on. However, these vary and they change. So, some of the younger 'career managers' such as Liza Potts are very much aware that they have been identified as part of a process of changing managerial thinking and approaches in their particular organisation. Also, organisations, within limits, do tolerate, or even welcome, different kinds of people doing the same job in different ways. For example, a number of people commented along the lines that 'they don't mind how I do the job, so long as I get the results'.

As we saw in Chapter 2, in applying for jobs, people usually focus on aspects of themselves and their experience that they see as congruent with the post, and filter out other aspects. Their CV is constructed to produce a 'good fit' between themselves and their understanding of the job (Metcalfe 1992). In an interview, they draw on their understanding of what will be acceptable ways of presenting themselves (Moir 1993). Thus, we are familiar with the idea of presenting ourselves in different ways. Processes of selection and recruitment encourage the would-be manager to present and emphasise a 'good fit' and to play down or conceal ways they feel less suited to the job. Once in the job, this understanding of the social definitions and expectations may well change. So, the person is involved in a continuing process of negotiation and adjustment between themselves and their role – their sense of how they see themselves as managers is emergent.

So are you typical? Moulding, cloning, distinguishing

We asked managers if they saw themselves as typical of those who got on in their organisation. In answering this, they are implicitly comparing themselves with others and drawing on their sense of the particular demands of their organisation. Marion Brown, for example, talks about how she had to work to make herself appear 'typical', in order to get the job. 'If I am [typical], it's because I've seen a mould and I've consciously tried to squeeze myself into it . . .' Having decided she wanted to become a headteacher, after a number of interviews she adapted her presentation of herself. 'I think I frightened a lot of heads . . . I know that I look and sound a lot more confident than I am sometimes . . .' Alicia Coltrane 'moulds' herself to what her boss wants for different reasons, she has seen the difference her manager has made to the area she works in, and to her own confidence in doing her job:

I think I'm pretty easy for Bill to manage, because I'm quite interested in hearing what he has to say! . . . he's earned that respect . . . we all felt out of our depths, and he came along and really gave us the confidence and gave us the skills and pointed us in the right direction.

Sally Vaughan and Betty Smith found it easier to identify themselves as 'typical'. Sally, with tongue in cheek, described the people working in her marketing division as 'clones'. Many are women, all work hard, are creative, have similar skills, pass through the grading system in broad age bands and so on – Sally sees herself as 'untypical' only in that her progress has been faster than most. Betty talked of doing an exercise with other practice managers where they all came out the same – patient, able to see all sides and viewpoints – characteristics she sees as important in enabling her to deal with the demands of the job. Others identified particular characteristics they saw as 'typical' of people in their position, for example, being young, ambitious, hard-working, enthusiastic, committed.

However, labelling oneself as 'typical' sits uneasily with our need to see ourselves as unique and different. It also sits uncomfortably with ideas of the successful manager as exceptional, outstanding and 'different from the average employee'. Most people did point to things that made them different. However, this is potentially threatening for the new manager if they are distinguished in ways that make them less suited to the job. One way round this is to draw on the idea that the 'typical' manager in their organisation is nevertheless a unique individual. So, people spoke of 'typical characteristics' such as 'having a strong personality and opinions', 'all have egos', 'being personable', 'flamboyant', 'thinking "outside the box"', 'able to stand alone' and so on – characteristics which can be read as marking a 'typical manager' who is, paradoxically, also a 'unique individual'.

Andrew Shepherd takes this up by pointing out that there is no norm. 'Everyone brings their own style and personality', 'many different kinds of people get on'. However, although everyone is different, 'the average Joe doesn't get on', which means that his 'difference' has a particular place in the bank. 'I think it is my own personal style throughout that has carried me through quite strongly . . . valuing people, yes, valuing people.' He also accounts for his rapid progress by being noticeably different from the 'average Joe'. 'I was not a standard bank clerk, because I had long hair . . . upset one or two people, too cocky, you know. But I realise now that by being slightly unconventional, some people remembered me.' So, we see Andrew presenting himself as having a strong sense of being different, but in a way that it is useful and acceptable – that hasn't undermined his sense of himself as fitting the social category of manager.

Ron Scott takes this further, as he questions whether there can be a 'typical' manager in the prison service:

There's different types of managers and there has to be, because there's different situations that crop up that have to be dealt with . . . say, inmate on the roof, or inmate smashing cell up, or inmate setting fire to the library. There's no handbook you get out to solve that . . . you have to make sure all the right procedures are followed . . . but [beyond that], one manager would deal with it completely different to another . . . that's where personality comes in . . . you have to weigh all the situation up as it comes up. That's the beauty of the job, I think. That's why people that are in it like it. Because you don't know what is going to crop up from day to day.

In saying this, Ron argues that all managers are unique – being 'typical' becomes a matter of having personal qualities to draw on that enable one to cope with the range of situations that might arise.

Others saw themselves as part of a 'new breed' of younger managers, with new ideas – a shift away from the 'typical', part of a trend accepted and encouraged by the organisation that places them at the forefront of change. So, Kathy Westbrook identified herself as part of a new trend towards recruiting graduate trainee managers in Big Pizza: 'it sounds pompous . . . there just seems a different calibre there . . .' Also, she sees them as part of a change towards 'a more people orientated management style . . . more bothered if the crew are enjoying themselves, and they're creating a good atmosphere, and stuff like that'. Liza Potts talks of how her organisation expects its graduate trainees to be 'flamboyant, enthusiastic, growth thinking, new age managers . . . sports car drivers who race ahead of everybody else and are all store manager calibre from day one'. So, these young career managers feel quite isolated, 'untypical', different, alongside more established managers. As newcomers to the organisation, they have been set a difficult task, to challenge and change established practice. They are helped in dealing with this difficult position by their sense that they are recognised as 'untypical' of the current breed of managers. This marks them as special, as part of the future.

As they draw comparisons between themselves and other managers, we see Andrew Shepherd, Ron Scott, Kathy Westbrook and Liza Potts defining 'difference' in ways they can reconcile with organisational definitions and needs – even though they all feel they meet some resistance to their 'difference' amongst colleagues. However, some differences may be challenging or threatening to the 'social self'. The exceptional speed of Liz Carter's promotion to a senior managerial role marks her as having potential which has been recognised and acknowledged, and for her, this difference is positive. However, because she has been promoted so rapidly, her 'identity project' involves dealing with her vulnerability about her limited experience. She makes up for this by being very careful to 'do her homework' before making decisions, familiarising herself with legislation and procedure, consulting more experienced personnel staff, liaising and talking to a wide range of colleagues where she works. In these ways, she is demonstrating to herself and to the listener that she does 'fit'. In part, she does this by showing how characteristics of 'personal self', her ability to involve and consult with others, her hard work in 'doing her homework', alongside her openness about her limited knowledge and her willingness to seek help from colleagues, enable her to deal with the limitations of her 'social self' that make her feel vulnerable.

For some, the reality of 'being a manager' in their organisation may be threatening to their 'personal self'. Ken Pine is clearly disappointed with many aspects of his job as a management trainee with a restaurant chain, as are many others in his company, for the position has a high turnover rate:

A lot of trainees come and go. They all come into the job and think, Assistant Manager of a place like ours, brilliant. But it's not as good as it sounds. You've got to have dedication and something about you to stick at it. You've got long hours, you take a lot of crap and I think the failure rate's about 80 odd percent who quit . . . so if you get on so far, then you must have something about you to stick at it.

Ken grew up with a sense that he was an able student, destined to do well. He trained to be a civil engineer. He is clearly working to reconcile the reality of his life in the restaurant with his view of himself as someone who is 'going somewhere'. Here, Ken redefines his disappointment with his job as success – the majority (who leave) are failures. The 'untypical' ones who stay have 'something about them'. However, this is a difficult position to sustain in the longer term. By the time of the second interview, Ken had also left.

So, as people draw comparisons between themselves and other managers, there seems to be tension between a desire to recognise themselves as possessing the attributes that fit with belonging in the social category 'manager', yet also being significantly different.

For some people, it is important to see themselves as 'untypical'. Although Charles Parker wears the 'grey suit' and blends in, in some ways, with the senior managers he has to deal with to get his work done, he also emphasises that he is *not* a 'man in a grey suit', and does not want to be. He is conscious of himself as different – and this is important to him. Will Evans is also at pains to emphasise that he is different, that he is not 'driven by the job', like other ambitious and successful teachers he sees around him. 'I don't think I work hard enough', he says. Yet, he also makes it quite clear that his department is very successful, that he takes a lot of the credit for building it up. As he talks, he works to distinguish himself from colleagues in similar positions, presenting himself as 'lazy', 'not totally committed', 'not bothered whether I work in teaching or in something else' – his personal self is 'untypical'. However, despite this, he presents his achievements as exceptional and he presents himself as someone who is looking to move forwards, or upwards, in his teaching career 'because it's there'. In some ways, the outcome is indistinguishable from, or even superior to, that of his more 'typical' colleagues – but it is clearly important to Will that he sees himself as different. Will links this, in part, to his rebellion from the pressures of his family, who are all artistic and able teachers – he chose a different route, and came into teaching later, via industry. 'I did sciences and what not. I'd probably have done best to have done the arts . . . yea, a rebellion. It seemed like a good idea at the time.'

As we listen to these people, we see them presenting themselves as 'fitting' the role of manager, and working to show that the ways in which they are 'untypical' can be viewed positively, or can be dealt with and do not undermine their claim to the post. In these ways, they are doing 'identity work', they are shaping their presentation of self in ways that do not fundamentally challenge their claim on the role – explaining and reconciling their limited experience, their difference, or whatever, in ways that are acceptable to themselves and, they hope, to the listener. However, in listening to them, there is a strong feeling that some people have more, or different kinds of 'identity work' to do than others.

The ideal job for you: 'but everyone has a love hate relationship with their job don't they?'

As Diane Washington says this, she questions the idea of a perfect fit between a person and their job. She is checking her assumption that we all share her ambivalence. As we saw in Chapter 2, the discourse of a 'career' holds out a possibility that somewhere out there is the ideal job, the 'perfect fit'. This is still a powerful idea against which people judge their situations.

The idea of a 'fit' is complicated, something which we have already touched on. Are we 'a person', or a complex of different 'selves', sometimes in conflict with one another? Could a job fit comfortably with how we see some aspects of ourselves, but sit uneasily alongside others? Are our personalities 'fixed', or do we change and develop over time – is the search for a 'fit' therefore endless? Can we even make choices and work to change ourselves – through reflection, assertiveness training, counselling or whatever? And what of 'being a manager'? Is what that means open to change and negotiation in organisations – can the job be adjusted and shaped to fit us? As we saw in Chapter 3, 'being a manager' is ambiguous; even those doing the job are not entirely clear what it involves. As Jack Dodds puts it:

I don't have a very, very clear cut picture . . . you know, the various attributes, what the ideal manager should be. I think management is a whole range of different aspects and different personalities and so on.

Also, as Julian Adderley points out, any sense of a 'fit' has to be worked out over time, it 'emerges' as people find ways of dealing with situations they encounter.

I think it's the approach you adopt really, you know. Not everyone can turn round and sort of shout at people. And I'm not a great shouter at people . . . I tend to take . . . a sort of different approach to dealing with issues. And you know, it works, and sometimes it doesn't work. If it doesn't work, then you have to change your approach. And I think every manger should develop their own approach and their own way of dealing and managing . . . I think managerial skills don't just happen over night. They happen really through experience, a lot of it. OK, you can . . . know a lot of the theory of management and so on, and how you should tackle certain situations and so on, but the really sort of day to day bits and pieces are – are down to experience really.

Stan Jordan takes up this idea that any sense of a 'fit' is transient, it can change:

I suppose success in management must be like everything else, a retrospective view of life. And when do you say, 'this is the point at which I look back and say whether that is a complete management phase or not?' I think it's ongoing . . . So when you became bored with the type of people you were with or the type of business that you and the team are managing, or that particular part of the business, then yes, that particular management role would be boring. I think you grow into things in life.

Yes, I do fit

With these kinds of concerns in our minds, we asked our managers whether they felt, when they made the transition into managerial work, there were any bits of themselves that they were concerned might not fit with 'being a manager'. In their responses to this question we see people identifying things about themselves that make them feel they are the 'right person' for this job. For some, these are personal characteristics, attitudes, philosophies – 'wanting to involve people', 'I treat people like adults', 'I like responsibility', 'I get on with people', 'openness', 'being cheerful', 'I communicate with people at their level'. Others demonstrate their awareness of what is expected and demanded by the organisation: 'I always try to meet my targets', 'Now, I don't have any doubts about what I am doing or about my ability to do it.' Others see the 'fit' in terms of having the right background and experience, 'I know the department and the hospital'; 'I know the shop floor people'; 'It was in a sphere where I've had quite a bit of practical experience. The senior nurses, a lot of them know me and know the way that I work, and I think that's its credibility, really.'

So, we can see the ways in which people show 'fit', in terms of personal characteristics, appropriate background and experience, awareness of expectations and ability to meet them. However, their responses are moderated.

Things fit here, but not there . . .

Mary Rainey shows how the job itself might suggest a need for different 'selves' to deal with different elements in it. This is something she finds hard to reconcile with her sense of self. She doesn't see herself as someone who adopts different styles or different personae to deal with different circumstances. Her sense of herself as consistent comes across as important to her, something she is reluctant to compromise. An important part of this is that she is someone who 'calls a spade a spade'. Although she feels this should fit with the proclaimed culture of 'honesty and openness', she is aware that on more than one occasion, the way she 'calls a spade a spade' has not been well received by senior managers. On the other hand, she feels it is part of her credibility with the nursing staff she manages: 'they know I mean what I say . . . I think it has its positive sides as well . . . for the ward staff, I think they actually believe it gives me some credibility.' So, Mary feels clear about the kind of person she is, and always has been – but finds it 'fits' well with some of the people she works with, but not with others.

Which me?

Other people are more conscious of their different selves. Earlier, we heard Jean Holliday reflecting on which aspects of herself she thought were more important in her job – the technical aspects in which she excelled as a young accountant, or her life experience as a parent, a person outside work and how this had changed her priorities and outlook, making her view of managerial issues in the health service 'less black and white'. Thus, Jean traces how her 'accountant self' has been overlaid and softened by later experience.

In the first interview Marion Brown talks of how she is 'different people' at one and the same time, and of her equivocation about what she wants. When we first met her, in her first year in the job, she was aware her feelings about herself in her job could swing dramatically, depending on how things were going at any moment. So, 'there are times when I think this is wonderful; I was born to do it' and other times when 'I've thought, my god, I've been promoted beyond my capabilities here'. As Marion talks, she also shows how the conflict between different managerial discourses is reflected in her own feelings about herself and her job. The manager is a leader – however, this is an aspect of her job as a head teacher that she felt ambivalent about. On the one hand, she knows how she wants her school to be, 'I have a strong vision and view of how I want things to be in this school, and I think I'm strong enough and persuasive enough for that vision to affect a lot of people.' On the other hand, when she first came into the job, 'it did worry me that I'm such a follower. How would I cope when there was no one else to sort of sound ideas off?' The idea of 'the leader', who fulfils a new vision for the school, also sits somewhat uncomfortably alongside other ideals of a more democratic management style – especially as Marion feels many of her staff are not fully committed to the kind of changes she wants to see. So, 'I know that people work best when they feel they have got some decision-making power' but on the other hand, 'it sounds very negative, getting people to do what you want. And that is what I mean really.' The 'democratic' discourse suggests a team of equals, ideas of consensus, possibilities of shared responsibility, 'they're responsible alongside me for managing the school'. However, at the same time, she *is* different, her job puts her in a position where her ideal of joint responsibility is limited: 'I feel very definitely the buck stops with me and that I'm ultimately responsible for everything that happens in my school.' In some ways, it is *my* school for Marion and she is there to work to get others to share *her* vision for its future. She has strong feelings about how it should be run, and sees herself having reached a stage in her career where she is ready to 'plough my own furrow'. This contrasts with her sense of herself that she has lived with throughout her teaching career, 'I was always one of the girls before, the in-crowd, if you like'. In contrast, as a new head, 'I've found it very hard this year, I've found it lonely'.

These glimpses of how Marion Brown talks about her role as a manager and contrasts it with her earlier experiences as a classroom teacher and deputy head, show how she is living with conflicting ideas about herself, about how she would like to be doing her job and what others are expecting of her, about the kind of relationships they want to have with their 'head'. These conflicts are at the level of the structural, contractual relationships between her and the staff – the way these set her apart and put particular responsibilities upon her. They also show her struggle to reconcile conflicting managerial discourses – the manager as inspirational, the manager as democratic leader; the manager as a person with special skills of working with and through others, but managing staff on whom they are dependent, who can resist and refuse to change. At yet another level, she is working with a view of herself as a complex person, who sometimes feels secure and confident about her abilities, at other times insecure and uncertain; who is both a leader and a follower, who has always belonged, as 'one of the girls', but who no longer fits quite so comfortably in her new position. As we listen to Marion, it becomes clear that any notion of 'fit' is complex.

Changing selves and changing situations

Lucy Armstrong focuses on how her experience has made her the kind of person who is able to take on and deal with difficult issues, able to influence people and change things, rather than the detailed knowledge and skills it has given her.

I think I'd built up a kind of – a sense of experience, and I suppose it's a sense of self confidence as well that goes alongside it. I realise that over the two years I was seconded, when I look back, I'd done some really hairy things, you know. I'd gone in and sort of confronted head teachers [*laughter*] and got them sorted, you know.

Lucy also feels this gave her an awareness of what is involved in bringing about changes in further education that she feels are important: 'you can't pick up one thing, you are actually generally dealing with a whole tranche of things – quite often student values and priorities and attitudes'. She feels her secondment was important because it came at a time that marked a significant change in how colleges are dealing with student support services.

I mean, the way colleges care for students is a big issue, and it's shifted tremendously over the last few years. And I was very much in it at the point at which it was starting to shift, and I really felt, you know, that I was there giving it a push in what I did feel and still do feel is a very important direction ... I could see it coming, if you like. I knew it was going to happen, so I was part of it from the very, very beginning.

So, Lucy shows how she 'fits' as a person able to bring about the kind of changes colleges are having to make. But even more important, it seems, is her sense that within this climate of change, she fits because it offers her opportunities to work on developing services that she has seen a need for, that fit with her own philosophy of student support, that she is committed to. Lucy puts her emphasis on ways in which the job fits her and the experience and values she brings to it.

Fits over time

As Colin Hawkins talks, we come to see the complexity of his sense of a 'fit' between himself and his job. As he answers our question, he talks at some length and in the process, raises many issues. Colin, you may remember, left the armed forces to develop a career in social work. He has recently moved from 'mainstream' social work to become the manager of residential accommodation for people with mental health problems who have left hospital. His recent move is a major leap forward in his career and he is clear why he has been appointed. The post had been vacant for some time and his boss wanted to bring in a strong manager, someone who would be able to 'turn round' the project, from caring, supportive, homely, long-stay residential accommodation to a more dynamic environment, 'empowering' residents, enabling them to make decisions, equipping them to live independently in the community, and providing the support to enable them to make this transition.

Colin feels quite strongly that military life had shaped him into the kind of person his boss was looking for to take on this task. However, he is also clear that the 'self' he presents is far from the whole story. One of his supervisors, as a new social worker, warned him that his confident exterior might mask his lack of experience. He too, is aware that the way he appears to others conceals another self, nervous, sensitive, less confident, less sure of himself. Although this 'appearance' is part of him, it is only part. He talks of how the development of the confident, forces self may have been at the expense of 'other selves'. So although, in some ways, it has helped him to achieve and get on in his career, in other ways 'I've never really achieved what may have been potentially there'. He goes on, 'I think the forces were, for me in particular, wrong. I think there's part of my own personal self and it's never really developed, there's parts of me that are missing.'

This sense of a mis-fit between the self-in-role and the deeper, more private self has been a source of unhappiness in Colin's life, something hidden away, undealt with:

I'm still surprised that I'm in a management position . . . because of my own frailties and my own – the confidence. But I think I manage to hide it, I don't think my staff would [realise]. I manage to cope with it in that way . . . There's parts of me appear very confident and that's something that I've learned from the forces, to take on the role and the responsibilities, I've never been comfortable with it.

'Becoming a manager', for Colin, has happened to coincide with a new relationship, in which he feels able to express and deal with some of these underlying concerns and anxieties:

it's been a relief to me, to show someone that side of me . . . not to have to hide it, the vulnerable side, the weak side. And it allows me to actually come out and be that person that I want to be, the confident, out-going person that I want to be, full of life – it's given me the confidence to actually do it.

So, we can see how the 'self' he learned to present in his military career has enabled him to cope and to get on in the world of work, and outside. He has appeared outgoing, confident and capable, but all the while felt nervous, unconfident, out of touch with part of himself. He talks calmly and openly about this – 'it's quite easy, in self-analysing it all' – but at the same time, it is clear that Colin is talking about a mismatch between his sense of himself and of his work role that has caused him considerable insecurity and unhappiness in his life which, it seems, for many years he has had to hide and absorb.

Another layer of concern is Colin's growing sense that the style and appearance his boss has appointed him for – the decisiveness, the 'ability to cut through the crap and get things done' – qualities that have served him well in the military environment – may not be so appropriate in the very different world of residential care. The contrast was less stark in other social work jobs, where decisions had to be made quickly in crisis situations:

[Here] I had to physically remove myself, and say be a manager, let them get on with it . . . They'll bring their problems to you . . . It's been quite a transition. And it's quite interesting, because in social work, you can actually be quite reactive in crisis. And that suited me down to the ground, because that was what I'd been trained for in the forces. Especially crisis work. It's up my street . . . also child protection work, it was very procedural, you're given clear guidelines, and there is a structure there. I knew what I was meant to be doing, I knew what was expected of me. So, that fitted very nicely with my experiences in the forces.

In the environment he is in now, often he has to hold back, and allow others to reach their own decisions in their own time – to do otherwise would go against the principles of 'involvement' and 'empowerment' that are central to his philosophy of how he believes the service should be run. At the same time, this runs against all his learned instincts of how a manager should behave.

I think those attributes from the forces can be quite dangerous in social work. I'm having to read-just and rethink some of the more dangerous bits of things, or methods, or experiences, or theories, that I've got from my own past. You'd jump in . . . you'd say, get it done, and that would be it. No arguing. And I have to remember that my staff haven't had that type of experience, or that type of structure. And there's times when I say, 'could you do that please', and I just forget it. And a week or two later, I say, is it done?' 'Oh, I haven't had time', or 'I've been off'. And I get quite irritated with that, from a manager's point of view . . . in the forces you could just forget it . . . It's also a different way of dealing with people. In the forces, you become quite firm, and say 'that's enough'. And you had a punishment there. And there is a procedure. Whereas here, it's much more about participation and consensus, and trying to get your workers to work the way you see – well, within your own procedures and guidelines.

So, there are helpful and useful qualities he brings from his time in the forces, such as 'my ability to make decisions and to be comfortable with making decisions'. But at the same time, he is aware that he is having to change his own style to fit the environment he is working in, and that this is moving away from his manager's expectations of him:

There's the dilemma of what my network manager wants me to do, and me at the work floor, starting off saying 'Yes, that's what I'm going to do' and that's how I came in, and created hell. And now mellowing a little bit and understanding some of the more subtle forms of management. So there's a problem for me there. And balancing what my manager was saying to me, what he expects and wants, and me agreeing with him to begin with, and now saying, 'well hang on a minute, let's slow down a little bit'.

Colin is having to adjust his manager's view, 'renegotiate' his expectations and also shift his sense of the kind of person and manager Colin is. At the same time, he is having to renegotiate with staff, colleagues and clients, their initial impressions and 'traces of the forces . . . traces of my personality that come through, and that is not helpful'. For example, there is his reputation of 'being a straight speaker':

People can't deal with that, being open and honest . . . yes, there's some bad bits, a bit painful some of the time. They find me quite threatening. But that's more to do with the confidence that the forces gives you. Actually being up-front and being able to talk to people. Because really I'm not like that. I'm not at all.

Are you surprised that you have ended up as a manager?

In Chapter 2, we saw that 'children don't dream of being managers'. However, some people are more surprised than others to have ended up in managerial positions. For some, their route into management, their paths to where they are now, have been shaped by unforeseeable and unexpected circumstances. Ellen Fitzgerald explains how getting divorced has changed her orientation to work and her expectations of her career, how, moving away from her 'traditional upbringing', she was 'almost forced down a different route that I would never have chosen'. Unforeseen changes in organisations also play their part – unanticipated opportunities arising, being in 'the right place at the right time'. Mike Davis charts his career through a series of mergers and takeovers that have taken him in unplanned directions, tracing an unlikely path from printing, to working in hotels and the leisure industry, into bingo. Others are less surprised. Dan Tracey is only surprised that his ambitious plan has worked out so far; he is still on track to achieve his goal of becoming a managing director. For Julian Adderley, management has 'always been a goal', but at the time he was a student, 'there was only one computer', so 'there were no ideas about going into computing . . .', as he has since done. These glimpses give an impression of people moving through a changing environment, seizing chances, responding to changes, adapting to fit – a picture of emerging lives and emerging selves that bring people to more or less unexpected places. Amidst this change, people are also able to construct a sense of continuity, what Giddens calls a 'trajectory of self' (1991), to present a picture of themselves moving through, bringing things from their past, redefining and coming to understand past influences in different ways, explaining how they have come to change in the process. Our emphasis now turns to how people talk about self and change. However, although everyone's story is one of change and adjustment, we now look at some groups who arguably have more 'identity work' to do, who seem to have a sense of having particular issues to deal with as they look back over their lives and talk about how they came to be managers.

Professional and managerial identities

I trained to be a physiotherapist, I didn't train to be a manager.

As Diane Washington says this, she emphasises that she sees herself as a physiotherapist, albeit one who has come, gradually to take on managerial responsibility for her department. The absence of career paths in many professions is problematic. People reach a point where the next step takes them away from the profession they trained to follow, onto a managerial ladder. Amongst our managers are a number, like Diane, who have dealt with this by attempting to retain their professional interests while taking on managerial work. Diane Washington feels it is important to retain her clinical role and to use and develop her knowledge and experience – not only in terms of her sense of herself as a professional physiotherapist, but also, to make her a more effective manager, more in touch with changing knowledge in her field and with the experiences of those she manages. Jack Dodds continues his research, and is delighted to have been invited to make a keynote address at an academic conference. Mary Rainey is doing a job that is unquestionably managerial, but still sees herself, first and foremost, as a nurse. All these people present their sense of professional identity as central to their sense of self.

Although Diane is currently determined to retain her dual role, she is finding it a struggle. Jack Dodds is clear, as he looks around at jobs, that one direction for progression involves moving into roles that are more exclusively managerial. At the time we first met Lucy Armstrong, she had come to the conclusion that, much as she loved her teaching role and felt it contributed positively to managing student services, combining the two, 'it's killing me'. She had come to feel that the solution was to shift the balance of her work towards management:

I mean, I don't want to stop teaching. I have got into a bit of a conflict in myself actually at the moment. I really do enjoy it . . . some of the things I do, in a way, to me are just kind of life blood. But it's very difficult when you're tied to a teaching schedule.

By the time of the second interview, Lucy had clearly been thinking about this further. She was considering new opportunities for placements in industry, identifying her generic 'transferable skills' and looking at jobs outside education:

there are a very strong set of ideological values attached to (working in education) . . . and one of those quite often means that you put in a lot of your own steam for not a lot of reward, frankly. And I think it's got worse, I think colleges are trading on that more and more.

This is difficult for Lucy. She has always worked in education, her 'ideological commitment' is strong. However, people at all levels are having their teaching loads increased, 'it's just happening automatically . . . because of the FEFC funding mechanism'. So, Lucy is beginning to look for a better effort–reward bargain.

Despite the benefits they see of having professionally active and professionally aware people in management, we meet people beginning to question whether this is feasible or sustainable in their particular situation. This raises further questions about whether organisations could do more to enable people to combine these tasks – and whether they consider it important. However, here, we are more interested in the dilemmas people face as they have to redefine their professional identity.

Some have come to accept that they are now primarily managers. Marion Brown is quite happy with this, she feels the more managerial job of being a school head 'fits' her better than being a classroom teacher:

I had to leave class teaching . . . It was that burn-out factor . . . you couldn't go on caring – you could, but it was so hard to go on giving what you needed to give and being dynamic and changing and growing . . . And I'm not a natural – you know – it's November, so it must be bonfire night – and I've found a picture for nature! After twenty years of classroom teaching, I found it hard . . . I mean, the very nature of the job, the routineness of it, no, I would not say that I was a real close fit with that. It was necessary to get where I am now, which I think is much more of a close fit with me.

Marion has a sense of having made an important change in her career. She knows she is now a manager, and says 'I've never enjoyed a job as much in my life.' Marion talks of many other ways in which the transition is difficult and uncomfortable. However, it seems to extend and build on, rather than threaten, her professional identity:

I love the variety of it. And you see, now I have the opportunity to practise all those classroom skills, all the skills I learned in teaching, but then loads of others as well . . . I feel very matched to the job that I'm doing at the moment.

Colin Hawkins is clear that he is now a manager rather than a social worker. He talks about this transition in terms of a 'strategic exchange' (Watson 1994a). He sees himself sacrificing the 'kick-back' from being directly involved in helping and relating to people with problems for the less direct rewards of being involved in building a different kind of service, 'enabling, empowering' its users.

It's not visible on the caring side, which again is a dilemma for me, because I think that's part of my nature, and why I came into social work . . . you need a kick-back, you're a human being. And I'm actually missing that in my management role, because they see me very much in a negative way . . . a lot of the time. Because I'm the one they see as making the decisions . . . I actually do make good things happen. But they don't see it, because the ones that stick in their mind are the negative ones. And for me, that's a real dilemma, because part of me coming into social work was I wanted to be seen as a caring person . . . So it's a dilemma, a personal dilemma for me.

So, although Colin is clear he is now 'here to manage' and says he is comfortable with that, there is still the part of him that chose to be a social worker, 'wanting to be seen as a caring person', that conflicts with the way he feels he is often seen as manager – disrupting and changing comfortable routines, making tough decisions about who can be accepted, or remain, as residents. As he puts it, 'it's a dilemma, a personal dilemma for me'.

Arthur Blakey and Mark Taylor both started out as engineers, but saw they had hit a 'log jam' at the top of the technical grading, along with many longer-standing and very highly skilled engineers. Both recognised that a way forward in their company was to move into production management, onto a managerial ladder with more scope for progression. As Mark puts it, a move from an 'office mentality' to a 'very different shop floor mentality – it's rough and tough, basically, rough and tough'. The link, for Mark, was that he would be managing an area using machines he had been involved in buying and that he knew well. However, having tried it, he decided '10% of the role was machine knowledge, 90% was people-based stuff . . . I didn't actually think it was for me'. Mark has returned to manage a new project in engineering. Arthur Blakey, on the other hand, said 'It was a step out into – almost into the outside world . . . it just happened to be an ideal one that suited me.' He has made rapid progress, he has enjoyed the challenge of developing a plan or strategy for the tool room he manages, and the reward of seeing it happen. He feels his background as a successful engineer gave him credibility in that environment, but he now sees himself as a manager. He is looking for bigger managerial challenges and is looking towards general management.

These experiences show people with very different feelings about moving away from their professional backgrounds, into managerial work. For Marion Brown, it is positive, she feels she is moving forward after twenty years of classroom teaching. Becoming a head teacher is clearly very different, yet, at the same time, the move from a professional to a managerial identity is less stark than it seems for some other people. Arthur Blakey and Colin Hawkins welcome the opportunities that their job moves have opened up. Nevertheless, for Colin, there is also a sense of loss, of the 'kick-back' of direct involvement in social work. However, others are much more reluctant to define themselves as managers. We see Mary Rainey saying she is 'first and foremost a nurse', but doing a managerial job. We see others struggling to maintain professional involvement alongside managerial work, and questioning whether this is viable in the longer term.

'A big thing is being a woman and a manager': gender and managerial work

Many of the women see their gender as marking them as 'untypical'. No men say this. Marion Brown was 'gobsmacked' to see the number of men at her first meeting of primary heads. Carrie Bley feels she was 'not well received' as a young woman in a senior position. Alicia Coltrane says 'I think what is a big thing is being a woman and being a manager. And also being quite young.' While all new managers have some 'identity work' to do in working out how they see themselves as managers, it seems that there is additional work for women, in reconciling being 'a woman' with being 'a manager'. Marshall and Wetherell found that students training to be lawyers all had to work to make their sense of themselves as people fit with their ideas of the qualities and characteristics of lawyers (1989). However, there was an added twist in this for the women, because the characteristics of lawyers also tended to be seen as 'masculine' characteristics.

A similar dilemma could be proposed for women entering managerial work. Marshall discusses how characteristics seen as stereotypical of the 'successful manager' also happen to be characteristics that tend to be seen as 'masculine' – being decisive, rational rather than emotional, taking initiative, being a 'leader' and so on (Marshall 1989). Lucy Armstrong and Shirley Stitt talk about their struggle to find a way of being a manager that they feel comfortable with. Finding role models from the previous generation of women managers was difficult, because 'they did it by being like men'. Furthermore, Shirley found that, as a woman, her behaviour was 'read' differently from that of a man: 'If I'm strong, and stand my ground, I'm seen as being aggressive and stroppy. And if it's a bloke, then he's just doing his job, you know.' Shirley talks at some length about how no comfortable model is available for her, in the 'macho' world of production where she works. Lucy Armstrong stresses the importance of her secondment to a project managed by a woman, who at last offered a role model that she could identify with, that made the managerial posts she had dismissed from her own plans suddenly appear feasible.

As Marshall points out, some have argued that 'feminine' characteristics fit better with current ideas of management that emphasise skills such as communication, team working, nurturing and developing staff – however, she also questions whether these could confine women to particular kinds of managerial jobs, and how far they are accepted as fitting people to senior, strategic management roles. Marion Brown talks about how she brings 'how I am as a woman' to the way she manages:

But I think that's good, I think that's positive.

What do you mean by that?
In [*laughs*] the way that I've been taught and conditioned to care about other people's needs. And I don't think it's good that I've been taught always to put them before my own, and I don't. I don't because I've rationalised some of that out. I still do it far more often than makes me a healthy, whole person . . . the bits of me that have been taught to communicate as a woman, and to care about others and to empathise with others and to put their needs first – I think I do that very much as a manager.

Marion recognises that, as a woman, she has learned to listen, empathise, care about others' needs. These qualities come across strongly as part of her managerial style. She wants to operate in an open and democratic way, but also sees herself having a role as a leader, a person with strong views about the direction she wants her school to go. Leadership and democracy are in tension in managerial discourses of 'teams', 'involvement' and 'empowerment'. This creates dilemmas for all managers. However, listening to Marion, she presents a parallel dilemma at a personal level. While valuing her qualities of listening, caring and empathising, it has been important, as a 'healthy, whole person', to 'unlearn' her readiness to put others first.

Colin Hawkins talks from the 'other side', of being male in a predominantly female managerial group in residential social services. He is conscious of how being a man affects how others view him. For example, 'It's quite easy to be used as the group spokesperson', he points out. From his own experience, he senses that, as a man, he is received differently, that he is listened to more carefully, he is afforded greater credibility, 'when I deal with professionals like psychiatrists or GPs'. He recognises that these characteristics may be an advantage when dealing with relatively powerful groups, and when acting decisively to bring about change. However, he questions whether they fit with other elements of his work, and how far it is being a man, and how far it is being a manager, that becomes the issue:

There are times when [clients] don't want to discuss things with me, especially if they've been abused, that has an impact . . . it's quite difficult, because what I'm trying to assess is how they perceive me as a male – but there are times when I think the role of manager gets in the way. So therefore, I think they're tied up together, being a male manager actually has an impact on how they see me and perceive me. They see me as very powerful in making decisions, because invariably, if things are going wrong, I'm the one that actually goes and sits down and makes the decision about whether or not they should be staying, or how to resolve issues . . . I can't be specific, but in a generalised way, I think being male and being a manager does have an impact on how they perceive you.

Mike Davis sees women managers in bingo as a recent development: 'they've always sort of, like, associated managers with being a man'. He goes on to argue that this means 'they need to prove themselves more so than a male', in various ways – for example, 'with the customers', 'in achieving the budgets', at meetings 'making sure their presence is felt'. Mike makes sense of this in terms of his own experience of being in a minority, as a black manager, and how it has made him more conscious of his behaviour, although in different ways.

I mean, some of them are quite hard, in the sense that they're very tough. And I think they've had to be tough to get where they are. I suppose it's not the wrong approach or wrong line to take, but I think they have sort of like wanted something and have had to go all guns out for it.
So they behave like men managers, or do they behave differently?
Oh, they behave different, but they are very sort of assertive, very assertive. And I think that's something they feel they need to be, assertive and in control of situations.
Can you understand that?
Yes, I can. Because sort of like from a race point of view as well, there' s not many blacks, Asians, whatever in the industry. And so, from that point of view, I can understand it, because I'm continually sort of thinking, am I creating the right impression? You know, am I looked upon in the same light as the others? So yes.
So does that influence how you behave?
Oh very much so, yes. Because I always think, well if I misbehave . . . or act in a certain manner, I mean it could be frowned upon . . . And that fits with my personal viewpoint.
So, in a different way, the women have the same issues?
The same, yes – issues, yes.

'I still feel my class quite strongly . . . I do know where I've come from'

Tom Smith remains amazed that he, a 'council estate kid' from a 'benefit family' has ended up where he is. Jack Dodds says 'I marvel at it', and jokes 'my sister calls me a snob, she doesn't understand'. Others, who describe themselves as coming from middle class backgrounds, express surprise that they have ended up where they have – because they have drifted into it, or because they never imagined themselves doing what they are doing now, or because luck and chance have produced outcomes they couldn't have foreseen. However, when Tom and Jack use words like 'amazed' and 'marvel', they hint at a different degree of unlikeliness.

Sally Vaughan talks of her family background as 'very working class . . . they're all skilled, but it's skilled manual work'. She traces how this led her into a degree in engineering, and how her class marked her as 'different' even as a student:

For me, coming from a working class home and then going to university was quite difficult . . . at the Polytechnic, I found, you know, there was a definite attitude amongst some kids that they were, you know, from a particular background . . . they had been brought up better than you had and you didn't speak properly and all of that . . . so yea, I mean, I still sort of feel my class quite strongly . . . it sounds really corny, but I do know where I've come from.

She goes on to talk of how this affected her relationships with people in ways that have taken some time to overcome:

I just think that now I'm mature enough, that I'm just comfortable with myself and I know who I am and I know what my place in the world is. I know that I've got the right to be where I am and all the rest of it and I don't think I have any hang-ups now. But I think, you know, I have had them . . . you might be at dinner with several men and . . . you know, you feel like you're with the old boys . . . I think, you know, as I'm getting older, I'm just growing in confidence and as I say, I'm just comfortable with myself and who I am and so therefore it's not a problem any more.

So, it is no longer a problem, but clearly it has been an issue for Sally. As she talks, we can see that gender and class have come together to make her feel out of place in some of the situations that she has encountered in her work.

Another aspect of class is codes of speech and behaviour. Sally has already touched on this, as she talks about having dinner with the 'old boys'. Mary Rainey links her personal style with her working class background, which has taught her to 'call a spade a spade'. For Mary, her openness and honesty are part of her, and important in establishing her integrity with nurses whom she manages. The hospital promotes 'this culture of openness and honesty', but ironically, Mary comes to realise that she is sometimes more 'open and honest' than they intend. It reveals, to Mary, the hypocrisy of the hospital 'culture', and Mary 'can't be doing' with all this. Shirley Stitt also feels she has grown up strong-minded, voicing her opinions openly and forcefully, as both her parents do. Shirley links this with class, contrasting it with a friend's middle class family: 'they're very reserved with their comments, and very considerate', 'you keep your opinions to yourself'. Shirley feels she has had to work at how she communicates with people, 'for work, but also for myself as well'. As she contrasts herself with her friend, Shirley explains it in terms of how their backgrounds have influenced the way they communicate and deal with people. 'I envy him, in the way he deals with people, and it's frustrating because I'm not a bad person, it's just things come out wrong sometimes', 'it's difficult to break the mould'. The 'mould' of her partner's middle class upbringing has, she feels, given him certain advantages in handling situations at work.

'I had a chip on my shoulder about education'

I felt I had a bit of a chip on my shoulder [about not having a degree], if I'm honest. That I hadn't done it when I should have done it. And I knew I was of that calibre. But I didn't have that bit of paper to say, yea, I'm the same as you . . . I felt I hadn't proved myself, and it was about time I got round to it. (Shirley Stitt)

I can't tell you the satisfaction my degree gave me, personally. I think I did it for my father . . . he actually moaned at me, and complained that I threw away my education. And if I did it for anyone, it was for him. Just to tell him, yes, you were absolutely right dad! (Colin Hawkins)

I took two professional qualifications [while working] when I was young. One because I wanted to prove myself better than the men . . . I was aware that if I was away for ten years to bring up a family, I was going to be fighting in the market, it was going to be very difficult to get back into it . . . Since I've been back, I've taken an MBA. Again, really, a question of proving my credibility. (Jean Holliday)

Of the managers in our sample, roughly half left school to go to university or to undertake professional training. The other half went into jobs of different kinds. Of these, all but four studied part-time, alongside work, at some later stage to get degrees or other professional qualifications. For example, Arthur Blakey did a BSc and MSc in engineering; Tom Smith qualified as a barrister; Harry Lyttleton took various courses connected with computing and process control, as part of a conscious plan to move away from being an electrician. The comments above all come from people who didn't go into higher education after school. They reveal something of the importance of education to them, and how it affects how they feel about themselves. Shirley Stitt always felt that she was capable, but had to prove it to herself and others, to get rid of 'the chip on [her] shoulder'. It has settled something for Colin Hawkins. It has made amends, in some way, for wasted opportunities when he was younger. For Jean Holliday, it has been important in her sense of credibility and security. It is perhaps no accident that almost all the people who have done MBAs in our sample were people who didn't go to university from school. In one sense, it is simple. Qualifications are helpful, or even essential, for people looking to move forwards in their careers. They are part of the 'standard biography' that justifies their claim to a professional or managerial 'social identity'. However, as we listen to Shirley, Colin and Jean, we can also see it is more complicated. Education is important to their sense of themselves in different ways. No doubt this is true of everyone in our sample. However, it is those who have not followed the standard path of going into higher education from school who talk about its significance most. We focus on how Eddie Hayes talks about the graduates he trained in his previous job. His account illustrates how, in complex ways, education has been an issue for him, in how he relates to others he deals with in his work and how he sees himself.

Eddie was glad to leave school with the four O levels he needed for a technical apprenticeship: 'I failed everything else, didn't bother to revise for them.' He went on to do an ONC and an HND while in work, and was thus technically well qualified. Eventually, in the job previous to his present one, Eddie found himself training graduate entrants:

I used to see all these graduates coming through the door, and I'd say, you know, that some of them were as thick as oak. You know, because they'd got no common sense. They knew their subject inside out, but actually trying to apply that subject, they had no chance ... I had some problems with some of them, because they believed that because they were graduates they were supreme and they were all singing all dancing. And it wasn't the case. Some of them were very, very bright and I would consider them to be a lot brighter than me. But it was very difficult for them to catch me out. And as long as you could stay one step ahead of them – and I was always good at doing that – then they respect you for that. But no, it was I think, a case of, you know, treating them as equals still, even if they believed they were something they weren't.

Listening to Eddie, we can see him 'working himself out' in relation to the graduates. 'They knew their subject inside out' and some were obviously 'very, very bright' – others were as 'thick as oak'. However, they lacked common sense, they couldn't apply their knowledge. Eddie was able to 'keep a step ahead', 'not get caught out', 'earn their respect' – his 'social identity' as their trainer is secure. However, their qualifications are clearly significant, they seem to represent a potential threat. In organisational terms, Eddie was taking part in a training process through which they were destined for higher things than him. He seems to feel that their qualifications gave them a sense of superiority, which, at a personal level, he is still questioning and resisting in these words.

Eddie has moved on to a senior position in personnel in another company, still with responsibility for recruitment and development of graduates. He seems confident he does this well. At the time we met, he was awaiting the results of an MSc in Human Resource Development. To the outsider, his HND, along with the MSc, should go some way to settling his concerns. However, he is still debating with himself how important degrees are.

I'm still not convinced that I would have done a degree level qualification by exam – there was no exam as such at MSc. Whether I would actually have sat down and revised. I know how much work I put into my dissertation and the other pieces of work ... I still can't believe how much time ... perhaps it takes me longer to, you know, put things down. I'm quite particular, you know, each chapter read and re-read, re-read and tweaked and tweaked and tweaked.
They're big pieces of work though.
So you know, I'm not sure whether that meant that I'm now their equal or not. [*laughter*]

Well, if you've got an MSc?
Well, but does it mean a great deal? . . . I think, well, if I can get one then, you know, is it all it's cracked up to be?

Eddie, at this moment, is not going to let this internal debate with himself rest, despite his achievements as a manager, and in education. But he has a 'part to play' in his work. We take up this theme in the next chapter.

CHAPTER 6

MANAGING THE SELF AND PLAYING THE PART

We have been listening to people talking about the process of coming to see themselves as 'managers'. We now move on to hear something about their experiences of acting as managers. Most of the managers we met were aware of ways in which they had changed or learned to control the way they acted and the way they presented themselves at work. In itself, this is not surprising, it goes with taking on a new social position – being 'the manager'. People arrive with some ideas and expectations of appropriate behaviour for a person doing that job. However, as we have seen in Chapter 3, these are by no means as clear as one might expect; 'managing', and how it is accomplished, is often ill-defined and ambiguous. So, these understandings have to be actively worked out and adjusted – they are negotiable and changeable. People's understanding of themselves as managers is being shaped by experience and by reflection on that experience. Again, as managers, they are 'emergent'.

The second time we met, we asked people directly about the ways in which they felt they had to 'manage themselves' to do their jobs. We also described the idea of 'emotion work' or 'emotional management' – that in work, people may be required to present themselves in certain ways that suppress or conceal their feelings, or allow them to be expressed only in certain situations or in particular ways – in accordance with the 'feeling rules' of the organisation (Fineman 1993a; Hochschild 1983; Putnam and Mumby 1993). In most organisations, there is 'emotion work' to be done, and 'emotion rules' that require that people present themselves and deal with their feelings in particular ways (Fineman 1993b). For the flight attendants in Hochschild's study, this involved putting the passengers first, dealing with their needs, fears, complaints, while concealing their own frustration and anger with passengers who may be acting unreasonably or offensively. In such work, this becomes 'emotional labour', a 'commodity', passengers are 'buying' their concern, their smiles, their even-tempered response to irrational or even insulting behaviour (Hochschild 1983). However, Hochschild talks of how this alone is not necessarily enough – customers are looking for 'sincere' performances, signs of genuine warmth and concern, not just a fixed smile and mechanical 'have a good day'.

Managerial work is not just a matter of 'doing the right things', consulting people, holding appraisals, making oneself available and so on.

Some people recognised this immediately. For example, Mary Rainey was well aware that, as a nurse, 'when you put on your frock . . . it's a whole new persona that's there . . . there's expectations around that role and the profession that you're in'. She was also aware that as a nurse manager, she was very much involved in 'managing herself'. Managers do a great deal of 'emotion work', controlling themselves, taking care to present themselves in appropriate ways to achieve a particular effect, dealing with the feelings of others, addressing and trying to resolve conflict, motivating and encouraging others. There are questions about the burden this 'emotion work' places on them, what happens to the feelings they absorb, suppress and conceal (Fineman 1993b; Höpfl 1994). This emotion work can also be seen as a form of 'emotional labour'. Are managers paid, in part, to use themselves, their feelings, their personalities, their skills as warm, approachable people, good listeners, persuasive talkers, to help secure the cooperation of others, in pursuit of some larger goal (Hochschild 1983; Turnbull 1996)? As Mark Taylor put it, to behave in such a way that people are 'motivated and wanted to do the job *for me*', rather than being directly motivated by achieving the goals and targets set by the organisation they work for.

We now go on to look at what might be involved in the complex process of managing the self and 'playing the part' of a manager.

Acting a part and being real

Concealing, controlling, performing

I think I am very open . . . I wear my heart on my sleeve, people know how I feel, although I don't bite in the office. I never bite, I walk away . . . If I get wound up at work, I'll cap it and walk away from it. It always looks different tomorrow. (Andrew Shepherd)

In everyday life at work, there are constant decisions about how to present ourselves in order to achieve the result we want – in persuading others, getting them to take our views or feelings seriously, concealing our anger, calming a heated situation, or whatever. There are cues from seeing how others act, and the reactions they get. We learn what does and doesn't work, we distinguish situations and individuals and adjust our performance to suit. We are conscious of what is expected or seen as appropriate in different situations. Much of this behaviour becomes habitual, we learn to do it 'without thinking', it comes to feel relatively spontaneous. There are, however, situations that make us more aware of our 'performance'. These may be occasions when things go particularly well, or badly. They may be new or difficult situations, when we find ourselves 'rehearsing' in our own minds how to approach the boss with a request, how best to voice a complaint, or to confront a difficult colleague. In doing this, we take account of our understanding of 'norms' or 'rules', our sense of acceptable limits within which we have to operate. We also bring to bear our understanding of the particular people involved, their likely reactions. We also use what we know of ourselves, what we can 'pull off', the safest ways for us to approach a situation, to minimise the risk of personal threat or damage.

The new manager is working with a heightened awareness of themselves and the situations they encounter – much less can be taken for granted, familiar patterns of behaviour may have to change. As people talked about 'managing themselves', they were clearly conscious of ways in which they were trying to control, or manage, their performance as managers. Sometimes, this means holding back, thinking carefully before speaking, deciding to leave things unsaid. In other situations, it means pushing oneself forward, forcing oneself to enter discussions and debates, or to address difficult situations.

'Biting your lip'

A recurring theme was that of 'biting your lip', holding back, being much more careful about what you say and how you present yourself. This may seem an obvious managerial skill to develop and an important aspect of 'managing oneself' in what, as we have seen, people perceive as a visible and vulnerable position. However, it is also clearly a form of 'emotional management', or 'emotion work', and also reflects a sense of changed relationships.

'Biting your lip' takes different forms. In various ways, it leads to less spontaneous behaviour. For Diane Washington, it means being 'much more careful what I say', thinking how people might interpret flippant remarks, being 'less mischievous' – it affects how she behaves in everyday social situations at work, and when she socialises with her staff out of work. She presents these as relatively small adjustments and changes, but is clear that they do affect social relationships – things that she might have said as an equal and colleague are 'read' differently now her position in the department has changed.

Colin Hawkins has had 'to change quite a lot', to make sure that he conceals some of his frustration with the way he gets drawn into day-to-day crises and events, 'the seemingly never ending crisis or chaos' of residential social work that gets in the way of his plans.

I've actually made quite a determined effort that if things go wrong, that staff don't see that I get frustrated with it. So, I've had to change. Whereas opposed to wearing my heart on my sleeve, so to speak, I've had to stand back and adopt a managerial type.

Colin is conscious of 're-channelling' his spontaneous reactions. For example, his armed forces self sometimes wants to 'tear off a member of staff a strip'. However, he realises it will have quite a different impact in the world of social work, where it is not accepted as 'normal' behaviour, and where staff are more likely to get upset and don't expect to be 'told off' in that way . So, as Colin talks, he shows how 'spontaneous' behaviour is shaped and learned in different contexts. He is conscious of re-learning and controlling some of his immediate feelings and reactions.

Alicia Coltrane talks of how she has 'changed in the way that I manage myself'. When she first became a manager, she felt under great pressure to have all the answers: 'I used to be stressed at not knowing an answer'. She presents an important lesson that she has had to learn not to answer questions 'off the top of my head'.

However, learning to do this has not been easy. Kathy Westbrook has had to work out that there is more risk to her integrity as a manager by making bad decisions 'off the top of my head', than there is from saying 'I'm going to have to think about that', or 'I'll ring you back'. She talks of how her previous expectations of herself led her to make some 'silly, silly decisions' and how she would then get 'into a right mess trying to back-track'. Now, if she made a decision then changed her mind, she says she would be open about this. ' "I'm ever so sorry, but I've thought this over and really I think we should do this instead." I think it's far more productive than thinking you can do it straight away, because you can't.' She talks of how this lesson involves 'knowing something about myself': 'I'm not always that good off the top of my head.' Also, Kathy is accepting a discrepancy between herself and her earlier expectations of the sort of person a manager should be – decisive, able to think and weigh things up, able to respond to situations quickly. She is 'negotiating' a new model of a manager with herself, giving herself permission to take time to think, not to know, and to get it wrong sometimes.

For some people, 'biting your lip' can mean keeping quiet about things that they aware of in their organisation. Eddie Hayes, working at a senior level in the personnel division, is 'privy to a lot of information', things he may not agree with. Although 'you may not know the full reasons why that's happened or why that's been put in place, you can have a damn good guess . . . you do have to control yourself emotionally'. Carol Laine also talks of having to keep a lot of things she hears in management meetings 'very confidential'. This is in contrast to information she picked up when a clerical officer, 'you could just spout off about anything, say exactly what you think, you know, it didn't matter'. She finds this a difficult part of her relationships with her ex-colleagues:

'there were never any secrets as far as I was concerned before ... I've never really been used to that before now'. Again, this may seem an obvious fact of managerial life. She can see the dangers of 'scaremongering' before definite decisions are made, of worrying people over hypothetical problems that may never materialise. Also, she talks of how she can now often see both sides of a situation. However, for Carol, it is uncomfortable. It is made complicated by her relationships with ex-colleagues that are not straightforwardly managerial, relationships where she would previously have had no dilemma about telling.

Feeling responsible for the 'happy shift', the 'happy office'

Despite the fact that, you know, I do want to be close to people and I don't see myself as a distant manager, I do feel that I need to present a non-emotional front really. And it is a front as well. And that I need to be the same for them all the time, whatever I might be feeling. And obviously that isn't possible all the time. But yes, I do feel that I need to manage and control myself because I have a role to fulfil which is nothing to do with the person that I am really – I don't know that it's *nothing* to do with the person that I am.

As Marion Brown talks of managing her emotions, she describes how she has to 'put on a front', she cannot be emotional in front of staff, she has to manage and control herself – but 'obviously that isn't possible all the time'. At the same time, her 'preferred style' is not to be distant – as she acts out her 'role' how far is she detaching herself or bringing herself into the 'performance'? Again, she raises important issues about the demands of managerial work on the person – and leaves us with concerns about what happens to 'the person that I am' in the process, to all the things that she has to deal with, that are left unexpressed as she presents her 'non-emotional front'.

Other managers talk of similar experiences, of how they assume a considerable sense of responsibility for the way their staff experience work. Charles Parker feels he needs to 'appear optimistic at all times', even if he is really feeling 'incredibly pissed off', otherwise staff may feel responsible.

If you sit grumpy in your office and you barely talk to them, they don't think, oh he's preoccupied because something else has happened, they think, oh what have I done? I reckon, anyway.

Or, he talks of another occasion, at the time of a budget meeting, when a member of staff was voicing her pessimism 'knowing our luck, something worse will happen tomorrow'. Charles was 'quite conscious of the fact that you need to appear optimistic, because you're leading the department', so, he was quick to point out 'our luck's changed, I've just got an extra x thousand'. However, he goes on to say,

I only did that because I felt as if I ought to. Not because I would have disagreed with what she said, because there are times when things go badly and you're entitled to gripe about it. But I felt as if I had to counter-balance, so that the others didn't get dragged down with what she'd said.

Kathy Westbrook also talks of her sense of responsibility for setting the mood of the shift in the pizza restaurant. In this, she places a considerable burden upon herself. Elsewhere she identifies many other things that might affect how a particular shift goes – but here, she focuses on her part:

It's such a kind of quite intense environment. And especially as manager, they see you as their sort of centre-piece, you are the set-piece of the restaurant, and everybody looks to you for guidance. If you come in, in a bad mood, it sets them in a bad mood and the whole shift then is sort of ruined, because you won't operate as well, the mistakes start happening, and the pressure starts piling on.

Lawrence Young also talks of his extreme disappointment when he was turned down for a job he wanted. He 'bottled it up' in front of his team:

So, it was very much a case then, of having to manage my instinctive emotional feelings. 'Oh bugger 'em, I'm really not bothered about this job any more, I'm feeling completely deflated, nobody's come to console me', and I was feeling pretty down in the dumps about it. But I made sure that I didn't let that shine through for the people who I'm managing, hopefully, fairly successfully.

Having 'put on a brave face', then 'I basically poured my heart out to my wife and felt a lot better for it'. As Lawrence recounts this event, he raises important questions about the 'feeling rules' in his organisation. He has taken on board the message (given in his appraisal a few weeks earlier) that he must be aware of how his feelings affect members of his team. He was careful, in this instance, to conceal his disappointment and resentment, but also quite angry that no member of senior staff had yet taken the trouble to talk to him, to recognise that he needed an opportunity to deal with his feelings and frustrations. It had been made quite clear to him that, as a manager, he had to manage himself and his emotions in front of his staff – but it would seem the organisation provided him with no alternative outlets for his feelings. The 'feeling rules' help to deflect conflict and maintain calm, yet clearly there were strong feelings that Lawrence had to deal with. Often, a lot of emotion work goes into expressing such feelings in a reasonable and rational way at work. Outbursts of emotion from someone in Lawrence's position would be labelled inappropriate. Like many other people we spoke to, it was his spouse who received the 'unbottled' version, who gave him the time to work through his feelings and the implications of this incident.

Exploding at work, letting it out

So far, we have heard managers talking about their efforts to obey the 'feeling rules' of their organisation. In bureaucratic organisations, these 'feeling rules' elevate the rational, the controlled and reasonable, rather than the emotional or intuitive expression of feelings (Putnam and Mumby 1993). From the accounts we have been listening to, it is clear that a great deal of work and energy goes into controlling feelings, presenting oneself appropriately as a manager, dealing with things that are distressing or disagreeable in an appropriate way. However, as Fineman points out, expressions of emotion are also part of the experience of organisational life (1993b). There are, of course, risks in displaying emotion, especially to more senior people or people who have become very skilled at 'emotional management' themselves. However, for the person, this may sometimes feel a 'healthier' way of dealing with these feelings. Mary Rainey talks of how she 'certainly felt better' after a row with her boss, when she'd said 'exactly what I felt like'. However, she senses that this incident was risky for both of them. Her boss 'gave her a bit of a shout back', she momentarily lost control of her temper, which placed her in a vulnerable position, and gave Mary a sense of power, that she had had this effect on her.

I had a row with my boss, and I told her that I felt she was being unrealistic in her expectations, and if I was so bloody bad, send me back to the ward. She's been different since then ... she seems one of these ice cool women, always in control, you know, and she gave me a bit of a shout back. And I think that shocked her, because I don't think she liked being out of control. For them few minutes, she was out of control, she was losing her temper back, and I don't think she liked that. So I think she's a bit more careful now, because I think I have the capacity to make her do that at any time now ... I don't think she felt comfortable with not being able to control her own feelings.

For Mary, there was also a price to be paid:

I certainly felt better, because I'd said exactly what I felt like ... I just snapped, and said my piece, and that night, I sat at home and cried all night. Then I went back to work the next day, and I just sort of thought, well, keep your head down, keep out of the way.

Putnam and Mumby raise questions about whether organisations would be more comfortable, more productive places if they created opportunities for people to share and express their feelings more openly. This may be so. The story of Mary and her manager may have been different if they had been able to engage in a dialogue about their feelings, rather than waiting until the pressure built up to a point where Mary 'snapped'. However, such openness also requires skills of 'emotional management', it is not easy. Mary and her manager are now locked into a relationship that makes this very difficult. As Mary suggests, controlling and concealing her feelings, and encouraging others to hide and suppress their feelings, has become a major part of her boss's 'ice-cool' persona at work. In this relationship, sharing feelings would not necessarily achieve a moment of honest communication, it also has important power dimensions – Mary senses her power, but also, her boss retains the power to 'label' Mary as emotional, unable to cope, or whatever.

Charles Parker describes an incident where he lost his temper, in his case, with a member of staff. When Charles moved into his job, he had expected to be able to manage people in a 'reasonable' way, getting them together, 'putting ideas on the table', 'taking a consensus point of view'. However, he found his staff unresponsive to this style, meetings were like a 'zoo', they were more like 'badly behaved children'. There was a lot of underlying resentment to the changes which had led to Charles being there, and he was working with some people who, he later realised, brought a lot of problems to work with them. However, initially, he was unaware of much of this and thoroughly frustrated with their behaviour and their attitude toward him. Eventually, he snapped.

I had a big argument with somebody – not very professional, supposedly, for a manager to do – but I got so stressed out with the whole thing that I had an enormous row with this chap . . . I mean it was dreadful. The sort of thing you never want to get involved in . . . it was dreadful, believe me . . . the things he came out with went back even further than I thought they would . . . all to do with the move . . . I'd no idea he was so bothered about it.
So it was a useful row?
Well it was – it was eventually . . . it took a long time to sort myself out.

Charles retains his 'preferred theory' of how to manage reasonable people. However, he speaks now of 'the theory', taking account of the possibility that one might not be dealing with 'reasonable people'. He imports ideas of a body of managerial knowledge to support his revised theory. 'I suppose the management theory is, if you're going to be tough, you should be tough at the start. You ease off as you go on.' So, with hindsight, he would approach such a situation very differently; like others we spoke to, one of the things he feels he has learned as a manager is that difficult situations have to be confronted, they have to be managed.

If I was the line manager now, I would approach it very, very differently now . . . I would walk in and be [arrogant] enough to say look, you know, there are obviously some problems here, let's sit down and talk about them. There's things under the surface which are not coming out.

So, he would begin by being reasonable, and seeing 'what people *do* about it'. However, if necessary, he would be prepared to take disciplinary action much more quickly. When it reaches that point, 'It's not good. But it's not good before, you see. You have to make the decision that things are not getting better.' 'Life is just too short for it. Two years of misery is something that I'm not going to go through again. And if people don't accept that I'm in charge now, then they will have to.'

Again this incident reveals a complex set of issues Charles is having to manage with his own staff and in his own mind. He has since had more positive experiences of working constructively with teams, which reinforce his 'preferred theory'. This remains relatively undamaged. However, he has come to build a much firmer view of disciplinary action into his managerial repertoire. Charles's 'explosion' was one way of dealing with his feelings towards a particularly 'hard to manage' member of staff. In part, it could be seen as a consequence of the gap in his 'preferred theory', he hadn't really anticipated having to deal with 'unreasonable people', people who, for whatever reason, didn't share or respond to his style. He has now built this possibility into his 'theory in practice'. He doesn't suggest that confronting issues and taking disciplinary action is easy, he has had to 'manage' and change himself in different ways to accommodate this. Also, he has come to adjust his view of himself as a manager and a person to incorporate his revised theory about how he would deal with such situations. 'I've never been what you might call a natural leader. That's not the way I function – I'm not aggressive . . . I don't go forging ahead all the time, and bullying people into what I've decided is going to happen.' However, Charles recognises that 'I'm showing another side of myself that I didn't – it never occurred to me that it existed. I find it quite hard sometimes, but I never thought I was like that.' This 'other side' involves, in part, accepting the power that goes with being a manager and behaving appropriately. It also involves adjusting to others' expectations of a person in that position,

You've got to get rid of any sort of reticence you've got about making difficult decisions. Because that's what you're paid to do. You're in a situation where you're damned if you do and damned if you don't. If you don't make a decision, people will say you're shirking your responsibility – why's he paid so much money if he's not doing anything about it? If you make a decision, there's always going to be some people who don't like what you're decided on. So the only thing you can hope the best for, is to carry as many of them with you as you can. And do that by consulting.

Acting out a character . . .

In describing their 'emotion work', we have heard people talking about how they have learned to control what they say, to hold back their feelings, 'bite their lips'. However, there are also occasions when they actively project a different image or persona. For example, we heard people talk of how 'dressing the part' has helped them. Tom Smith has always seen himself as a performer, from his early ambitions to become a musician, to his present involvement in amateur dramatics. He still works in court once a week, with a 'stage' (the courtroom), props (different clothes) and a cast of people in different roles (the magistrate, the court officials, the various 'villains' and 'victims') – this environment invites a 'performance' and for Tom, it can be therapeutic,

In a way it's nice, my job, because you can take out your frustrations in a hidden way. Because you get someone who doesn't pay their fines, you can then feign a loss of temper saying 'well why on earth should the magistrates accept this, because you haven't paid!' So you can get out your frustrations that way. But those courts only happen once or twice a week. It's like the whole five days' worth of temper building up!

Tom talks of using his acting skills as a way of dealing with his feelings in many exchanges at work. For example 'years of experience' have taught him that 'if you're nice to someone when they're losing their temper, they don't know what to do with you'. Tom, like other managers, talks of how he's learned 'techniques' and 'games' to deal with particular situations. For example, he describes his 'soft soap' technique:

So part of the chipping away process in trying to get someone round to your ideas is . . . 'well just go away and have a think about this for a while, see what you think' . . . and then say, well, OK, but how about doing it this way? And I like to try and make people think things are their idea rather than mine. But I'm still trying to perfect that!

Or, Diane Washington has her 'smile technique', which is openly recognised by her staff:

If you walk up to someone and you grin like this [*big grin*] they go, 'oh no, Diane's smiling . . . what do you want now Diane?' They're well used to me. Diane smiling, standing by your desk is bad news. You're going to have to do something.

These are, of course, examples of people finding ways of getting people to do what they want them to do. They can be seen as working on more subtle techniques of control, which they find more comfortable to use, which they feel 'fit' them. As Tom Smith says, 'I'm still trying to perfect that.' Carrie Bley also recognises that she has learned to 'play the game':

I used to see things more black and white . . . I'm a lot more appreciative of the other person's point of view now. And I've changed, just slightly, how I would go about things. Only subtly, but it makes a big difference how you're received. Perhaps I'm getting cleverer at it, you see. I do know more how to play the game . . . I used to think you could . . . just be totally honest, and just say, you know, 'this is how it's got to be', full stop. And now I know that's not the – that doesn't work, because you're working with people and the reality is that you've to actually negotiate through.

. . . or acting out of character?

As these managers describe the kind of 'techniques' they have learned that help them in their task of getting others to comply, we recognise them – we may have used them ourselves, or have been conscious of others using them on us. However, for the new manager, this is not always comfortable. Learning to behave in different ways can raise questions of how 'learning' and 'self' sit together. There are questions in Andrew Shepherd's mind about how much of the way he operates is 'him', reflecting his nature and his beliefs, and how much is learned. This discomfort raises doubts about how it appears to others – does it look as 'genuine' as he feels it is? Andrew is questioning how 'authentic' his behaviour is.

It's almost like, you know, I'm the next one off the production line . . . my number two sits there grinning occasionally. And I know what he's thinking, and we talk about it afterwards, and it's – he says to me, 'you know' he says, 'I've done all these courses, but you're the first one that does it.' So I take it as a compliment, because I think it's natural, but it's not, it's trained. So maybe, what I'm saying to you is that I'm not – you know, that's not necessarily me that they're seeing, it's what I am as a manager – which is not always compatible with what I really am.

A number of people took up this theme, of how they had 'learned to be different', and how this could be unsettling for their sense of their 'real self'. Often they spoke of this as a change in themself, that carried across into areas of their lives in ways they saw as positive – increasing confidence, assertiveness or whatever. However, for some managers, it also left them with a sense of learning a performance that they used in work, and a distance between their sense of self inside and outside work. Jean Holliday holds the view that personalities are 'fixed', that although we can be 'taught' to behave in different ways, this remains a performance, somehow at odds with the 'real' self.

Underneath, people don't change. But our personality gets trained rather than changes . . . Although I say to you I'm introverted, it doesn't quite fit in, does it?
Not quite, no.
It doesn't fit in, and yet it's true. The introversion is the personality, this is the training. So what comes over is not necessarily the basic personality type. I can do this in the work situation very easily. I can be really pushy in the work situation and I can negotiate a really good deal in the work situation. But you send me outside, to buy a car, and I just cough up what they ask for. I don't negotiate *anything* in a personal situation. I'm just too timid.

Using learned techniques and approaches can also leave uncomfortable feelings that these may be more subtle forms of control, rather than simply 'better' ways to manage people. As Andrew Shepherd puts it:

Occasionally it can make you feel manipulative. And by creating this being that wants to be all things to all men, and deal with it properly and follow all the text books in terms of how to involve people, and say hello in the morning and wander downstairs and manage by walking about. And you have teams and you have a dialogue – you don't discuss things . . . but at times I do feel that playing this game at times is a game. And sometimes that devalues it a little bit. And I wonder sometimes if others can see through it. Whether that really is me, or whether it's something that I created that fits the bill.

As they describe their experiences and their feelings, these managers show that beneath what may be quite accomplished and effective performances in the workplace, there are uncomfortable questions about whether this is, indeed, a 'performance', or whether it is authentic behaviour. Tom Smith is clearly conscious that sometimes he is acting. Andrew Shepherd feels he is doing his best to manage in a way he feels is 'right', but is not so sure that it always does feel 'right'. Jean Holliday feels she has been 'trained' to act in ways that produce results at work, but has a sense of herself as quite a different person underneath, and outside work. Mary Rainey argues strongly for maintaining her sense of personal continuity and integrity:

At the end of the day, you haven't got to lose sight of yourself. And that management style might not be the in-thing in three or four years' time, because they change all the time. But underneath all that, I'm still the same person, and I've still got to work with these people. So, you've got to stay true to yourself, because all these theories and everything else change, whatever's the in-thing at the time. So, no, I'm afraid they have to take me as I am.

Like Jean Holliday and Colin Hawkins, Mary holds a strong sense of a 'real self', but unlike them, she doesn't talk of how it has been overlaid and moulded by the demands of different environments she has worked in – she sees herself carrying the 'real self' through, a self which is deeply rooted in her working class upbringing, where a spade's a spade, you 'don't get owt for nowt' and fools are not suffered gladly. Managerial styles may come and go, but Mary says she resists taking on behaviour that isn't 'true to myself'. Here she raises an important issue about whether people experience their selves-as-manager as 'authentic'.

Being human – empathising, swearing, caring

We have heard people talk of 'emotional management' or 'emotion work' in terms of controlling their feelings, 'biting their lips', finding ways of avoiding confrontation and 'explosions'. We heard Jean Holliday describe how she has 'been trained' to behave in a tough and assertive way at work, while remaining her introverted self underneath. Mary Rainey had a sense of power when she found she could make her 'ice-cool' boss lose control. Tom Smith 'acts' in court. Harry Lyttleton struggles to get the right style for different people. In these and many other ways, people talk of how they 'manage themselves' in their everyday work as managers. In Hochschild's terms, these examples are 'surface acting' because the managers are conscious of how they are using themselves to manage situations, to achieve particular ends. As we have seen, this 'surface acting' can run into conflict with people's 'preferred styles of management', they have to work to reconcile how things are with how they feel they should be. The burden of this discrepancy can be assumed by the manager – it is they who have failed to build a cooperative team, involve and inspire people, to generate commitment and a sense of working together with a common purpose and so on. In terms of the adverts we saw back in Chapter 1, it may raise questions as to whether they have 'what it takes' to achieve excellence as a manager. Although many people present such aspects of their work as difficult, as things they are still learning to deal with, this is rarely expressed as undermining their sense of 'having what it takes'. We heard Andrew Shepherd talk of how he feels he does the 'right things', but feels uncomfortable about whether it is 'real' or 'learned', 'genuine' or 'manipulative', whether people can 'see through it'.

I think one thing that sometimes I do feel uncomfortable with is that, at times, I *think* I'm verging on the manipulative by playing games to achieve what I want to achieve.
Do you think that's an inevitable part of being a manager? Or do you think it's something that you can handle in a more comfortable way?
... what I'm saying is that maybe I'm not a natural – maybe there's not a natural manager, I don't know. But I have to do it that way. So, I use all my experience and things that I've seen to achieve what I want to achieve.

Andrew Shepherd's question of whether he is a 'natural' manager links with his concerns about how 'real' or 'authentic' his behaviour is. He is aware that managers use themselves as a 'resource' – working to build loyalty and trust, creating an environment in which 'we enjoy what we are doing'. Others are also conscious of how they do this, but don't question, to the same degree as Andrew, the instrumentality and authenticity of the 'techniques' they draw on.

Presenting himself as a 'real person' is very much part of Arthur Blakey's approach to managing his 'hard to manage' staff, but like Andrew Shepherd, he also talks of consciously adopting a particular style and behaviour. There is a tension between himself as a conscious actor and a 'real person'. For Arthur, it is important that people see he is human: 'I can swear and shout.' He talks of 'doing the trust and respect thing' in the early stages. Being supportive, getting them the tools they need to do their jobs, 'being the nice guy', sitting down and listening to their problems, answering their questions honestly and openly. Arthur's strategy for the first six or twelve months was one of 'winning their trust and respect'. This also means being honest about his concerns and misgivings about their work. He's now 'completely comfortable' about telling someone if 'they're not pulling their weight . . . essentially they know that anyway, you're only bringing them in to tell them what they know'.

For Arthur, one of the pleasant surprises of the job has been:

I didn't think I would have got as close to the people, possibly, as I have . . . you can walk out of here and you can have a laugh out there, with some guys and so on. At the end of the day, they know you're the boss, and they don't mess with me . . . they can say to me f--- off, you know, tongue in cheek, and I wouldn't take offence . . . [I can say] 'you can just piss off will you, and give me chance to work' . . . being able to do that's nice, as a manager.

So, arguably, Andrew and Arthur entered their jobs with similar 'ideals' but with very different expectations of how far they would be able to realise them with the particular kinds of staff they had to work with. Arthur is pleasantly surprised, Andrew is somewhat disappointed.

In many ways, we have seen that people are aware that they use themselves as a resource to get things done. Mark Taylor was pleased when people 'wanted to do the job for me'. Andrew Shepherd was aware that his encouragement to the woman attending the training course was a kind of 'investment', he would reap the goodwill in other ways later. Arthur Blakey also talks of the 'pay-offs' of being seen as a nice person. On the one hand, he talks of dealing with staff facing crises and tragedies as 'a hard part of the job', how he found it 'very, very hard' to deal with staff coping with death and bereavement. These things just are hard parts of life; 'you get a personal sadness'. He talks of the genuine difficulty he faces in dealing with such situations, but at the same time, he is conscious that, in his position, it can be more than dealing with a tragic human situation. Giving them time off, or allowing them to come in late to leave children at the child-minder's when their wife is ill, affects his standing with his staff.

You have to show them a bit of empathy. And again, it probably pays you to do things like that – that's not why you do it, but you know, that probably does you a lot of good too, and gets you respected with the guys.

So, 'being yourself' and 'being a manager' can be complicated. The 'good manager' is a humane and caring person. This is hard to dispute. Being seen as a 'nice person' is important for the personal self, but it can also have pay-offs for the managerial self. As Arthur Blakey says, 'that's not *why* you do it'. But Andrew Shepherd is left with uncomfortable questions about whether the way he behaves as a 'good manager' is genuine or 'verging on the manipulative'. Managing relationships and 'doing the right thing' are connected, but not in a straightforward way, as we see in the next chapter.

CHAPTER 7

MANAGING RELATIONSHIPS AND DOING THE RIGHT THING

I've been able to get some people to work together in groups, that didn't happen beforehand. And I feel quite pleased with that . . . Certainly the communication and accountability has been much, much, improved, so I'd like to take some credit for that . . . I do like meetings and I do like talking to people . . . trying to get everybody to believe we are genuinely all in this together, famous last words! (Jack Dodds)

I enjoyed actually – being actually capable of making things happen for the men . . . for instance, if they had problems with their tools . . . there's something that they need to get, and the only person that could get it was me. You know, because of my budget . . . I was the only guy that could provide them with those things, that get them going. That was very fulfilling. I mean, I don't know why it was so fulfilling for me, but it was really enjoyable to actually get the things for the guys . . . you know, they were buzzed at that, and I got the feedback that they'd been motivated and wanted to do the job for me, you know. I liked that feeling. (Mark Taylor)

I like the fact that sometimes people come running to me for a decision . . . it makes you feel quite good that people are leaning on you for some assistance . . . It doesn't give me a sense of power, or anything outlandish like that. I don't know, I just like the feeling that I – that I can be there and that people respect my judgement . . . So I suppose, you know, it's quite a confidence thing really. (Lawrence Young)

I just love team projects, because I've now built a team. It's actually caved in a bit, because one of them got another job and left . . . But I'd reached a point where I had got this really tight, lovely team . . . it was, for me, the opportunity to do lots of things that I wanted to do, but I couldn't do on my own. (Lucy Armstrong)

It was convincing them that I had their interests at heart, and I wasn't the grim reaper . . . Things that were surprising was the closeness of people . . . Turning people around, the sort of problem children, if you want to call them that, turning them around to be high flyers. That's enjoyable . . . I haven't changed everybody, you know . . . It isn't easy working with them, that's the hard side of it, you're working with very hard-to-manage people. (Arthur Blakey)

I think people . . . having accepted your salary, your terms and conditions of employment, you end up doing a job of work, whether you're pitching tents, or working in a factory, or a pub, or a solicitor's office, in a court of law, what have you. Being once you're all in there, I think yes, then basically you all accept that you're there for that common purpose. And then the relationship develops, the agenda is what the business dictates . . . there is a common denominator, and that's the business. (Stan Jordan)

In Chapter 3, we heard people talking about some of their difficulties and concerns about the 'people aspect' of managing. However, when we asked them about the satisfying and rewarding aspects of their work, elements of what Dick Thompson called 'the smooth side of the people thing' frequently came up. So, Mark Taylor talks of making things happen, like buying new tools, which motivate and please his staff. Others find satisfaction in seeing people develop and progress, or 'turning round' the 'problem children' or 'awkward sods' of Chapter 3. Jack Dodds, talks of getting people to work together more effectively – improving communications, accountability, bringing a stronger sense of focus to the group. The idea of a 'team' is important in all this. Diane Washington would rather see herself as a 'team captain' than as a boss. Lucy Armstrong talks of having a 'lovely tight team' which is, together, able to achieve so much. There are also concerns to build a sense of shared goals, common interests. Arthur Blakey has worked hard to convince them that he 'had their interests at heart'. Jack Dodds hopes that 'we genuinely are all in this together'. Stan Jordan echoes this by talking of 'a common denominator', in his case, the demands of the business.

Theory and practice: doing it right

Underlying what these managers say, we can begin to see ideas or 'implicit theories' that can be seen as their 'preferred theories of management' (Watson 1997). They hold out the possibility of 'teams', more open and fruitful communications, motivated and committed staff, people working together with common goals, achieving improved results. In these brief extracts, people draw on their experience to demonstrate to themselves and to the listener, that it is, with the right people, in the right circumstances, possible to manage people in ways that fit with these 'preferred theories'. This optimism is, indeed, reinforced by drawing on 'discursive resources' from human resource management – which holds out the possibility that increasing performance and achieving organisational goals can sit easily with a concern to 'manage people better' (Guest 1987). Teams, involvement, commitment, a sense of shared goals and common purpose, empowerment are elements in managerial discourses that underlie these 'preferred theories' and offer managers the reassurance that the 'unmanageable' can indeed be managed. However, many of these work as line managers, in positions in organisations where they have an important part to play in the task of making these ideals work in reality (Guest 1987). They are in situations where they have to build teams, motivate staff and secure their cooperation, establish effective communications and so on. If they succeed, there may be personal rewards.

The recognition that Diane Washington or Lucy Armstrong have particularly close and effective teams may well be seen as partly their achievement, a demonstration of their managerial skills and abilities. If they fail, they may be 'marked' as lacking team-building skills. More than this, the new manager may well rely on their team for achieving the goals and objectives they have been set – to increase output, develop new services, or show improvements in quality, whatever. The manager is dependent on them for their own success.

As they describe their achievements, the way they have 'managed' people towards satisfactory outcomes, there are glimpses of ways in which the managers as people, with futures and identities at stake, are caught up in a very personal way in these relationships at work. For Jack Dodds, they may yet be 'famous last words', one cannot be sure of the outcome, it may yet go wrong. Or, as Dan Tracey puts it 'you're only as good as your last success'. Managerial performances have to be maintained, if not improved. As Lucy Armstrong talks, personal and team achievements become entwined as she talks of her dependence on them for achieving all the things she wanted to do. Also, her 'lovely tight team' is vulnerable, it 'caved in a bit' when one of the members left. Lawrence Young talks of liking the feeling that these 'well motivated and capable' people who work for him respect his opinions: 'It's a confidence thing really.' Mark Taylor found it fulfilling to be the one who could help and motivate his staff, so 'they wanted to do the job for me'. He isn't sure *why* it was so fulfilling, but he 'liked that feeling'. Arthur Blakey talks at some length of how he feels he is able to gain people's trust, of how he saw the need to change people's attitudes and approaches to their work, in order to achieve his goals for the department. He came to bring change, but had to work hard to establish himself as a person who 'had their interests at heart', rather than 'the grim reaper'. So, in building up his relationship with his department, Arthur not only had to establish himself as a particular kind of person, he also had to deal with his staff's ideas about him, for example, as the youngest manager in the company or as 'the grim reaper'. Diane Washington finds it easier to see herself as a 'team captain', rather than a 'boss'. We begin to see here how the manager's sense of themselves, as a person, as a successful manager, as a capable or likable human being, is closely bound up in relationships with those who work for them.

However, there are also glimpses of how this relationship takes place within a particular structure – a hierarchy of inequalities of status, power and influence. Mark Taylor is 'the one with the budget', the 'only guy' that could get the tools and equipment the men needed to do their work. He had the resources to make these things happen. Carol Laine, on the other hand, talks of her surprise at being unable to get the parking permit that one of her staff wanted. It proved much harder to meet this apparently simple request than she had anticipated. These relationships take place in a wider context over which the new manager may have little control. They also have a history, of which the new manager may have limited awareness. Arthur Blakey is aware his job was made easier because he followed in the footsteps of 'a bit of an idiot'. It took Charles Parker time to change and undo the patterns of behaviour his staff had developed under their previous manager, and to realise that their obstructiveness and hostility were not personal. It was the legacy of having had, reluctantly, to move offices and, in some cases, to personal problems that had nothing to do with work. As Stan Jordan talks of a 'common purpose', he goes on to present this as 'given', beyond his control: 'the agenda is what the business dictates'. Harry Lyttleton is involved in implementing major changes within a multinational business, over which he has little influence or control, but which he has to make work.

These are structured relationships, yet at the same time, personal relationships. They are relationships that are shaped not only by 'the manager', but also by those 'being managed' – everyone is 'managing' (Collinson 1992). They are 'relationships of production', whose primary purpose could be seen to achieve larger goals through consensus, cooperation, or control of conflict. However, they also 'produce' and shape the managers as people, they influence how they feel about themselves and those around them. Managers are aware that they can influence these relationships, they can make them better or worse, they can handle them 'well' or 'badly'. However, the manager also gets particular things from them – whether it is 'the opportunity to do lots of things that I wanted to do, but I couldn't do on my own', or comfortable feelings of being respected, or people 'wanting to do the job for me'. For the new manager, working relationships have changed. Where they differ from their 'preferred theory', the new manager may feel responsible, that they have, in some way, failed as 'managers of people'. On the other hand, these discrepancies may require adjustments to managers' 'preferred theories', to accommodate their awareness that they are managing structured relationships.

Managers, of course, rarely talk in terms of 'preferred theories' and 'implicit theories' of management. However, we go on to look at how they talk about their position and their relationship to their staff. From this emerge a number of 'lessons' that they have learned. In some ways, these may seem unsurprising. However, these 'lessons' do not appear as things that people could have told or warned them about. They are presented as the outcome of lived experiences, of trying to bring together their 'philosophies' and values as managers with the reality of what it is possible for one person to do within the boundaries of a 'job'. Their learning about the structural position within which they operate, its constraints on relationships and ideals is, arguably, all the more potent and powerful because they have reached these conclusions themselves. They are things they have learned through having to deal with difficult situations, through conflict with others and within themselves, through finding ways of 'managing themselves' in new and challenging situations. This is not to say that these internal debates have not been informed by ideas encountered in company rhetoric, management learning, discussions with other people. However, in the process of reconciling their 'ideals' with their experiences, their 'theories' or ideas about management and about themselves emerge.

Being a figurehead, being the centrepiece, being on a pedestal

'Being a figurehead' on the prison wing, 'being the centrepiece' of the restaurant, 'being put on a pedestal' are some of the different ways people described how, as 'the manager', they felt separate from and more visible than those around them. They go on to talk about what this means, and how they manage it. In apparently simple ways, some people have changed their appearance and behaviour. Charles Parker wears the 'grey suit' to fit in at senior management meetings. Ron Scott is aware that as a 'figurehead' he has to set an example, making sure he's not late, that he's correctly dressed and looks smart. Carrie Bley is careful to dress in a way she feels is acceptable to all who use the college, she 'would never wear jeans or leggings' to work, for example. Colin Hawkins has 'taken to wearing ties more and more, being smart', but at the same time, talks of how he likes to 'subvert the image' by sometimes appearing in jogging pants.

These managers go on to describe how 'dressing the part' connects with and eases other aspects of 'being on a pedestal'. It goes with 'setting an example', establishing norms for other staff. Her care over her appearance gives Carrie Bley permission to let her staff know when she feels they are dressed inappropriately. By being on time, looking smart, taking care to 'put myself about' and be available for staff and inmates, Ron Scott says 'You manage yourself to make sure that they realise that they, as inmates, have got responsibility as well . . . you've got to put that point over, that you've got standards, you expect them to have the same standards.' Having set these standards, Ron describes how they have to be maintained and worked at, 'if somebody comes and talks to you in the wrong way, or approaches you in an aggressive manner or whatever, you've got to leave them in no doubt that it's not on, and this is how it's done. And they're going to get more response from you if they do it that way.'

Here, we see these simple examples of paying attention to appearance and presentation of self are not just a matter of 'looking the part' or 'obeying the rules'. They also, in small ways, help the manager feel more comfortable with significant and difficult aspects of the job – changing the behaviour of others, setting standards and boundaries, appearing consistent. They show managers engaging in 'dual control', presenting themselves in particular ways to ease the task of controlling how others act.

'Being on a pedestal' was a phrase used by a number of people. It encapsulates their awareness of being at a distance from others, also, 'above' them. It also conveys something of the isolation of the role, of its power, a sense of being watched and visible, and also vulnerable, there is a risk of toppling off. It acknowledges their awareness that they are in a different social position from those they manage. We now go on to look at how people experience and see themselves managing themselves in this exposed position.

Accepting the distance: 'you're not an equal member of the team'

I would definitely say – one of the things that I have achieved is that there is a sense of team. But that I am not an equal member of it. No matter how much I might try to be or, worse yet, think that I want to be. In the end, I want to see the team where I want the team to go.

I do feel that I need to manage and control myself because I have a role to fulfil, which is nothing to do with the person that I am really. I don't know that it's nothing to do with the person that I am – my personality obviously affects what sort of manager I am . . . I mean, this isn't clearly formed at all and it is still a great confusion to me. Something I found difficult, certainly in the first year of the job, was the – the feeling I was no longer one of the girls. I wasn't in the in-crowd. And I've got over that really and I accept that I will never be accepted as one of the crowd . . . I feel that there is an expectation that the head is different in some way. Yes, they do want you to be approachable and considerate and different to the person that they had before – but you are not, at the end of the day, one of the staff. And that's true, you're not. You have a different role. And the buck stops with me and so does the ultimate power really. And that does make you different. Whether that is acceptable to you or not is another matter. I think it perhaps wasn't to me initially, but it is now.

In these passages, we hear Marion Brown trying to identify the different elements she has had to deal with in 'managing herself', issues that come up in other managers' accounts of their transition. There are questions of assuming a role, or a particular social position, of 'manager' and dealing with different understandings of what this involves. Marion describes how this negotiated understanding changes everyone's understanding – and how, in this process, she has had to accept and work with some of the ways her staff view her role, just as they have had to come to terms with some of her expectations of them. She has hopes for change, but her staff also have limits as to how far they're prepared to change. She has certain powers and responsibilities which mean she is not 'one of the girls', and her staff don't see her as one. Yet, at the same time, they do have expectations of her, they want her to be 'approachable and considerate'. She has a role to fulfil 'which is nothing to do with the person that I am' – but at the same time it is; she is clear that her personality, the way she sees herself, does affect the kind of manager she is. Marion has come to accept that she is 'different', but it has taken time. These insights are the product of experience, of gradually coming to feel more at ease in what has, at times, been a difficult and uncomfortable position. In the process, she has identified a number of tensions, discrepancies and contradictions in her position. This reflection helps her to understand why she initially found the transition to being a head teacher so difficult although 'this isn't clearly formed at all and it is still a great confusion to me'. However, as she talks, she demonstrates how she has had to engage in a 'debate with herself', which takes account of her 'preferred theory of management', the ideas and behaviour of those she manages and the constraints of her structural or social position. She has greater power, and responsibility, she's the one 'with whom the buck stops' and one who has been appointed for her vision for the school – a vision she hopes others will come to share and support, but a vision which is not fully negotiable, despite her ideals of open and democratic management.

Distance, demands and boundaries

Initially, because I was sort of like one of the girls gone up, everybody wants you. The slightest problem, they're ringing you, instead of trying to sort it out for themselves. And so, I had to learn to be a bit hard . . . And then when, sort of when I'd like done some more boundaries there, I'd got to sort of like cut my apron strings type thing . . . that made it quite a lot easier, really.

As a nurse manager, Mary Rainey believes it is important to keep in close touch with things that are happening on the wards, to be aware of the issues they are facing and of how policies are working out at that level. This is an important part of her philosophy or 'theory' of management. Also, having worked with the ward staff over many years, she wants to do something about the things she knows cause them problems. However, she quickly came to realise she would soon be overwhelmed if she didn't detach herself from day-to-day problems and her sense of obligation to longstanding relationships – if she didn't 'cut the apron strings' and 'learn to be a bit hard'. It is clear to Mary now, that she was taking on too much in the initial stages. However, it was something she had to learn, at the expense of working very long hours, feeling drained and exhausted by her job. We see Mary's 'preferred theory of management' adapting in the light of experience. The values that underpin her personal philosophy are as strong as ever. She is still clear that as a manager, she wants to remain sensitive to how things affect people 'on the ground', to be aware of their problems and their perspectives on changes being implemented. However, she came to realise that she could not sustain her level of involvement, or her staff's dependence on her: 'I had to learn to be a bit hard.' These are perhaps familiar issues for longer-standing managers. However, Mary had to experience the pressures and the work load she was taking on before reaching her own conclusion that something had to change. This is, undoubtedly, not only the experience of someone new to management; accepting one's limitations and negotiating acceptable boundaries are continual challenges.

Keeping some distance – what does it mean?

It may seem obvious that 'becoming a manager' sets one apart from other staff. It carries a different grade or job title, certain formal powers, status and so on. Between people's 'preferred theories of management' and their emergent theories of management in practice, certain discrepancies and tensions emerge. One issue is the question of how 'close' a manager should be to those they manage. Listening to the managers in our study, we see that many of them are engaged in working this out for themselves. Although many have arrived at the conclusion 'you've got to keep some distance', this is not something that is easily defined. It means different things to managers in different situations, with different individuals; it is negotiable and changeable. It conflicts with ideas of open communication, of the manager being approachable and available. It feels somewhat at odds with ideas of teams, and of people working with common purpose. The experience of 'distance' for Diane Washington, who has gradually taken on more managerial tasks in an established department of committed young professionals, is very different from that described by Ken Pine, who talks of his battle, as a newcomer, to get the respect of older, experienced restaurant staff or Mark Taylor's shift from working with professional engineers to managing shop floor production.

Familiar identities: 'one of the girls' or one of the managers?

Mary Rainey and Carol Laine have both moved into managerial posts in places where they are already known. Mary has to work to create

some distance, to make it clear that her role has changed, and to establish boundaries to protect herself from becoming overwhelmed by staff
who are used to looking to her to solve their problems. For Carol, there
are rather different problems of establishing herself in a more senior
position and redefining her relationship to those who were previously
her friends and colleagues. She finds the distance surprising and hard
to come to terms with. Her own view of her position is having to
change, as it doesn't fit with that of her ex-colleagues or the managerial
group of which she is now part.

Carol Laine 'felt awful' and at the same time 'very pleased' to have
been the one promoted amongst her workmates. Carol's is not an
unusual situation, but one she clearly found difficult to handle: 'I
thought, how can I tell these people what to do? We've all worked
together as friends, if you like.' In many ways, Carol still felt more like
'one of the girls', she felt she knew 'how their minds ticked over'.

I still felt like one of the girls, if you like. And I knew exactly how they thought, because I was
one of them. I knew how their minds ticked over . . . and I used to say to them, 'look . . . I know
how you're feeling' as if I wanted to say, 'look I am one of you'. And I wanted to be sort of with
them . . . but I think they felt distant. Whereas one time, they'd be able to tell me how they felt,
and how they thought, I think they used to think, 'well, we can't say that to her now, because
she's one of them'.

In many ways, Carol still felt more like 'one of the girls', than one of
the managers. As a newly appointed manager, her way of seeing things
was more deeply shaped by her years as a clerical officer, than it was
by her new managerial role (cf. Salaman and Butler 1990). Like Mary
Rainey, she was concerned to do something about the things she knew
concerned and bothered those she had worked so closely with. Looking
back, she can see that, initially, it was easier to think of her role as their
spokesperson, rather than their manager. 'It's as though I'm feeling it,
we've already spoken about things, and I know that other people have
had the same impression about things, or they've felt the same, they'd
want the same thing.' However, she can see occasions where this has
left her vulnerable: 'The reason it back-fires on me is because nobody
gives me any support.' Carol was having to manage herself through this
dilemma. In her new position, she wants to think she's 'working for
people', 'helping people', trying to 'achieve the best for them', this is
part of her 'preferred management style'. She wonders if they saw her
as 'wet behind the ears' and ineffective, in her efforts to do this. She
clings to the rare occasions when someone makes her feel they respect
her for trying: 'I really admired what you were saying, I wanted to clap.'
However, she is clearly struggling with feelings of whether she is
behaving appropriately. As a manager, is it her role to speak up for
others? Or 'should I let the person that's got the problem speak up for

themselves?' On occasions, she's got it wrong, 'they're not thinking those things'. Sometimes it has led to confrontation in meetings, she's been seen as a trouble-maker: 'I've learned, probably, that I should try and keep a bit quiet sometimes.'

'I can't be me any more': being a person and being a manager

Others, like Carrie Bley, face a rather different problem. Coming from outside to join a college as a senior manager, she found herself definitely 'placed on a pedestal', being seen in a particular social position. The first time we met, this was an important issue for Carrie. She was clearly uncomfortable with the distance between how others saw and treated her as a manager, and her sense of herself as a person in a particular job: 'I'd always been chief organiser, chief Christmas organiser, "let's go out and have a drink" organiser ... I'd love to do it ... go round and get the pounds every week off somebody.' Suddenly, she couldn't do this, she was not expected to make coffee for people, people weren't eager to discuss football with her. For Carrie, this is uncomfortable, she feels constrained, as a person, by others' expectations of the position she holds:

You can't be social any more. I can't be me any more. I hate that. That's the biggest drag about it. I don't have a laugh any more ... they don't open up because they don't trust me.

She recognises that it goes with the job, that she has seen it happen to other senior managers. She knows that she has, herself, kept her distance from senior staff. Nevertheless, 'it was a real shock to me personally when it started happening to me'. For Carrie this is problematic not only to her sense of herself as a person. As a manager, she is working hard to develop a more open, approachable style; she wants people to be honest with her about problems they are having, so that she can take steps to help them. She is willing, as Finance Director, to keep them informed about changes that are happening and to debate openly how the college should respond to them. She wants them to question things that are happening, to challenge things they don't like, to express their concerns and misgivings to her, but they don't. She finds her power 'scary', 'it's like I've written this bible ... anything I say goes'. So, for Carrie, it is uncomfortable that the way she sees herself as a person is not reflected in how others treat her. As she talks, she seems to feel that if only they would see and respond to her as the person she sees herself to be, things would be different. 'That's people's perception of power, isn't it, I think. And the status with the job.'

The second time we met, Carrie seemed to have accepted this gap, and can see that the distance has its usefulness. She says she no longer finds it hard to manage because 'they created the division to start off with'. She's open to discussion, debate, but she returns to the issue of dress, and accepts that someone has to make a final decision about 'what's inappropriate for the customer', then 'at the end of the day, I might have to say, well, I'm sorry, but I don't want you wearing it'. Nevertheless, at the same time, she is also working on a management strategy to narrow the distance, by making a point of meeting with groups of staff to explain policy. She is still bothered that people make assumptions about her, as a person, because of the senior position she occupies, as Finance Director. For example, they assume she's 'somebody with a lot of money', but she decides, although she doesn't like it 'there's no point biting' when they make such comments, 'it only makes matters worse'. However, other assumptions seem to bother her more:

People automatically assume, because of the position I hold and what I do, that I vote conservative ... but the political thing is interesting, because their perception is phenomenal. I'm a lot more left wing than the majority of people here. I really am ... it's not as if I'm secretive about my political persuasion ... I've got very strong views about education and health, particularly. And I'm always making jokes about what I'd do if I was prime minister, that type of thing. Very strong messages, but they still perceive me as a conservative. They do, I'm sure they do.

This is clearly difficult, and annoying, for Carrie, to feel so misunderstood as a person. It could be her strategy of making more effort to go around to explain to staff what is happening in the finance area has a dual purpose. She presents it as a genuine attempt to inform, communicate, debate with staff – to narrow the distance between the staff and herself. However, she is 'really surprised' and clearly pleased, when she heard the reaction to her as a person, 'Oh, Carrie's really nice, isn't she?' She finds it difficult that people cannot distinguish between the 'hard things' that she has to do, within the constraints of her position, and her personal commitment to the survival of the college and its contribution to the local community.

Then I think it's more difficult for me, because I have to actually justify it to myself as to what I'm doing, perhaps, rather than them. Yea, perhaps it isn't for them, perhaps it's more with me.

So, we have seen Carrie struggling with how people's perception of the job interacts with their perception of her as a person. We can see that at times she feels misunderstood both as a person and as a manager. Also, in the quote above, she ends with an interesting observation – this discrepancy means that she has to feel much clearer, in her own mind, that she is happy with what she is doing in her job. What she can do, within the constraints she operates in, may not be ideal, but she has to justify it to *herself*, as much if not more, than to others.

'I haven't fully absorbed the power that comes with my role':
discipline, control, being seen to use your power

Whether that's a good thing or a bad thing I don't know. I haven't yet fully absorbed what power there is that comes with my role now. (Marion Brown)

You're working with other people, so you have to learn to manage each other. Having the authority over other people means you have the power to control the environment under which they can produce and actually relate to you. So there is a greater responsibility to actually peg out the boundaries of how people can function. And when you have that sort of power, you can actually develop them quite quickly, because they're intelligent people who want to develop. It's human nature. (Stan Jordan)

Most of the managers spoke of a 'preferred style' of management that aims to be democratic, consult, discuss, reach consensus. However, as Marion Brown puts it, they also have to come to terms with the power that comes with their role, with their awareness that they occupy positions where others may well acknowledge their power, expect them to be responsible for making decisions, for confronting problems and issues and so on. Coming to terms with this is not easy or comfortable. Initially, Alicia Coltrane felt obliged to act decisively, answer questions and make decisions quickly. Carrie Bley describes her power as 'scary', 'it's like I've written this bible . . . anything I say goes'. Power can, of course, be positive and enabling. As managers, they have scope to 'make things better', or to offer people opportunities. However, it also has a more difficult side, of having to confront and deal with problems.

Nurturing and developing: the smooth side of the people thing

We have already heard people talking about what Dick Thompson, in Chapter 4, called the 'smooth side of the people thing'. Many of the managers describe people whom they have seen move on and develop and the satisfaction they get from encouraging and 'nurturing' their staff by offering them new experiences, opportunities to develop new skills, providing training and so on. As Ellen Fitzgerald points out, she is where she is today because, earlier in her career, her manager took an interest in her, pushed and encouraged her. In terms of relationships with their staff, these are ways in which people find their power positive and enabling. However, although they emphasise the rewards of seeing others develop, this is not purely altruistic. Ellen Fitzgerald gets a 'real buzz' out of seeing her staff develop – passing exams, putting training into practice, 'seeing them actually achieving the results'. There is, however, also an important sense of personal achievement, 'knowing that I've had an input into that – either by putting them on a training course, or coaching them along'. This introduces a sense of indebtedness, a more subtle form of power that cannot be voiced.

I think also, that managers ... have to be quite unselfish, and they have to be able to stand back and let somebody else achieve, and then say 'well done'. And probably knowing that it's them that's actually got the person to achieve in the first place. You've got to let go. Yea, and let them think otherwise. Yes. So, I think that you do need to be quite unselfish in that respect.

However, at the same time, Ellen has an underlying sense that it is also her achievement, that without her good management, it would not have been possible.

Andrew Shepherd also talks enthusiastically of developing the potential of his staff, encouraging them to take on things they may have felt were beyond their scope. He is pleased with how he persuaded a member of his staff, 'a young lady here who's got far more to offer than she's been delivering', to take up a place on a weekend course. She was very nervous about doing it, and Andrew put himself out to go along and see her over the weekend, to offer some support.

One, I wanted to go and support her, but two – I hate to say this – I *know* what the impact was that I went to support her ... I know that she'll volunteer for something else next time, and I'll get it back. So I almost saw that as an investment, not only in her but for me as well ... That's what I mean, that's the slight dilemma. Because she thought how wonderful to see you, and I was thinking yes, how nice to see you, but there's more to come ... somewhere in my mind, I was thinking 'well, she'll go to the wall for me now', and that's nice to have ... (Andrew Shepherd)

As he talks, Andrew takes us back to the complex motives we heard managers talk of in Chapter 6. He has a genuine interest in supporting this woman's progress; he is aware that he has enhanced her view of him as 'wonderful' by offering this support. However, at the same time, he is aware that, as a manager, he can later draw on and benefit from the goodwill he has accumulated. Andrew is struggling with some discomfort. He is questioning whether he is acting as a 'genuinely nice person' or engaging in a subtle form of managerial control or manipulation. 'She thought, how wonderful to see you, and I was thinking, yes, how nice to see you, but there's more to come.'

Dan Tracey is more conscious of how he uses staff development primarily as part of his strategy for 'managing the unmanageable', 'people who want to get on', 'people who think they're underpaid', 'people who don't get as much personal development as they should do', 'people who are just basically pissed off with what they're doing'. A mass of hopes and expectations which are impossible for Dan to fulfil within available resources and opportunities. Dan talks of how he tackles these competing demands as business decisions. 'Recruitment is an expensive business . . . and training them up.' 'I've got some fairly key staff here who I can't afford to lose.' 'I have to manage their expectations within the fiscal constraints that I've got. But that's all about resources management and I suppose that's a fairly fundamental part of being a manager.' So, Dan focuses on staff development in terms of 'business strategy'. He presents himself as able to reconcile ideas of himself as a supportive, helpful person *and* a 'good manager' without Andrew Shepherd's misgivings about authenticity or motives surrounding his actions, or Ellen Fitzgerald's implied indebtedness. Maybe it is clearer for Dan, because he presents it in terms of a solution to a business problem he faces.

So, rather than trying to keep them, you know, in a box, where this is their set job, it's all about introducing new concepts to them, giving them different challenges and different responsibilities and allowing them to grow within the role that they've got, all be it at a fairly limited level. But yes, there is the opportunity to do that – and by that way you can offset some of the expectations that they've got without costing too much money.

So, it could be something as simple as 'yes, I will buy an extra word processing package for you and you can learn it or use it', or,' we will allow you greater autonomy', say, in managing the stationery budget or the way they communicate with stores, or some accountability for one or two other members of staff. Dan is consciously 'managing expectations', 'you give them a bit of autonomy, a bit of responsibility and people think, yes, that's quite good, you know, he knows what he's doing.' So, he retains his key members of staff, they feel they are not 'stifled', they are acquiring skills that make them feel 'a more rounded person . . . more employable, if they decided they wanted to leave' and thus more secure. He is negotiating mutual benefits. 'You will ultimately get the best both out of them, and the business as a whole.'

In looking at these managers talk about aspects of the 'soft side of management', we see them using their enabling power in ways that undoubtedly benefit and develop staff. However, relationships are made more complex because they may be interested in them as people, but they also rely on them as key members of staff, for output and results. Andrew Shepherd is the most experienced of these managers, yet interestingly, he expresses discomfort with this dilemma most strongly. Although managers may, at one level, be learning to understand and deal with relationships at work in a more accomplished way, on another, more hidden level, there are questions about whether these 'interpersonal skills' could engage the manager in more subtle ways of controlling and manipulating people. Rather than coming to terms with and getting used to it (Hill 1992), we find managers like Andrew continuing to ask questions about the nature the relationship between themselves and those they manage.

Using power: the 'rougher' side of the people thing

A difficult side of 'making things better' is the recognition that this not only involves making 'good' things happen, it also involves confronting and dealing with difficult situations and relationships. Charles Parker spoke of reaching a point where he could no longer allow things to continue as they were. The situation was at odds with his 'preferred' approach, but there were also issues of his credibility, a danger certain individuals were 'running rings' round him. Tom Smith talks about a 'lot of gin and tonic' and a 'lot of sleepless nights' as he ponders over how to tackle a person who, he feels, is 'outmanoeuvring' him, as Tom can see he has outmanoeuvred others for some time. Mary Rainey talks of her frustration at seeing people 'working the system' by taking time off sick and not being able to see what she can do about it. Mary is 'absolutely infuriated': 'I feel as if I've been used.' A number of managers have similar stories of situations they feel they have to confront, that they cannot allow to continue. 'Working the system', pushing things to the limits, asserting the power of 'us' against 'them' can be seen as part of the structured relationships in organisations. However, phrases like 'being outmanoeuvred', 'used', 'running rings round me' suggest that such 'power struggles' are also experienced in a more directly personal way by these managers. *They* are 'being taken advantage of', *their* personal credibility is at stake if they handle it wrongly.

These are judgements, then, about organisational limits and boundaries as well as personal limits and boundaries. The manager has to make decisions about where to 'draw the line' in both senses. Also, there are judgements about how best to assert oneself. There are questions of knowing the people involved, of judging how best to deal with individuals. Harry Lyttleton talks of 'the old saying, different strokes ... it's exactly that'. Within his team, he identifies people coming from two cultures – the 'old culture' of authoritarian relationships, and a younger generation of workers who have 'fought hard to get apprenticeships', who accept the moves towards a more flexible workforce, who are more responsive to the ideas of 'empowerment' and taking responsibility for their own work that Harry is promoting. Harry talks of some from the 'old culture', having a 'severe mentality problem'; skilled tradesmen of a 'certain age', who 'think they can get away with anything':

They'll do anything, they'll put one over on you. It's like a game, they come to work, but it's a game, it's role-playing for them – let's wind up the manager today ... And they'll take everything literally ... we've just had a staff handbook and it says in it that you can't take anything home. And when I asked them, have you read it, they say no, we haven't, because you wouldn't allow us to take it home ...

What's behind it?
I don't know, years and years of being treated like crap, if you want to use their words. The old indoctrination of companies like this, where the way that they were treated is that you will say nothing, do nothing except when I tell you. And they just continue it on, because they don't see why they should change.

Harry recognises and understands this behaviour as part of a long-standing culture, part of the pattern of life in the chemical plant where he works. However, it is a problem, not only because *he* is now the manager to be wound up as part of the 'game', but also, because it gets in the way of his plans. It doesn't fit with the style of management and attitudes to work he is trying to introduce. At the other extreme, he finds people who don't even take their break. 'They have got so much sense of affiliation with what they're doing . . . you have to drag them away from the place because they're so intent on making sure that things go right.' This leaves Harry having to work with conflicting approaches:

I know I won't get this person to do anything if I don't shout at them . . . you just do it, at the end of the day . . . you just yell at them, you know. And you use a few expletives and then they'll respect it and they just get on with it then. Then you'll get somebody of the same trade, but if you raise your voice above a certain level, they'll burst into tears, virtually, you'll see tears welling up and their bottom lip starts to quiver. And what you've got to do is get the judgement between the two. And if you use the opposite . . . you're really struggling. [*Harry laughs*] It does happen.

Harry is having to operate a complex control strategy, spanning the continuum from 'indirect' to 'direct' managerial controls (Watson 1999). He is having to adjust his preferred approach ('indirect control') to fit the diversity of the situation in which he works. He is also, in the process, using himself to influence others. As he deals with his team, he is making judgements about how to present himself, how to treat individuals. He is aware that, if he gets it wrong, his credibility and his relationships as a manager are threatened.

As Harry points out, people do, of course, get it wrong. Lawrence Young works with a team of ambitious 'young Turks' in the Head Office of the bank, in a culture of long hours, where people work 'beyond their jobs' to be recognised. If there is a control issue, it is about making sure that people don't neglect their core tasks for more innovative projects, in their efforts to be noticed. He describes an incident where he 'cracked the whip', after he had been in the job two weeks. Someone brought in their wedding photographs, and Lawrence 'bit his lip' for half an hour, as people looked at them 'while I had work piling high' before he said 'would you mind waiting until lunch time to do this . . . we've got some work to do'. As he talks about it some time later, he is still weighing up the judgements that were involved in this intervention. In the 'long hours' culture he works in, he is aware his staff feel they have a right to some autonomy over how they organise their work, 'what does it matter if I've wasted half an hour this morning . . . I'll take it home'. He doesn't mind people relaxing and having a laugh at work . . . 'but there has to be a line drawn somewhere'. 'Perhaps it came over more bluntly than I meant it to . . . [but] I felt justified in speaking my mind'. 'I regretted it quite a lot . . . but it may have been quite good that, in a quite ham-fisted way, I kind of exerted my authority.' 'For a while, I got a bit of a reputation for being a bit of a tyrant' . . . 'perhaps I'm a little too soft at times . . . somebody said to me, you want to be careful you don't get taken for a ride'. Some time after this incident, it still crystallises dilemmas Lawrence recognises in his managerial role and uncertainties about how to deal with them.

Arthur Blakey, on the other hand, working in the very different environment of the tool room, is much clearer about the need to assert his power before he can move his staff towards taking on more responsibility for organising their own work and solving their own problems. The workers in the tool room were used to being 'bawled out': 'I'm the boss, I know what I know about it, sonny.' So, in this environment, when a new manager arrives, the staff have to find 'what the limit is'. Arthur felt, especially because he was young, it was a case of 'we'll see how far we can push the kid here'. So, initially, he felt he had to be very tight about rules and boundaries. He describes how they used to go for their tea break early. He went up to the canteen, 'there's a minute to go, out you get':

That was actually probably a good – quite a good thing that I'd done . . . I was probably overly-hard with them. But I let them know I'm not going to put up with a lot of shite with them on that.

Like Harry Lyttleton, Arthur wants to change the nature of relationships in his area, he wants to build greater trust, he wants his staff to take on more responsibility for their work. However, the way they manage is constrained by the expectations of their staff and the culture they are used to and are re-creating.

Being honest, making decisions, hurting people's feelings

Alicia Coltrane talks of how she has learned that being a manager involves confronting and dealing with issues. This might mean being honest with people when their performance is not up to standard: 'In the past, I was a bit wishy washy, not wanting to hurt people's feelings.' Or, if she is aware of disagreement, she 'makes time to prepare for things' and think her position through. 'I'd say, you know, I understand what your position is, but my position is this, this and this, for these reasons.' Alicia has not found this easy: 'I think I had to make myself do that.' It is a lesson she has learned the hard way, when 'I didn't have the confidence to fail somebody on their probationary period'. Neither Alicia, nor the person's immediate manager 'wanted to take that responsibility'. With hindsight, she sees 'it's not doing them any favours, they're absolutely stressed out because they're just not up to the job' so the person was on the verge of resigning anyway. 'You learn from your mistakes . . . you've got to follow it through, and you've got to make decisions.' Alicia 'theorises' her change in approach. 'I decided that you don't necessarily hurt people's feelings if you're up-front.' 'You've got to be honest with your staff, it's no good being not happy with them, if you don't tell them, because if they don't know they need to put it right.'

Rules, discipline, making it easier on yourself?

These managers have just been talking about how, as managers in different situations and different workplace cultures, they are involved in constantly shifting processes of building relationships, drawing boundaries, self-presentation and self-reflection. This is part of every-day life, as they work on developing relationships and achieving results as managers. Organisations also incorporate rules and procedures that spread the responsibility for making some of these judgements and decisions. So, in hospitals, routine checking of procedures, recording of actions taken help 'make manageable' individual responsibility for patients' well-being. Expectations of 'professional' relationships between different groups of staff and between staff and patients help to 'manage' emotions and potential conflict. In many organisations, disciplinary procedures and HRM practices provide guidelines within which managers handle the 'rough side of the people thing'. So, Liz Carter talks of how disciplining and dismissing staff was a 'real big fear' that 'turned out to be unfounded', if you 'follow the book', 'make sure you keep good notes', 'don't make any silly mistakes'.

You build up this sort of awful disciplinary interview, where you're going to dismiss somebody. But when you actually come to doing it, if the manager's done their job properly . . . it's really very clear cut. And the individuals that come to you, they understand exactly why they're there and they know what the consequences of them being there are, and it just generally makes things a lot easier.

As Liz Carter argues, 'good HRM practice' can ease the discomfort of having to discipline or dismiss an individual member of staff, by providing clear procedures, which, if carefully followed, make the outcome of 'shortcomings' in performance or behaviour inevitable. The responsibility is shifted onto the employee who has failed to respond to warnings, to agreed action for support, or whatever. As a personnel manager, it is part of Liz's role to create the frameworks within which disciplinary processes take place. However, in Harry Lyttleton's experience, such procedures take the manager into 'us and them' territory. He describes getting involved in proceedings that could lead to dismissal as 'putting your hand in the fire'. If you don't know exactly what you're doing, and don't 'apply the letter of the law', and have watertight evidence, 'they'll take you to the cleaners' and 'probably you're a laughing stock as well'. Harry has seen other managers avoid the risk of taking this route: 'why should I make myself go through all that, you know?'

Shirley Stitt describes a situation where she accepts, and is locked into, the inevitability of the 'business decision', and where procedures have been followed which leave her in a position to sack a member of staff whose work has been unsatisfactory. However, carrying out the 'sound decision' was clearly done at some personal cost to Shirley, who felt 'a real bad person'. She is aware of the impact it will have on the person's life. This is part of the 'emotional labour' of management; managers are paid to do these difficult things and Shirley has to see it through and deal with her feelings herself. As a manager, she's doing what has to be done 'for the best of the company'. As a person, she 'felt lousy for days' and has to come to terms with strong feelings, with roots that go back to her own experience of the impact of unemployment on her own family.

I had to let her go . . . Once I realised I had to do that, I had to get it over with quickly, because I knew I wouldn't sleep at night-time. So as soon as I'd done the final assessment of whether we keep her on or not, I'd checked with personnel, and I'd checked with one of the bosses and they said, yes that's the right decision . . . within an hour, I had her in and told her. Because I'd have been too churned up, if I'd have left it. Now that – that has a direct impact on somebody . . . oh I just felt a real bad person. But I wasn't, I was making a management decision for the best of the company. But as a person, I felt lousy for days.

As Shirley describes herself, caught up in the process that led to this woman's dismissal, we see that an unintended consequence of 'good practice' in HRM terms, could be to lock managers into a process with a logic and momentum of its own. Alicia Coltrane describes a situation where she felt uneasy, because the objectives and targets set for managers of her housing projects didn't address her view of the organisation's 'real' goal. She talks of a case where it was not difficult to show that the person facing disciplinary action had failed to meet their targets and objectives. They had clearly failed to achieve targets for introducing new procedures, implementing a new computer system and so on. This propelled Alicia into a course of action which she felt ignored other underlying questions about the 'fit' between the person and the work. Did these objectives actually address the really important aspects of the job? Alicia felt not, 'Her best areas are in supporting her staff and ensuring a high quality service to (clients), but what she's not good at is finance and admin . . . and it took us a long time to identify that that was pulling her down.' For Alicia, the objectives and targets got in the way of identifying the 'real' problem.

Alicia was 'worried to death' until she identified the problem and found a solution. She managed to find some money to provide an administrative assistant, to allow the woman to concentrate on the aspects of the job that she was good at. However, despite the happy outcome, this had clearly been a very stressful process for those involved. It involved Alicia in questioning the logic of the organisation's practices and procedures and how they defined the 'performance' in ways that she felt ignored more important issues of quality. It demanded an analysis of the situation that identified an alternative course of action; funding had to be secured to make that feasible. It had required Alicia to question rather than follow the organisation's procedures and practices, and to take some level of personal risk in doing this.

Dan Tracey steps back from issues of rules and procedures and justifies 'getting rid of staff' as one element in a cluster of business decisions, in the longer term interests of staff and customers:

You have to be flexible to the changing needs of your customer. And if that means sacking – getting rid of people, making people redundant, yea? And if it means opening new facilities . . . or building new warehouses, then you do that, yea? Whatever it takes, you do it, you have to do it. Because at the end of the day, your customer is your bread and butter. Without them, everybody's out of work.

However, although the 'business decision' may be clear, Dan has to deal with the discomfort of actually carrying it through:

We all have bills to pay and houses to run, families to support . . . if anybody can sit across the desk and say to you, look they enjoy getting rid of people, making people redundant, or sacking people, then they'd be a bloody liar, I think. Either that or a sadist. I don't like doing that, I'll be honest.

Being 'in the middle'

'The man in the middle' has provided a way of describing some conflicts and tensions of lower management roles. Roethlisberger recognised the position of supervisors sitting between managers and workers, with loyalties to both groups, but not fully belonging in either (Roethlisberger 1945). In various ways, the managers we talked to could also be seen as 'in the middle' – between workers and more senior managers; responsible for implementing policies and decisions that have been decided at more senior levels; feeling responsible for making firms more efficient, more profitable, but possibly with little to gain personally from this; responding to external influences such as 'the market' or government policy, over which they have very little control. Such characteristics of their position mediate the notion of managerial agency, power and control. They also complicate ideas of 'shared interests' and a common view on the organisation as they place the manager in a position where they are in contact with groups with potentially different perspectives and orientations to the organisation. Thus, we were interested in whether the managers we interviewed experienced themselves as 'in the middle' in any respects. When we asked whether or not they saw themselves as 'in the middle' in any way, we received responses such as:

I've normally been part of the decision-making process that has made that policy. So that's the difference, and that's why I say I'm not in the middle. Because I think that's what happens to people that are in the middle, they are stuck with implementing policies that they might not have a direct say in. So they've got no ownership of it. (Carrie Bley)

I mean, I'm with a big company, but no I don't feel that I'm in the middle at all ... There are obviously many more senior managers at much higher levels than I am. But I still think that I'm, you know, involved to some extent, in setting strategy and that yes, I might be given some strategy to implement and carry out. But I feel that I have all the information surrounding it and not that I'm just kind of being blinkered and told to do that little bit of it, if you see what I mean ... we all share a vision and we all share – we know where we're going and we all know what we've got to do to get us all there and that sort of thing. (Sally Vaughan)

Some people would probably say that just because you've got a team of people below you and you're reporting to someone else, that you can be a bit isolated, in the middle. But that's down to the individual really, how they get on with their team and how they get on with their superiors. I don't really see myself as sort of being stuck in the middle at all, not within our organisation, because it's quite a flat structure really. (Julian Adderley)

Carrie Bley, Sally Vaughan and Julian Adderley all recognise ways in which managers can be 'in the middle', but don't see themselves in this way. Carrie and Sally link this with their involvement in decision-making. Carrie is a member of the directorate in her college. Sally feels that although she is only involved 'to some extent', she is working with people who have a 'shared vision' and that she has all the information she needs to see how the bits of strategy she has to carry out fit within a broad picture. Julian Adderley doesn't see himself 'in the middle' because he works within a 'flat' organisation, that has been de-layered – he argues that the uncomfortable aspects of 'being in the middle' can be eased by the individual themselves, their skills of 'getting on' with people. However, Julian does, like most people, go on to identify rather different ways in which he does feel 'in the middle'.

Round tables, fulcrums and spiders' webs versus pyramids and pedestals

We're having another mini restructuring . . . and one of the lads on my team said, 'does this mean you're still going to be our boss?' . . . I don't like the word boss, and I said jokingly 'I prefer the word friend or something like that', which caused some amusement . . . Behind it was a genuine reason for saying this, which was that I don't like to be seen as this figure at the top of the pyramid. I do like genuinely to be part of the fulcrum of the team. I don't necessarily mean be at the centre of it. Be the one that everybody looks to for guidance – I do very much like to be there and be part, rather than being up on a pedestal, as it were . . . in an ideal world, we'd all be sat round one table . . . preferably a round one, so that there's none of this sort of hierarchical overtones to it.

As Lawrence Young answers the question of whether he sees himself 'in the middle', he turns it around. He defines 'the middle' as a good place for a manager to be, as part of his team, in a position that minimises hierarchical differences, that eases relationships and communications. Tom Smith feels to be 'in the middle' would be preferable to his current position, which he sees as at the 'top of a pyramid'. He would like to be 'in the middle of a spider's web', getting all the sections to talk to one another. Lawrence and Tom, initially, use the idea of being 'in the middle' to present their 'preferred' view of the manager's position, rather than the inherently problematic position Roethlisberger (1945) identified. They do this to make the point that this would be preferable to the hierarchical position they find themselves in at present. However, both go on to illustrate ways in which they are 'in the middle' in more uncomfortable senses. We now go on to hear some of the rather different ways in which managers recognised themselves as 'in the middle'.

Making other people's policies work

We get given projects and we have to make them work, basically . . . so yea, you're sandwiched there . . . Even if you're not thinking that it's the best idea in the world, you have to sell it as that to the staff, you know. But I can also see that our project managers are very in the middle as well, because they have their staff groups to manage and yet they've got us as well. So I appreciate it's not just me. And I think my boss is 'in the middle'. Because he's got us and then he's got our director coming in as well. (Alicia Coltrane)

Well, you are making sure that directives which have been made from above are operating on the shop floor. Terminology! The shop floor! This Investors in People is a good example . . . Now I am in the middle because I am having to organise and arrange the timetable of interviews within the department. A classic example there of where I'm in the middle . . . I don't try and 'sell' things, but if I feel – it comes back to goodwill again. If I feel that something is . . . to the collective advantage of the department, then I'll push it as hard as I can. If I am totally convinced by it. (Jack Dodds)

I think when there are regulatory requirements that you think are absolutely stupid, but you've got to tell people, you know, this is what we need to do. And they think, do we really have to do this? Yep, sorry, yep, there's a law, you've got to do it. And you think [*whispers*] 'what a load of rubbish'. And you've got to hold yourself back from saying, 'yea, I think it's a load of crap as well, but you've got to do it' . . . you've got to play it down the line, even though you think, oh this is ridiculous, why are we doing this? (Shirley Stitt)

Sometimes you have to do something which you don't want to do, awkward things like reducing hours, or things like that. And you do feel a little sort of aggrieved about doing it . . . you know, it's that person's job and should you really be doing it? Sometimes you do question, you know, the decisions that have been made . . . I sometimes feel piggy in the middle over that . . . there are outside influences which I have no control over. I mean, the staff do understand to a certain extent, but there is an extent where they don't understand. (Mike Davis)

As these people talk, we see them using the notion of 'dual control'. Whatever they think of the policies they have to implement, they have to find ways of getting others to comply, to achieve the necessary result. They also have to think about how they are going to manage themselves in this process. Jack Dodds surprises himself as he slips into the language of 'the shop floor' as he talks about the staff in his university department. He acknowledges he pushes things harder if he feels convinced by them. Shirley Stitt 'plays it down the line', she holds back from saying she thinks the regulations are a 'load of crap'. It's the law, it has to be done. These reactions illustrate how these managers are engaged in concealing and suppressing their real feelings, using themselves, their skills of persuasion (or, as a last resort, the power of their position) to get people to do things they themselves may question. All these managers seem to feel an obligation not to question or undermine the policy they have to implement. This is one way of dealing with the conflict between policies they have to implement and their personal feelings about them.

However, for Arthur Blakey, loyalty to 'the company line' is potentially threatening to his personal credibility, which, as we have seen, is central to his relationships with the men in the tool room, and his ability to 'get them on-side', to cooperate with the changes he wants to make there. So, he takes a rather different approach:

I suppose I would never – very rarely – let things that would ruin my credibility happen. If there was an announcement to be made to the people which I didn't agree with, I would tell them that before I made the announcement . . . A personal credibility . . . I probably get a kick out of that.
So you express your view of what comes from above?
I may not express my view, sometimes I may not be allowed to express my view, so I'll *say* that. Say this isn't my opinion, but this is the company line on it. Again, it's all around my own credibility, and I have credibility I want to protect.

Arthur balances the 'company line' against his personal credibility, a credibility he believes is essential in his building cooperative relationships with his staff. He presents himself as in control of himself, his credibility, able to handle discrepancies between the 'company line' and his personal opinion – telling them 'this is the line', but that he doesn't agree; pointing out when he isn't allowed to express his view. This is clearly a more difficult tight-rope Arthur is walking. For his staff, it leaves unanswered the question of what his view actually *is*. It is problematic, in terms of relationships with senior management, that he isn't giving wholehearted support to policies. So far, Arthur has given priority to managing his credibility.

'Piggy-in-the-middle', 'sandwiches': managing conflicting demands

We're called, in our organisational structure, 'middle managers' . . . we've got one level of management that's looking at three to five years hence and doing the planning forward stage, then you've got what they call the middle managers that manage the day-to-day and planning for twelve to eighteen months hence – which is things like your staffing levels and all this sort of thing. And then we've got the level with the people actually working and providing the service on a day-to-day . . . the manager's job that I'm in now is very much middle management. You've got the pressures from the people above saying you've got to get this job done, with this amount of money. Then you've got the people that's actually to do it, saying we can't do this . . . you do feel very much like the jam in the middle of this sandwich, being squeezed from both ways. (Mary Rainey)

The sandwich filling. The way I would describe it is, you've got a very old culture and you've got one at the other extreme. I'm caught between the two. (Mina Mangeshkar)

When Mary Rainey was asked in what ways she saw herself 'in the middle', she responded immediately by pointing out that, in her organisational structure, she's called a 'middle manager' – so clearly, she must be. She then goes on to think through what this means. There are levels of 'strategy', 'forward planning', medium-term planning to day-to-day implementation. There are pressures from 'above', asking for maximum output from given levels of resources and from 'below', saying they need more to do their job properly. Mina Mangeshkar adds the possibility of being 'between cultures', between caught up in change, between 'old' and 'new' ways of seeing and doing things. As Alicia Coltrane pointed out earlier, these are not exclusively characteristics of people in particular positions in organisations. She could see how other managers above and below her in the hierarchy could also come to feel 'in the middle' – but in different ways, as they come into contact with different groups, face different kinds of pressures, have different goals and targets to meet and view the organisation from their different viewpoints or perspectives. In this sense, 'the middle' comes to represent the position from which a person might come to recognise or experience conflicting demands to be managed. It has suggestions of divided loyalties, being able to see different viewpoints, being a 'buffer' absorbing and mediating the tensions between opposing groups. Thus, there are many 'middles'. However, it is a powerful notion, as it acknowledges conflicting interests and demands within organisations and at the same time recognises that these are experienced and dealt with by individuals in particular relationships to others. Here, we are interested in how these new managers defined and dealt with 'being in the middle'.

As Mary Rainey identifies levels of strategy, 'forward planning', short-term and day-to-day implementation of policy and strategy, she suggests that these may be in tension, pulling in different directions, focusing on different concerns. Other managers talk with greater certainty of '*the* strategy', of a clear sense of strategy or direction in their organisation. Mina Mangeshkar talked of falling between the 'old' and the 'new' cultures. Liza Potts also feels she works in an organisation where there is a clear sense of strategy, or 'the way the business needs to go':

Due to my own inexperience, at the moment I do [feel in the middle]. But at the personal level, from a business point of view, I know I have strong attributes which tend to mirror those of the top management that I see . . . I see people as people regardless of their positions and I will stand up to a store manager who I don't respect – and I will tell him why. I will respect someone with less power more, if I regard them with respect as a person who sees the way the business needs to go.

Liza seems to share the top management vision for the future of the company. Her sense of 'being in the middle' is her inexperience. She stands up to experienced store managers, but as yet, her influence is hard won, it is based on others listening to her ideas and respecting the way she works. She gives her respect to those, at whatever level, who can see 'the way the business needs to go'. As a graduate trainee, she knows her role will be to lead the organisation in this direction, she seems confident she has the attributes to do this, that 'mirror those of the top management'. However, for the moment, it is 'my own inexperience' that leaves her 'in the middle'. She seems clear where she will fit eventually, with the top management, with those who 'see the way the business needs to go'. She is, for the moment, 'in the middle' at 'the personal level'.

As they talk of 'being in the middle', other managers see 'strategy' in a more diffuse way. So, Mary Rainey sees different time-scales or 'levels' that sit together uneasily. Julian Adderley is struggling to make his strategy or plans fit with everything else that is going on around him and with 'the overall strategy of the organisation':

There are times when you make decisions thinking, well, what's the line manager going to think? So being in the middle does and can affect your decision-making because you know what your manager expects from you . . . so yes, you are very much in the middle, because there's lots of other things happening all around you and everything has to fit together with the organisation, so that the organisation does go forward in one direction.

Other managers emphasise how 'being in the middle' involves them in mediating pressures from 'above' in the interests of their staff and of the areas they manage. So, Lucy Armstrong manages the growing demands on staff to take on tasks 'as part of the larger organisational issues', by making them 'as straightforward as can be' or,

I try not to pass them on to the people I line manage . . . I've got the experience and I know the areas I'm dealing with, I can probably do it 99.9% of the time . . . if it is ever necessary, I've got the kind of staff who will understand, respond.

Will Evans also gives examples of how he tries to mediate demands on his staff. He's in the middle in the sense of,

'Them and us'. I sort of see us as the 'us' you see.
And who's the 'them'?
Them that make the decisions . . . who's got the power to spend the money really, because it all revolves around the money – how many staff you have, what you teach, those sort of things. How people are treated. For example, a lot of my staff are off doing other things, whereas really they should be here in technology. But because we're such a late priority, they've been used to teach English elsewhere . . . Keeping our department happy and being dumped on from above, without passing on the dumping, if you like, trying to absorb it, cushion the blows . . . you do what you can.

As well as protecting staff from pressures from above, some managers talk of how they have to deal with pressures for increased resources from below. Lucy Armstrong, for example, says,

There's a lot of pressure from the staff I line manage, for resources of all kinds, whether it's time, money or whatever . . . And then I've got people above me saying 'no, you can't have any more of that'. And I've got people below me saying 'I can't do this job unless' . . . I sort of mediate, I suppose, essentially, between one set of pressures and the other.

It may not just be 'us' and 'them' or 'above' and 'below' that have to be 'managed'. Like Lucy, Dan Tracey is mediating between different sets of pressures. He has control over a large budget, but he sees himself as the one who is having to decide where priorities lie.

You have to set budgets and you only have a certain amount of money to spend . . . at the end of the day, it's all accounted for and so there isn't an awful lot of slack in it really. And I have my own personal objectives, because if I don't achieve my own personal objectives, then I won't progress, OK. And then I've the people who work for me, yes, and I've got all their expectations, all their needs and all their personal desires and dreams to try to cope with as well. And unfortunately I cannot meet all these people's personal needs and desires always within the budget and the objectives that I've got. So I'm in the middle, yes. I'm managing expectations at a people level, as well as against the financial constraints that I've got in terms of the budgets and the finances. So I guess you could say I'm in the middle of that, yes, I don't know.

Mike Davis describes himself mediating between customers and changes from head office. For example, he is the person having to explain why prices have risen to customers who see little or no improvement for the extra money they are paying.

The customers say, you need to do more. And I would agree with them. Then the company's saying, business is not as good as it should be, you need to make cuts . . . or, every Saturday, you charge them a fiver to come in and you're being told, charge them £6. And you say, that isn't going to go down very well. And you do it, and then you're in the centre. The customers are having a go at you and the managers at head office are saying 'you will do it'. And you're thinking hmmm . . . Sometimes I can see both sides of the coin . . . sometimes head office cannot . . . they'll go, 'the customers will accept it after a while' . . . Head office are not as close to the customers and do not see the customers on a daily basis, as we do. I don't think they really fully understand.

Colin Hawkins feels a wider range of pressures, 'the carers, the residents, the budgets, you are in the middle'. In negotiating these different demands, Colin feels it is easy to lose sight of the goal of it all:

You sometimes wonder why you are here, you lose sight of that because of all the other bits and pieces . . . I mean I think I'd hold on to the fact that I'm a social worker and that I want to effect change in people's lives . . . all the other bits that I have to do is to achieve that one thing. That's what I try and hang on to. It keeps me going.

Betty Smith also sees her position, as practice manager and fund-holding manager, as one that, by nature, places her in the middle of competing viewpoints and demands:

Oh yea, you're very much piggy-in-the-middle in general practice. Because you have to support the staff, you also have to support the partners . . . you've sort of got to arbitrate between the two and you're also the first port of call if anything goes wrong for either side. And then you've got the additional Primary Health Care Team, who are the health visitors, district nurses etc. If anything goes wrong for them, they come to me as well.

Common interests and 'pyramid selling'

At the start of this chapter, we picked out some of the ideas that form part of our managers' 'preferred theories' of management. Amongst these were ideas of teams, with shared interests, working together towards a common goal. However, running through a number of accounts is also an implicit recognition that any 'common interest' masks the very different kinds of stake that organisational members have. Some managers were conscious that recognition for performance is unequal, not only in financial terms, but also in terms of visibility within the organisation. The 'team' is not as well recognised as the team leader.

to some extent, I find this a bit strange – but people within the organisation, in head office, will look at branches, and they'll look at me, at Newtown, and Newtown *is* Ellen Fitzgerald.
To head office?
Yes, I am Newtown, Newtown is me, and that's it. Now as a manager, I'm quite happy about that. As an office manager, first line manager, as a member of the team, I never realised that they thought like that . . . But if I had known at that level, I would not have been happy at all.

Although many of these managers are ultimately dependent on their staff for their own success, they are also influenced by them in terms of how they feel about their own performance as 'managers of people' on a day-to-day level. So, Alicia Coltrane's housing projects all produced excellent residents' handbooks. She is clearly delighted 'it's nothing to do with me, it was the staff that did it, but I felt really pleased that they'd done such a good job . . . I think that they know that I feel quite pleased and proud of them, you know'.

As new managers, many talk of their staff as a very important source of feedback. Marion Brown is aware of this, 'I judge how I'm doing by what others say'. So, if people are saying positive things, that's good: 'But a really poor negative of that is that any time someone grumbles about something, I take it to heart.' So, Marion is working to 'develop a tougher skin' as 'it's in human nature to moan, to argue, well, in my experience of teachers it is!' Diane Washington also talks of 'the way that staff react and behave with you' as her way of judging how well she's doing at 'managing people'. If they all 'suddenly stopped coming through my door' or 'talking to me at lunch', she'd begin to think 'oh maybe I'm doing something wrong here'.

So, we can see that these managers are dependent on their staff both for achieving their goals, and also, for positive feedback that makes them feel more at ease and competent as managers. Any discomfort around this dependence may be eased – or made more intense – by the realisation that they themselves are part of the same process. As Harry Lyttleton has moved up in his organisation, he has come to see that he is tied into a process which he calls 'pyramid selling' – his efforts contribute to the success of those above him.

People who you thought were very clever, you realise that they're not . . . you know he's sitting there twiddling his thumbs all day . . . you think, well 'all right, he's delegated' . . . you feel a bit used and abused by it, but you know, that's what they say is effective management anyway, isn't it? . . . I have targets to work to . . . my first target is to provide an efficient service to the production department . . . and then I have another five targets, let's say things like improve the safety record, or introduce a new system of work . . . And then you see your boss's targets, which his boss has given him, and you've got two of his targets! . . . So, he's using your targets, you see . . . but that's pyramid selling, isn't it? Or whatever you like to call it.
And you're using the people below you to achieve yours?
Oh yes, yea, of course you are, yes.

As Harry's comments suggest, feelings about this may change. This may feel acceptable as long as one is benefiting from, as one manager put it, 'hanging onto the coat-tails' of someone who is rising fast in the organisation. However, it may begin to wear thin or feel uncomfortable in other circumstances.

In this chapter, we have heard managers talking about managing changing relationships at work. Managers also, of course, have to divide their attention between a working life and a home or private life. Chapter 8 looks at this.

MANAGING A LIFE AT WORK AND AWAY FROM WORK: BOUNDARIES, BALANCES AND PRIORITIES

Do you think that the way you carry out or see your work as a manager in this organisation has been affected in any way by what one might call your 'other lives'?
What other lives do I have? I don't know.
Does it fit with the 'you' in the other bits of your life?
Does it fit?
Or are there any ways in which it conflicts with them?
Well, it's helped me with some things that I'm involved in, some of the committees I am on, some of the other things that are parts of my life outside of work. Oh, it obviously impacts on domestic bliss. So, I'm a pain in the arse and I don't interact with the kids perhaps as much as I should. Well, I think it's a job that puts quite a lot of pressure and strain on you and so therefore you – one is apt to take these sorts of problems home . . . I try not to, but they will obviously affect how you feel during the other hours when you're not at work. And of course, to do the jobs properly, like the pile of admin, often necessitates coming in when people aren't in, say a Saturday morning, or taking work home on an evening. And that is one of the evils . . . I think that's how it affects my other life, it eats into the time where I could be reading more, I could be interacting more with the family – although I have a stroppy wife who makes sure that I don't spend too much time . . . I play a bit of sport as well still. And we like to take weekends off and go walking and things like that. So it's a matter of perspective and balance.
So you've got to keep an eye on that balance?
Well yes . . . it would go too far in the other direction. But I sleep well at night, so I must have a semblance of control if I can manage to sleep OK . . . I'm able to compartmentalise things reasonably well. I don't wake up at three in the morning saying I should have done this, I should have done that. I can switch off. It takes a bit of time to do so, but I can do it and relax, in the domestic circumstance. But I think I'm coping reasonably well at the moment. I don't have an ulcer, I don't think I've got an ulcer. I'm not addicted to noxious substances . . . I gave up smoking several years ago. I've been tempted to take that back but I haven't. I like a drop of juice. But I think I'm reasonably in control.

In this passage, we hear Jack Dodds exploring the question of how his work fits with and influences the rest of his life. It is an account in which he seems to be constantly asking himself the question of whether he is in control of his life. He produces 'evidence' that he is managing the combination satisfactorily – he manages to get away for weekends walking, he still plays some sport, he sleeps well at night, he doesn't *think* he has an ulcer, he isn't too dependent on alcohol or addicted to

other 'noxious substances'. By the end, he arrives at a somewhat qualified answer, 'But I think I'm reasonably in control'. However, as he
works towards this conclusion, we see him weighing up many different aspects of the relationship between work and his life outside work
that have to be considered and managed. He begins by recognising that
work can have benefits for other aspects of life, for example, helping
him on committees. However, it is also demanding, 'it impacts on
domestic bliss', one can come home tired, preoccupied, 'a pain in the
arse'. Work also spills into the evenings and weekends, which affects
the time and energy left for other things. In these ways it 'eats into' the
rest of life, affecting Jack's family life, his social life, his interests outside
work. And of course, it also affects other people's lives, when they have
to live with the demands of the 'pain-in-the-arse-Jack', or the Jack who
'could be interacting more with the family'. So, they too are drawn into
managing the way Jack runs his life – his 'stroppy wife' manages its
effect on her life, making sure he doesn't spend too much time on work.
So, 'it's a matter of perspective and balance', of managing competing
demands and priorities.

In this chapter, we look at how managers present this 'matter of perspective and balance', at how they see their work 'fitting' with the rest
of their lives. Cooper (1981; Cooper et al. 1988) writes about the problems managers face in coping with the demands of high-pressure jobs,
problems such as 'management burnout', stress, long hours and the
difficulties of establishing priorities and striking a satisfactory balance
between work and other aspects of life. These matters are potentially
damaging both for their personal health and well-being and for
relationships and family life. Marshall's study of senior women managers who had left their jobs included a number who had said they had
done this to regain some kind of balance in their lives (1995). As Jack
Dodds hints, this is a constant and changing struggle. It shifts with the
demands, responsibilities and opportunities the individual recognises
both inside and outside work. Bailyn (1984) and Schein (1978) have
emphasised that the centrality of work in a person's life and their orientation to work varies between individuals and changes over time, in
ways that organisations often fail to recognise or accommodate. Also,
there are issues of how the individual manager's priorities and work
orientation 'fit' with those of others in their lives. Pahl and Pahl (1972)
and Rapoport and Rapoport (1976) have looked at how 'dual career'
couples manage and balance the demands of their working lives, and
Cooper (1981) shows how the balance struck between partners can shift
over time, as their orientations to home and work change, in ways they
may not find mutually agreeable.

We go on to look in more detail at how the managers we have met
see themselves managing the relationship between work and their lives
beyond work. First, we look at how they talk about the balance between

work and their 'other lives' in terms of time. Most talk about their early careers as managers as a time when they have worked long hours and been under considerable pressure in their work. This sets the context for the rest of the chapter, as it gives us a sense of the demands of work that they are having to balance and prioritise against the 'rest' of their lives.

We then look at how the managers talk about their sense of 'self' outside work. As Jack Dodds suggests, their work can have benefits for their selves in 'other lives'. Many talk of feeling more confident and at ease in situations outside work. Some speak of how they are 'different people' in and out of work, or of needing to 'switch off' when they come home. Relationships outside work also support the new manager in coping with the demands of their work. They may offer opportunities to reflect on their work more openly, or to view it from a different perspective. They may provide opportunities to recognise the 'emotion work' and 'emotion management' discussed in Chapter 7 and to express and explore feelings of anger, frustration and pleasure.

The third section looks at how managers see their work fitting with life out of work and the lives of those close to them. This raises issues of how they see themselves establishing priorities and balancing the different elements of their lives. So, for Jack Dodds, there were questions of how his job affected family life. We also saw how his 'stroppy wife' was drawn into 'managing' him. As Andrew Shepherd talks, he emphasises the benefits of his work for his family, but at the same time, recognises it has considerable impact on their lives.

Finally, we look at ways in which people question whether their present lifestyle is sustainable. Some suggest they might, at some point in their career, reach a 'level' where they may choose to settle. Most of the younger women managers feel there is no room in their lives, as they are at present, for children. Some of those with the biggest ambitions are asking themselves questions about how they can make them fit with the rest of their lives. Sally Vaughan sees others leave the competitive world of marketing suffering from stress and 'burnout' and wonders how far she will go in this pressured environment.

'I spend too much time there . . .'

I'd say that's probably the biggest frustration in my life is not being able to do other things like hobbies and things – because so many hours are spent at work. (Sally Vaughan)

There isn't really enough time, half the time, to do everything I want to do [*laughter*]. It's always a problem. I'd like to spend more time on certain things at work, and I would like to spend more time on things at home, so it's very difficult . . .

Does it move into time outside work?
Yes, it does, whether it's travelling, or whether it's doing work at home, or whether it's working late in the office. (Julian Adderley)

The hours do get me down . . . what I really hate is not having my weekends free any more . . . I don't mind it in the winter, but in the summer, it's like, my friends are all having a barbecue meal all day, and like I was at work . . . I thought, oh, I wish I was doing that! (Kathy Westbrook)

I just wish I could just – sometimes just come home at five o'clock, and go to the gym and, you know – actually plan my life . . . I find it very difficult arranging appointments with my friends in the week, because so often things happen which mean I can't go out for a drink in the evening, or something like that. So yea, it's definitely affected my life . . . At the weekend . . . I just have fun and socialise and do things I enjoy doing out of work. But it is now clearly the weekends when it happens. The week is really given to work. (Liz Carter)

I take work home every night of the week. I try not to work one night a week and I won't work at weekends . . . the Bank can have all it likes of me Monday to Friday, but Saturday and Sunday, I keep that for family time. (Andrew Shepherd)

Long hours seem to be part of working life for most of the managers we met, as they were for those in Vielba's study (1995) and other reported studies of managerial hours. Liz Carter leaves home at 7am each day and returns at about 8pm. Kathy Westbrook talks of working ten hour shifts in her pizza restaurant. Andrew Shepherd takes work home regularly: 'the pattern is I'll go home, be with the kids, bath them, put them to bed and I might start at 9pm and work till whenever'. Andrew Shepherd and Liz Carter echo other managers, who talk of how the week is dominated by work and how they try to keep weekends free for 'family time', 'having fun', socialising. Kathy Westbrook and Ken Pine, working as restaurant managers, or Stan Jordan and Mike Davis, managing bingo halls, tend to be at work when others are not – in the evenings, at weekends. Clearly, these long hours and patterns of work have a major impact on people's lives. The reasons for changing norms in working hours have been linked with economic recession; 'imported' cultures from 'more successful' competitors in Japan and USA; 'delayering' and organisational change; the need to 'prove' oneself in an uncertain and competitive labour market; information growth and overload and so on (Vielba 1995). Whatever the reasons, longer hours seem to have become part of the day-to-day reality of many managers' lives and have to be accommodated and 'managed' by individual managers.

We return later to how managers balance their work and 'other lives'. In the comments above, there are hints of regret, resentment even, and at times, uneasy questions surface about how satisfactory the balance feels. However, first we look at how they talk about the demands of their jobs. Herriot and Pemberton (1995) write of 'new deals', new psychological contracts, shaped in a context of reduced career opportunities, greater insecurity and increasing demands on managers. Similarly, Vielba (1995) identifies a group of managers who accept working as long as it takes to complete their task, but expect greater flexibility and autonomy about working hours in return.

Dealing with 'overload' has become one of the skills required of the modern manager – it is in their hands to manage the task, through time-management, negotiation, delegation, setting realistic goals and targets and so on. The manager is presented with a range of techniques and methods for 'managing the unmanageable', approaches that put them in control of managing their own work. As we saw in Chapter 3, mana-gerial work is often ill-defined, its boundaries are unclear, the manager is subjected to many competing demands. Part of being a competent manager is to be able to negotiate this ambiguity, to identify the pri-orities, to make one's mark – without compromising one's health, family life, leisure – 'working hard and playing hard'. Lawrence Young talks of how, in the bank, there is now 'much more emphasis on home and family, and getting that balance right'. Ellen Fitzgerald, Harry Lyttleton and Stan Jordan draw on the argument that working exces-sive hours is inefficient and counter-productive. Stan describes it as a 'personality problem', 'not being organised', 'their priorities must be somewhat confused'. Ellen makes a principle of never taking work home, prioritising her work: 'if you can't get it all done in 8 hours, then you're not doing something right'. She talks of 'working smarter, not harder', 'giving 110%' while at work, then not even thinking about it: '9 til 5 or 6 or 7 is my work time', on top of which she commutes 90 miles each way to work.

At the same time, managers want to be seen to 'do the job well', to make an impact, to effect change – expectations that often imply taking on additional work, widening their involvement, demonstrating their commitment, showing they can 'over-perform'. Managers have to negotiate conflicting demands that they 'do the job well', are excep-tional even, but do it with ease, without placing an intolerable burden upon themselves. In these ways, the 'problem' is individualised. In marketing, Sally Vaughan finds the attitude is 'sort of sink or swim', if you sink, 'you just couldn't hack it'.

In their accounts, most people work to demonstrate to the listener that they are indeed able to cope with a complex, difficult and time-consuming set of tasks. This is, of course, true. All are still working as managers and seem to be successful in their jobs. As people relatively new to managerial work, the interview provided an opportunity to reflect on and recognise this achievement. At the same time, most also make it clear that this has by no means always been easy. As they talk, there is often a sense that they need to account for how they come to terms with the demands placed on them and the effects these have on their lives – a need to explain to themselves and the listener why they accept this way of life and how they cope with it.

'It's the nature of the job': choices, commitment and 'doing whatever it takes'

Sally Vaughan accepts her very long hours as the nature of her job. She presents it as, in part, a situation that has arisen from choices she made, over which she had control. From the start, she willingly took on extra things she was interested in: 'I wanted to do them and that obviously helped me to progress quickly.' She has reached a level where she sees her job defined in terms of responsibilities, rather than clearly bounded tasks. She fits the group Vielba (1995) identifies, of managers who see their 'contract' in terms of 'doing whatever it takes', rather than working x hours a week. To her, this is something that makes managerial work different – if she doesn't do 'whatever it takes', a lot is at stake.

Now I've got no choice . . . I mean, I'm sure a lot of jobs are similar – that I've got this job to do, and I've got this brand to manage and I've got this profit to deliver and I have to do whatever it takes to do that. I haven't just got to turn up to work 9 to 5 and do x, y and z tasks. You know, it's having the responsibility. And if I don't do it, then the job won't be done, and you know, the brand will suffer and the company will suffer and what have you.

As a young, ambitious, successful woman, she says 'my job is a large part of my life and it's totally consonant with the rest of my life'. She has no problem with this: 'I guess that says I'm in the right job, I'm doing the right thing.'

Liz Carter presents another way of 'managing' the impact of her work on the rest of her life. We have already seen how, for Liz, 'the week is really given to work' and how she sometimes wishes she could 'actually plan my life' and organise some leisure and social activities during the week. When asked how she feels about this, Liz replies,

You just have to accept it. If you fight it, you know, it's something that could become a big issue . . . if you get too strung up about it and if it's something that really makes you an unhappy person, then you're not in the right job, because you do have to have that sort of commitment.

Her response is an interesting blend of 'having to accept it' (which implies there is something 'not quite right' here) and this being a sign you are the right kind of person for the job, because the job demands 'that sort of commitment'. She describes how she comes home just in time to see her partner, before he leaves to work nights. As she talks, there are questions of how far she *is* in control of her life: 'There are times when I think, you know, my whole life is being run by the company.' She then regains a sense of being in control by adding, 'it's what I want . . . you have to take the good with the bad'.

Mike Davis has to do extra shifts in his bingo hall when they are short staffed, or people are ill or on holiday. 'It does have its downsides', when he has to tell his girlfriend he can't go out, at short notice. However, it's 'to be expected', 'it's not as if when you take the job on, you're not told about the hours and what could possibly happen. They're very open about it and you're fully aware of it.' 'It's swings and roundabouts'; he too has holidays, he too might catch 'flu.

In these accounts, we can see that work plays a major part in establishing the priorities of everyday life – it has to come before other things, that is 'the nature of the job'. Ellen and Sally express regret that they cannot pursue other out-of-work activities during the week. Ellen is also prepared to 'jeopardise relationships' at the moment, to put her career first. 'I'm happy with that at the moment . . . focused on what I want.' Liz also talks of 'having to have that sort of commitment'. They present themselves as both in control and not in control. The job demands it, they chose it.

'That is the sub-culture, you know, in all these big organisations'

In many work organisations, long hours and working late are part of the culture – not to comply would mark one out as less committed than others, less suited to the job (Vielba 1995; Watson 1994a). Andrew Shepherd and Lawrence Young both recognise this culture in the banks where they work. Andrew is well aware of what is happening: 'You read all the articles, that is the sub-culture, you know, in all these big organisations.' 'I've played the game and done it, it's worked for me.' With hindsight, he is also clear that it is very much a game, and that by playing it, he has helped reproduce and sustain it:

It was a macho thing. I mean, if you left your room before quarter to seven at night, people would talk about you. I now realise that was a habit . . . I wish what I'd done was walked out at quarter to six one night, or several nights, and they'd have all followed. Because they'd have been the mugs and not me.

So, Andrew now has his own branch, and is 'trying not to generate that for my people here', but at the same time, he is still taking his own work home. Lawrence, on the other hand, is at an earlier stage in his career and still working in such a sub-culture. Like Andrew, he recognises that it is a 'game', but that he may be the loser if he refuses to play – he accepts it as 'short-term pain for a bit of long-term gain'.

It's crucial for me to show that I'm holding the job down, and that I can demonstrate the attributes that I'm going to need for my next management role, and the one after that, and the one after that. You could, with a bit of arrogance, say that it's a bit of short-term pain for a bit of long-term gain, if you're looking at it in terms of the purely financial or the progression way of looking at it.

But is there an end to that?

Potentially not . . . And no, I'm sure there isn't a need to do it. But that's just the way that it – it's expected that you do it. If you're not interested in using a bit of your own time, then you're basically written off as not being interested in getting on . . . if you work in a department where I do, where it's let's say full of the young guns, it's expected that you work your lunch hour and you work late, and you work at home, and at weekends.

So, Lawrence explains his compliance in terms of needing to demonstrate commitment to his job rather than getting essential work done. It is as much about showing you are 'interested in getting on' and 'a cut above your peers'. Although Andrew and Lawrence can see through 'the game', both recognise that, in the end, they have to 'play' it. This awareness seems to help them feel more in control of their situation, but it is only now that Andrew has his own branch that he is trying to challenge it in practice, by not recreating those expectations for his staff. Also, it clearly conflicts with Lawrence's view that the bank expects staff to keep a balance between work and family life.

'You do it for your own sake': feeling more comfortable in the job

Some managers we met come to terms with longer hours and an unclear boundary around work by arguing this makes it possible to do the work as they think it should be done. In this way, it makes them feel more comfortable in their job – they are the ones who benefit. Arthur Blakey, for example, mentions how he 'just pops in' on Sunday: 'I only live ten minutes away', 'that's just to give me peace of mind'. Betty Smith says, 'If I don't take the work home, I'm just at home thinking, well, I should have done this and I wish I'd have done that, and I could have done this.'

Others describe how they work longer hours to make time for things they consider important. Diane Washington describes her 'open door' management style and how this can conflict with planning and organising her workload. Coming in early buys her some time to sit and have coffee with a colleague, to chat about the weekend, their plans, or things that concern them – to relate to them as a person as well as a manager.

So, like Arthur, Diane talks of how 'you do it for your own sake'. In Diane's case, it makes her day slightly less pressured, it creates time to talk to people, something she sees as an important part of being a 'good manager'. Similarly, Mary Rainey feels, as a nurse manager, that she needs to be seen spending time on the wards: 'the fact you can see the conditions that they're working in, it gives you a bit more clout.' She doesn't feel this is how she is expected to spend her time, but does it anyway, 'even if I have to do that half an hour before official work time and half an hour after'.

Jean Holliday talks of her endless struggle to do a '140% workload', of how 'this starts to get a bit irksome, you can't do it, you have a heart attack, you have a mental breakdown, something happens'. So, she talks of setting clear priorities, and simplifies this by focusing on the aims and objectives agreed with her line manager, the person she is responsible to, rather than trying to accommodate everyone's conflicting demands.

Does it fit comfortably with you, in terms of your own feelings about what you should be doing?
I certainly do get problems that I want to do things that ... even my line managers wouldn't accept as my main priorities. If the crunch comes, I suppose I still end up taking some stuff home ... I tend to do what I want to do, which is not what my line managers would want me to do, in my own time.
So you have to pay a price for doing it?
Yes. I've got to admit I'm still strong willed enough to have my priorities. But I fit my priorities in, in my own time.

So, Arthur comes in on Sunday for his peace of mind. For Diane, working long hours is a practical necessity if she is to do her job in the way she thinks it should be done. For Mary and Jean, there is an added touch of defiance; it enables them to take control of their work, to give priority to things that they have decided are important.

'It benefits the business'

An obvious advantage of managers working longer hours for no extra pay is that it cuts organisations' costs. The managers who touch on this issue are the restaurant managers, who are keenly aware, on a day-to-day basis, of the performance of their units. Kathy Westbrook and Ken Pine find themselves doing very long hours to cover other managers' holidays and absences. Ken points out how his unpaid labour is used to improve the performance figures of the restaurant. In his company, managers control the staffing of their restaurants. Ken explains how his manager only has three assistants, rather than four and how assistant managers working long hours do some of the work of barmen on quiet shifts.

You save that much wages, don't you, at the end of the week?
And does that benefit you?
It doesn't benefit us personally, but it benefits the house, doesn't it?
You mean the performance of the house?
Yea, yea. If you've got lower wage percentage, that means you look better at the end of the week, don't you? Less overheads, more profit. At the end of the day, we get the same pay, it doesn't matter what we do. The barman comes in, you let him work, then you've got to pay him, don't you?

So, Ken comes to accept his long hours because they benefit the performance of the restaurant – and thus reflect positively on his management team – and because the other managers work in the same way.

The other side of Ken's argument could be that, as salaried employees, they are being taken advantage of. Surprisingly, few managers talk directly of feeling exploited or 'used'. However, Kathy Westbrook does some calculations and doesn't like the conclusions. She often works a 45–50 hour week. The week we met, she was doing six 10-hour shifts. She doesn't get overtime pay. She begins to draw comparisons between herself and her staff in the restaurant. On a Bank Holiday, they get double pay and tips:

You're thinking gosh, I've had all that stress, I'm knackered, and you know, I can come out not earning as much as they've earned in five hours. And you know, that can be really, really frustrating.

Will Evans talks of how he is 'alarmed' at the amount of time he spends at work, going in to events outside school hours, staying late to prepare props for school productions and so on. He does it. Yet he says 'I don't like to live and breathe it . . . I'm not paid for it . . . it's an odd thing to do in my own time . . . I'd rather be at home.'

Vielba (1995) found that managers whose working week included a fixed number of set hours were more likely to be conscious of the contradiction between their contracts and the reality of the job than those who saw their contract in terms of working 'as long as it takes' to complete their tasks. To some extent, we see this in our sample. As teachers, restaurant managers and production managers, there are core hours to be covered, there are parts of the week where they have no autonomy over when they work.

Putting hats on, taking hats off: continuities and discontinuities of self

In Chapter 5, we looked at how people 'manage' themselves in their working lives and how they are aware of having 'different selves' that come to the fore in different situations. This fits with the rejection of the notion of a 'real' or essential self and the replacement of it with the notion of an 'emergent' self. However, it still leaves important questions of how people experience these 'different selves'. For example, Harré's concept of 'identity projects' (1983) raises issues of the extent to which behaviour is experienced as shaped by external demands and constraints and whether it feels 'comfortable' and congruent with how one sees oneself. So, Jean Holliday accepts discontinuity. She argues for a 'basic personality type', seeing herself as an introvert who has 'been trained' to appear and act quite differently in work situations. In Chapter 6, we saw Andrew Shepherd questioning whether he was behaving in a way that was 'really him', or whether he was 'the next one off the production line'. Along with Arthur Blakey, he reflected on how his concern for his staff might at the same time be both genuine and instrumental. The 'self at work' is complex and many-sided. Here, we add yet another dimension that has to be 'managed': how people experience and talk about themselves outside work.

I'm not a 'manager type' outside of work. So maybe I've got to consciously put a hat on, if you like, every time I go to work. (Charles Parker)

I think my wife would say that I don't do anything but be a manager – hence the sleepless nights and the vast quantities of gin and tonic. [*laughter*] I still sing, I play the guitar. I'm involved in amateur dramatics. And going into court and performing, which after all, that's what it is, is very much the same as that. (Tom Smith)

I'm conscious at the moment that I talk to people out of work the way I do at work. You know, it's like 'just go and get that for me, will you please'. And it's like I'm expecting people to do things . . . it's hard to switch off sometimes . . . although I've always been a very, very patient person, I'm possibly a little bit more impatient, because you have to demand so much out of your crew . . . And I know that's starting to affect my personal life. I am more demanding . . . I'm a little bit tidier. I've raised my standards a little bit. (Kathy Westbrook)

These managers suggest, in different ways, that there are lines to be drawn between home and work. Charles Parker is not a 'manager type' outside work, and wonders if he 'puts a hat on' when he does his job. Tom Smith and Kathy Westbrook see a less clear line. Kathy is conscious of coming home talking to others like 'Kathy the manager', and that this is not always appropriate – 'it's hard to switch off sometimes'.

However, she also sees herself being changed by being a manager; she's 'possibly a little bit more impatient', 'more demanding', 'a little bit tidier'. Tom Smith is also conscious of the interplay between home and work. His wife says he carries on being a manager out of work; his hobbies and his work have similarities – all involve performing. In these brief extracts, we see possibilities of different ways of experiencing continuity and discontinuity of self inside and outside work that we now go on to look at more closely.

Changing hats, different selves: home as an antidote to work

You come to work wearing the hat and it's nice to go home and hang it up. It's – you sort of dissolve the responsibility when you get home. Yes, let somebody else take over and do the management side of it, because you've done that all day. I like to think somebody else will decide what we're going to have for the evening meal today or what we're going to do for the weekend, or whatever. (Betty Smith)

Outside work, I'm very laid back and, you know, enjoy my leisure time and don't actually have any team-leading things that I would do in my leisure time. I would maybe be a team player, you know, like say for instance rugby or football. I actually prefer in those instances to be one of the gang.
You wouldn't be the leader?
Och, yea, I can be if needs be, you know. There's not a problem. But I actually like to relax by not being it . . . I don't want to sort of be the one that's charging about trying to fire them and that, I want some time off . . . I possibly like actually doing things on my own in my leisure time, whereas in a big organisation, you've got to be in teams and cells . . . not be an individual, but be part of the team. And I think that's very important to be part of a team. But some of my leisure activities outside would run opposite of that . . . say fixing cars, or doing DIY – you know, oneman operation stuff, where I'm in charge of my own destiny . . . you're very not in charge of your own destiny here . . . it's a nice change . . . to have different interests in your life, and different ways in which you operate. (Mark Taylor)

Mark Taylor and Betty Smith show us ways in which they leave their 'manager selves' behind when they leave work. Betty is happy to take a rest from organising things, making decisions. Mark likes to have 'different ways in which you operate' and shows clearly how these counter-balance how he has to 'operate' at work – being a member of the team, rather than the leader; doing things on his own, rather than with a team. Outside work, they take a rest from the 'manager self'. Their leisure time selves are presented as a kind of 'antidote' to the responsibilities of work. As they talk, the 'self' and particular forms of behaviour are closely entangled. Some people say it is difficult for their friends and partners to imagine them in 'work mode'. Liz Carter describes herself as 'fairly light hearted socially', so it is hard for her friends to imagine her 'opposite some burly shop stewards' negotiating pay and conditions. Her work is mentally taxing, so by Friday night, 'I just want to have a good time and forget about it'. Harry Lyttleton's wife wonders how he 'ever got the job in the first place' as she is the manager and organiser in their home. 'I just sit back . . . and play with the kids and their toys.' 'Nothing gets done around the house.' He contrasts this with his 'dead efficient' self at work: 'I suppose after burning yourself out throughout the day, you just come home . . . you switch off, yea. Drives her mad.' Andrew Shepherd talks of how his family 'couldn't imagine me as a manager . . . they wouldn't take me seriously'. One of the ways he sees his work as a manager coming into conflict with the rest of his life is 'occasionally style, getting in the wrong mode' coming home behaving in ways his wife recognises as 'bank mode'. For example, Andrew says, 'I even talk differently as a manager. So, I'm deliberately slowing down when I talk to you.'

So, we see these managers drawing lines between themselves at work and at home, in ways that suggest they accept their 'different selves'. In particular, they show ways in 'which the self out of work' is, for them, as Mark Taylor puts it, 'a nice change', an antidote or rest from the 'manager self'. However, the 'manager self' is nevertheless part of them, a part that their friends and partners might be surprised to see.

Switching off, recharging batteries, leaving it all behind

If I can get out the gate and I can switch off, I know that I've done a good job. If I'm coming home and I'm thinking about it, or I wake up in the morning and I'm still thinking about that particular problem, or what have you, I know that I haven't achieved all that I wanted to do that particular day. (Ron Scott)

I'm doing much longer hours. I think about it a lot more out of hours. It's a lot more stressed, you know, pressurised . . . Sometimes I just can't sort of [*clicks fingers*] get in the car and switch off. (Liz Carter)

Dan Tracey suggests that, to him, it is also important to be able to 'switch off' and forget about work. Ron Scott goes home and absorbs himself in family life and in his DIY projects. Being able to 'switch off' in this way is, to Ron, a sign that he has done his job well, that he has dealt satisfactorily with issues on the prison wing, that he has informed the relevant people of unresolved problems they need to be aware of, that all the appropriate procedures and paperwork have been completed. 'Switching off' is a phrase that was often used. Not being able to switch off conjures images of continual motion, restlessness, stress.

Marion Brown links it with the need to 'recharge her batteries', a picture of being unable to switch off, but drawing on depleting energy reserves.

I've been surprised at how difficult I've found it to switch off . . . it's shocked me really. Because I used to traditionally use holidays as a re-charging my batteries time, and weekends as well . . . It's slightly easier now, after nearly a year. I mean, in the first term it was horrendous, I couldn't sit down at night, because I would think 'well, if you're not doing something, it's not getting done. It's you'. And that was quite a shock.

Others, like Ron Scott, seem to find it easier to 'switch off'. The first time we met, Dan Tracey said one of the surprises had been that he seems 'to be able to cope with pressure a lot better than I thought I would', that he can go home and 'completely switch off from it . . . I guess that helps in a way'. The second time we met, Dan was working long hours on a major new project and was finding it 'increasingly diffi-cult' to 'get home and just relax and spend time with my family and do things that I want to do'. So, managing stress and pressure is 'part of my personal agenda, for the next twelve months, say . . . because I have to get better at it'. Harry Lyttleton's situation has also changed. At the time of the first interview, his job was relatively contained, with set hours and overtime payments for additional work. The second time we met, he had a different job, with less clear boundaries, 'I'm on 24 hour, 7 day a week call, Christmas, all the way through, unofficial' as he works on a continuous production line. He was called on Christmas night: 'you're expected to carry that and advise over the phone, if not turn up and help.' He therefore has no control over when work impinges on his personal life, when he might suddenly have to 'switch on' to deal with problems at work, 'My wife will probably give you more about that than me!' Vielba (1995) reminds us that people differ in their reactions to pressure and long hours. What is acceptable to one person can be a burden to another. Dan Tracey reminds us that as the pressures on a person change, their sense of themselves as coping com-fortably can also change. Harry Lyttleton is aware that change affects not only him, but also his family.

Shoulders to lean on: to talk work or not to talk work?

We have just heard managers talk of ways in which they see themselves leaving parts of their 'manager selves' behind and 'changing hats' when they come home. However, in Chapter 5 we heard Colin Hawkins talk about the importance of home as somewhere he could deal with aspects of himself that sat uncomfortably with himself as manager – his less confident, more nervous, more vulnerable self. Earlier, we heard

Lawrence Young talk of how, at home, he no longer had to 'manage' his anger and resentment at being rejected for a post he wanted. In these ways, relationships outside work can support the 'emerging manager'. They may offer a space to talk more openly of their feelings about 'being a manager', people they work with, difficult situations and all their other concerns.

Carrie Bley's partner supports her by reinforcing her sense that she can do the job: 'He's always given me the security I need to think that I could do anything really . . . it's a fabulous feeling.' Colin Hawkins's partner is also a social worker. She 'drives me crazy' by wanting to discuss and sort out things that are bothering him and she is someone who can offer him both professional and personal support. He contrasts this with a previous relationship, where he kept work issues to himself, 'that's the way I wanted it to be . . . I always say it was protecting my family . . . She accepted that and I accepted that.' Looking back, he can now see 'it was quite lonely, dealing with all the problems yourself'. Kathy Westbrook's boyfriend also works for Big Pizza and is her 'shoulder to lean on'. He understands the demands of her work, unlike her previous boyfriend who resented the way Kathy's job intruded on his life. Mary Rainey sees herself as 'really lucky' to have the support she does at home, a husband who 'gets his earhole blasted'

My husband's the emotional support. The 'there, there', cry on my shoulder sort of thing. [*laughs*]
Does that have to be someone outside work?
I think that it does. Because otherwise . . . you can be the one that starts to demotivate people. If they recognise that there's friction and things.

Mary knows that this affects home life: 'I was hell to live with.' When Mary's relationship with her boss was difficult, her husband was 'sick of hearing that woman's name in this house'. He was also tired of Mary 'coming in absolutely worn out, no energy . . . you're flogging your guts out and all you seem to be doing is getting further and further down, more despondent'. However, his support was clearly very important to Mary in coping with her new job.

Not all managers describe relationships where both partners are so ready to talk about work. Alicia Coltrane lives with someone who 'doesn't feel as committed to his job', who comes home and 'doesn't worry', 'forgets it'. So, Alicia has given up asking him about his work, when he gets home 'it's finished for the day, it's boring to him', although Alicia would actually be quite interested to hear more about it. 'Because he sees it like that, he doesn't want to know what I do during the day.' Instead, Alicia turns to her 'very close friends, women friends' for support, people who also work in housing, or have made similar kinds of job moves.

Dan Tracey wants to 'completely switch off' from work when he gets home. 'One thing I don't like doing is taking my problems home, because my wife's a teacher, she has a tough job as well.' However, he finds himself 'managing' again at home; he has to 'manage the relationship with Rachel'.

Let's say you've had a bad day . . . the first thing Rachel'll want to know is, well, what have you done, have you had a great day and stuff – Rachel, I'm not interested, can we talk about something else here. And that's difficult to manage that, really. Manage the relationship with Rachel.

At the same time, she also wants to tell him 'about the trivia of domestic life . . . that's important, yea?' Also, they have a baby 'it's important – all my son's development . . . and I want to know about that as well. And Rachel is keen to tell me as soon as I walk through the door.' So, when he gets home, Dan has to 'manage' himself:

Managing that is sometimes difficult. You have to be, you know, attentive and 'there' and right on the ball . . . you don't always feel like doing that.

Mina Mangeshkar describes going home to her sisters and parents, and discussing 'all the things at work'.

Mum and Dad as well – they will say, have you thought of this, or that . . . a group discussion you could call it. It's great. [*laughs*] We don't get the flip chart out – it's not that bad!

So, we can see that relationships outside work are important in supporting the 'emergent manager'. They can provide a space where work is left behind. Or they can provide a place where people can begin to express and deal with the emotions that are managed at work, where the 'feeling rules' of the organisations they work in can be broken. They offer Mina Mangeshkar a chance to put issues that face her at work into words and to hear others' ideas and reactions. However, there has to be a 'fit', both sides have to want to take part in this dialogue, and this may not always be the case. So, Alicia Coltrane turns to her women friends for support. Dan Tracey has to balance or 'manage' his need to 'switch off completely', with his sense of the importance of his son's development and his wife's need to talk about his day, and her own work. Fineman (1993a) shows the importance of 'emotion work' in the workplace. Here we see different kinds of 'emotion work' going on outside work.

Benefiting from the 'manager self'

I think the sorts of skills I've just been describing have, you know, been as much benefit in my personal life as well . . . developing wider circles of friends and finding it easier to sort of, you know, talk to people in a group and what have you. I think it's all tied in together. And generally having more confidence. (Sally Vaughan)

Arthur Blakey gives examples of how this confidence helps him in everyday life, by helping him to be more assertive. In a restaurant, at one time, 'no matter how dreadful it was, I wouldn't open my mouth'. Or, if he had been given goods he was unhappy with, 'you went, "ah, hello, I think I bought this off you" [*hesitantly*]'. Now, 'you'd just put a constructive argument together, and a very persuasive argument and be a lot more confident that way, dealing with people outside of work.'

Earlier, we heard Jack Dodds talk of how being a manager has helped him on committees outside work. Will Evans says 'I do tend to take up things I perhaps wouldn't have done before', such as sitting on the committee at his sports club: 'it was always like the sort of thing that other people did'. Of course, 'that might just be I'm getting old, rather than becoming a manager ... the senior people tend to have those posts'.

Charles Parker sees himself able to relate to a wider range of people outside work, 'people I wouldn't have wanted to speak to'. For example, people in senior positions in their organisations, whom he might meet through his parents: 'I could relate to people who I mightn't have been able to before.'

'There's more to life': priorities, boundaries, juggling, balancing

In these accounts of managerial work and managerial lives, we soon become aware that there is a great deal to be 'managed'. The boundary between home and work raises important issues of the continuities and discontinuities people experience between themselves at home and at work. It also raises questions about the 'balance' in their lives and whether they have sufficient time and energy for all that is significant and important in their lives. This is complicated further by the way these things impact on others' lives and whether or not this is acceptable to them.

The problem of making the 'fit' between life at work and family life is an important issue in critical human resource management and careers literature. For example, people move from being young and single with relatively few responsibilities, to people with families to provide and care for; they find themselves 'plateaued', with limited opportunities to move on, they 'wind down' as they approach retirement. There are, then, questions of whether organisations recognise and adapt to the varying centrality of work in people's lives, or whether there are unwritten 'norms' and 'timetables' it is assumed they will fit with (Bailyn 1984; Schein 1978; Sekaran and Hall 1989). There are issues of how households and families 'manage' the balance of domestic life and life at work, for example, in terms of the priorities of each member of the household and how 'dual career' households negotiate and accommodate the competing demands they face.

We have listened to people talking about their working lives, and how they come to accept the demands it places on them and its impact on their day to day lives. They do this in ways that demonstrate some choice or control over the matter – that they are indeed 'managing the unmanageable'. However, for most people, this is not just a matter of individual choice, it is a lifestyle that has considerable impact on others, particularly those with whom they live. So, Ted Ellington talks of how his family accept the irregularity of his life – 'they've never known any-thing else'. He emphasises the advantages for them: he has the flexi-bility to organise his work to allow his wife to pursue her interests, and to travel abroad. Jack Dodds's wife steps in and 'manages' him when 'enough's enough'. However, Bailyn (1993) questions the assumptions of homogeneity underlying career patterns in most organisations – and expectations that home and family life will adjust to fit with work. In managing this diversity, it is usually the individual or the family, rather than the organisation, that adjusts to make it work. She presents this as an increasingly complex juggling act as changing organisational demands interact with changes in family life. She argues for a radical reorganisation of work that recognises the complexity of family life and the shifting patterns of career involvement over individuals' working lives. For example, she sees the notion of a 'family week' as potentially more relevant than the 'family wage'. However, the people in our sample seem to fit the rest of their lives around work, there is little evi-dence of organisations sharing the 'juggling act', or looking ahead to help these managers plan how they will accommodate the changing demands of life outside work.

We have already seen how people are able to present themselves as fitting with organisational demands yet also, to some extent, 'in control' of their working lives. We now go on to look at how they talk about how their lives in and outside work 'fit' together, at how people see themselves drawing these boundaries, balancing the different priorities in their lives and seeing different parts of their lives complementing or conflicting with each other. Of course, we only hear one side of this 'juggling act'; it may be their partners see things very differently.

'I don't have home time, I don't have work time, I don't have those boundaries'

Ted Ellington has a radical way of dealing with the problem of establishing his boundaries around work. He takes control of his time by allocating it to whatever needs doing at a particular moment – he doesn't draw clear boundaries between different parts of his life.

I don't have social time, I don't have home time, I don't have work time. I don't have those boundaries. If I need to, I work all day and all night. If I need to go to any part of the country, I go. If I need to have home time, personal time, I have it.
You have the flexibility to do that?
Yes, yes . . . tomorrow, my daughter's doing something at school, so tomorrow lunch time, I shall go . . . I mean, the whole building could be falling down, but I won't change that. So, I just have one time, and I do in that time what I need to . . . so sometimes, I'm heavily biased towards personal life, and sometimes work life . . . if I tried to have a boundary, and say 'this is work time, this is home time', then it would be a serious problem . . . I've got fax machines, all of the gubbins that one needs, so if necessary, I can work at home.

Ted holds a relatively senior position in his organisation. His view of time fits with Vielba's group of managers who see their job 'taking as long as is required to complete the task', but expect, in return, some flexibility and autonomy to accommodate their needs. This depends on his family accepting Ted's view of time, and being able to fit in with his flexibility. For some families, this could be extremely difficult. He claims this is no problem, 'it's always been the same, it's the way the family's grown up together'.

'It's the old adage of balancing your priorities between home and work'

As Lawrence Young talks of the 'old adage', we are reminded that there is nothing new here, people have always had to juggle and balance work and home life. However, some people have to juggle more than others, for example, lone parents and dual career couples or divorced people with responsibilities to more than one family.

We live in a culture where it would be problematic to say that work comes before family. The centrality of the family is seen in political rhetoric, in religious teaching, in social policy and its emphasis on parental and familial responsibility. This poses a dilemma in organisational life, where there have been criticisms of the failure to address and accommodate the diversity of family demands and responsibilities.

Lawrence Young shows how this is reflected in his experience in the bank. Earlier, we heard him talk of working in a sub-culture which expects him to work long hours and take opportunities to prove himself, which extend his work beyond his core tasks. At the same time, he feels the bank expects him to keep career success and family life in balance.

I think I've got that right. I think most people who get on have also got that right. Because most people have got wives and families ... So they must be doing something right, because they're managing to keep their home life, on the face of it, as happy as you could imagine it to be, and yet they are also, you know, getting on. You know, we are in the so-called caring nineties, where there's very much more emphasis on home and family, and getting the balance right. And I think I'm typical at the moment – but who knows? It may turn full circle again ... I know very few people who are very vigorously career minded. I think a lot of people are, like me, committed to a career, but they won't sacrifice what they've got outside to get it. I'm fairly certain that's typical, certainly in our organisation and outside as well.

However, this is not an easy balance for Lawrence; he regularly works late and takes work home with him: 'I'm acutely aware that sometimes I do it a bit too much.'

'I know where to draw the line'

Lawrence Young talks of having an 'alarm bell' that goes off in his head, as a warning that 'the balance is tipping too heavily in favour of work', that he has to do some 'adjusting of priorities'.

You basically just have to draw a line somewhere and say, well, I'll work this third night in a row, but that's it.

There is some discomfort in taking the night off, 'when you do it, you think, well blimey, I've left all that work for tomorrow – but you find the time to do it. It gets done.' We have also heard others, like Andrew Shepherd and Liz Carter, accepting that 'the week is given to work' while weekends are reserved for leisure and family life.

Dan Tracey, perhaps the most ambitious of the career managers we met, also talks about knowing where to 'draw the line'. He has a young son:

I now know where my priorities lie, very much, and at the end of the day, my family comes first. There are some managers that would not say that ... To me, my family's the be-all and the end-all, and the job is a means to the end, yea? But I'm also ambitious within that means, yea? ... if it didn't fit, then I think I'd do something about it.

However, this is clearly not easy. The second time we met, Dan was still ambitious, 'I still have a belief that in another four years' time I will be a Director of a plc, yes'. However, 'what I'm realising is – I mean, I'm married with a son, ten months old, and I don't get to spend a lot of time with my wife and child.' That week he was having to work Saturday, 'probably Sunday as well', because of problems with the important new project he was in charge of. 'All of a sudden, there's only so much time in the day for the things that really do matter, which is family, yes.' Dan feels lucky, 'I think I've got the lot' and if it wasn't working, he'd 'do something about it'. At the same time, there are questions about whether he has enough time for the things that 'really matter'. One way of bringing together these competing demands is in terms of 'wanting the best for your family'.

I've no great desire to change my lot at the moment, yes. I think I've been incredibly lucky and very fortunate in so much that I've got a lovely wife, a lovely house, a lovely car, a great son, I've got a good set of friends, I've got a good job . . . so I think I've got the lot and I'm incredibly happy with that, yes. But yes, you do strive for more. I mean, it's not necessarily a greed thing, you want the best for your family, yes. You want to increase the experiences that you are able to have, yes . . . widen your life to take more in, yes.

He uses the concept of 'life anchors' to develop this idea. He wants a good social life. His family are a 'real life anchor'. Where he lives is less important. He goes on, he wants to earn 'x' salary, drive 'y' car, 'I do want to be comfortable', 'have two or three children'. 'So, all of a sudden, if you put those life anchors together, yes, you can then start formulating what kind of job you want to find yourself in, in three, four, five years' time.' At the moment, Dan has 'got the lot', but this is not easy to manage. The first time we met, he felt in control, confident he could manage the stress in his life. The second time we met, his demanding new job was making it increasingly difficult to 'just relax and spend time with my family and do things that I want to do'. He was clearly feeling the stress, 'managing stress and managing pressure is a key part of my personal agenda for the next twelve months, say. Because I have to get better at it. At the moment, I'm maybe letting it get to me a bit too much, a bit more than I should.'

Lawrence and Dan both have wives with demanding jobs as teachers. Both have very young children. We hear little about how these women cope and their role in 'managing the unmanageable' or whether they are unhappy with where their partners 'draw the line'. As they talk about their own daily lives, one wonders whether these dual career families are managed by 'accommodation', where one partner's career dominates (Hall and Hall 1980).

'It's not all ego, it's doing the best for those around you. Making sure everything's nice and safe and comfortable for them'

I think being in the situation of having a family, having my house to run, I think you strive to get better for yourself and your family. And if that means that moving up the management ladder gives you more benefits and that, I think you carry that forward. And the thought's at the back of your mind, that you're not just doing it for yourself, you're doing it for your family as well.

We heard Dan Tracey talk of 'wanting the best for your family'. Ron Scott also uses this idea, presenting it as the driving force behind his own career. Andrew Shepherd is aware of how his own choices were reduced by his parents' limited means. This is why he joined the bank on leaving school, rather than going to university. He makes links between this experience and his view of his own job as he talks of his father's pride in his achievements and of how he doesn't want his children's choices to be constrained, as his were.

A career also provides me with benefits for me and my own – I'm very hungry for them. If they're going to be at university, these boys, it's going to be very expensive, you know, I need to plan for that.

So, he likens working in the bank to a game, a football pitch, with certain boundaries – a game that can be played to mutual advantage.

I've got to stay within the parameters, but they're quite wide. But like any game, you've got to play it to your advantage also. So, it's playing a game to mutual advantage, so that it's a bargain – they get their bit, and I get mine.

Andrew's wife has reluctantly been drawn into this game, attending functions, entertaining customers. However, she 'plays' it 'for me', 'our family':

She plays the role for me, if we're going to the theatre, or for a meal with customers, then she'll just switch into the mode. And she's learned – she didn't like it initially, she fought it. But she's realised that the bank provides us with our living. And if it means playing the game together occasionally, to give us more that we would want as a family – not just materialistically, but in every way – then it's a price you have to pay . . . she should earn a tally from the bank occasionally!

Harry Lyttleton presents the benefits to his family in a rather different way. As he talks about his early job choices, his father has clearly been a significant figure, pointing out the importance of 'getting a trade'. Harry now sees himself as a role model for his children: 'I really am a keen believer that kids pick up on what you do'. He hopes, from his experience, they will see 'if they want to do something, it's never too late', but also that it does take a great deal of work and effort.

My daughter picks up on the fact that you don't just go to work, come home, put your feet up whatever . . . to get anything, you've really got to put the effort in as well. It's not the major reason for me studying . . . But I hope that my children will see that if they want to do something, it's never too late to do it. But they have to work for it as well, it doesn't just land on their laps.

We have been listening to how people juggle the priorities of work and family life and how they are constantly striving to achieve a sense of balance that they feel comfortable with. This is something they are actively 'constructing'. As they talk, there is a 'dialogue' with them-selves, as they address their own misgivings and uncertainties. As they reflect on their lives, there are things they can feel pleased about. They are also conscious of things that need to be 'explained' to themselves and to the listener.

'It's my life rather than my job'

Not all the managers we spoke to have so much to juggle in making work and family life fit. So, Sally Vaughan is able to say 'it's my life rather than my job', in a way that Ron Scott or Andrew Shepherd or Dan Tracey would find difficult. However, even for the younger man-agers, work has to fit with the rest of life. Liz Carter talks of how her friends are 'all the same'. Diane Washington's partner also works very long hours. Nevertheless, as we have seen, although some of the younger managers accept the way that work dominates their life, they do voice regrets – about how this affects their social life, about not seeing friends, getting to the gym, and so on. When we first met, Alicia Coltrane said:

How it fits in with my life is that I don't have much of a life outside of work really . . . and I keep thinking I ought to do something about that, you know. I don't really have any hobbies, other than painting and reading, I do a lot of reading. I do very little exercise, which I feel is bad for me . . . it's a very unhealthy job really, sitting in an office or sitting in a car. I don't get a lot of fresh air.

Some of the young, single managers see their work affecting their relationships. Ken Pine describes how he often works at weekends and the evening, so sees very little of his girlfriend, who has a more 'normal' working week. Ellen Fitzgerald is 'very focused', and for the moment, willing to 'jeopardise relationships' to get on in her job. Kathy West-brook has 'lost touch with a lot of old friends'. Her longstanding boyfriend couldn't accept her pattern of work, or perhaps, she suggests 'he couldn't really handle the fact that I was doing alright, and working as a manager'. Her current boyfriend also works for Big Pizza and Kathy talks of how the company organises 'area dos', which is how she met him.

Betty Smith is married to a 'workaholic', which fits well with her own orientation to work. 'I married the right man. We eat and sleep together and that's about it, you know, we see each other to eat.' Betty works very long hours. We met late on a Friday afternoon – when asked what time she had to finish, her answer was, 'It doesn't matter. I finish whenever.' She talks of 'swings and roundabouts', deadlines and frantically busy times; quieter seasons when she can take time off. She relates her attitude to work back to growing up in the shop and post office, where the boundaries between home and work were never clear. She does draw some boundaries:

Obviously, you know, I like to work and I see the working life as a challenge. To achieve the goal that's been set, and that is part of my life. Obviously, yes, I like to go on holiday, I like to be at home. I dedicate, obviously, my weekends to my home life, and my dog.

But seconds earlier she had said, 'I think one of the problems I've got is I put too much into it and therefore don't spend enough time at home, enough time to relax. That is one of the big facts, you know, I don't like about myself. I do put too much into it and therefore neglect the home life, if you like.' For Betty, it is a fact about *herself* rather than her job.

Women, work and families

We have listened to people talking about how they balance home and family life. In doing this, we heard men draw on ideas such as 'doing the best for my family' and 'knowing where to draw the line', to make sense of how they managed this aspect of their lives. Although they were not entirely happy with the balance of home and work in their lives, these are ideas that sit comfortably both with discourses of 'the good father' and 'the good manager'. As the women talk, most of them struggle more with questions of how they combine being a mother and being a manager.

Jean Holliday has managed having a family by fitting it into a larger plan for her life:

Twenty years as a child, ten years building credibility in jobs, ten years retiring from the jobs and looking after the children, ten years ... settling into a job that I'm going to be content with for the rest of my life. Ten years content in your job, spending the money, watching the kids grow up, having the grand kids, and twenty years retirement ... you can see that I'm an accountant!

Jean is now in the phase of 'settling into a job that I'm going to be content with for the rest of my life'. By focusing on bringing up children for ten years, Jean's plan dealt with the conflict of being a mother and having a career.

However, readjusting to work was difficult. She had been well recognised as a 'highly qualified and technically accomplished accountant'. Because she was so well qualified, getting a job was not too difficult. However, 'you've got to admit . . . after ten years wiping noses, you've stopped being a viable accountant. I had not thought about it for ten years.' She found herself in an uncomfortable position: 'I was not confident, couldn't do the job, but was perceived to be terribly competent, purely on the terms of the academics.' She took an MBA, 'to prove my credibility', and made the move into managerial work when business manager posts became available in the NHS. This could be read as a not uncommon story of mid-career change, of re-establishing oneself after a career break. However, listening to Jean it is clear that her path from returning to work, to where she is now, had taken time and been difficult. It involved studying for the MBA alongside work, to restore her credibility in her own eyes; the discomfort of feeling unable to meet the expectations of others; analysing her situation and concluding that she needed to make major changes; repairing her confidence that she could tackle a difficult and demanding job. These are not minor tasks of readjustment, they are complex and difficult processes of self-management, of 're-constructing' her identity. So, while the 'career break' may ease some problems of managing work and family life, it brings others, that may not be visible, that are absorbed and dealt with, but nevertheless, have to be 'managed'.

Other women in our sample chose to carry on working. Carol Laine sees becoming a lone parent as a point where her attitude towards her job changed. 'I thought "Oh, I've got to be more responsible now, I've got somebody else to think about".' So, Carol worked when her daughter was three months old. However, she 'settled then'. She took promotion more seriously and looked at herself differently: 'I thought, I'm just as good as all these other people that have been promoted in the meantime.' Lucy Armstrong and Marion Brown had their children at a time when they had also become much clearer that they wanted to move forward in their working lives. Both talk of how, when they were younger, they had seen being a teacher as a 'career in itself', but had come to realise that they didn't want to remain a classroom teacher, they wanted to move on. Lucy got her promotion, then found out she was pregnant – 'it wasn't the best time!'

If you have got a child and a domestic situation . . . and you work full-time and you want any kind of life of your own – immediately you have to do time management and balancing and prioritising and delegating or whatever it might be.

Marion says:

From the time that Josh was planned, I knew that I wouldn't give up teaching . . . that I didn't want to stay at home, that teaching was important . . . I just took seven months maternity leave and went back and then I became much more together about thinking . . . yes, well I do want my own school. Well, if you want this, then you've got to start thinking about when you're going to apply for things and how, and by what age, you've got to have done things. And if you like, I developed a career plan for myself then. But that was post thirty.

So, as Lucy puts it, both have 'done most of the real career shifts' since they have become mothers, 'which is hardly the time when it would have been easiest in terms of managing life, as it were, and time and energy'. These women all contrast with Bailyn's (1980) 'slow burn' career pattern, of women whose careers slow down until their children are older. All have 'slow burn' careers in the sense that they worked for some years with little hierarchical progression. However, unlike Bailyn's 'slow burners', major changes and moves forward in their working lives coincided with having children, a time when there was more to be managed at home.

Lucy grew up with a working mother who also 'did it all herself' in the home. Lucy was 'sort of politically ill-at-ease' with the idea of paying people to help in the home. She tried to remain fiercely independent when her baby was small, but,

I guess I just recognised that I can't do it and I feel much more at one with myself in recognising that. And if people offer to help me, I say yes! [*laughter*]

Now, her mother says, 'Don't do what I did. There's more to life. It's taken me a lifetime to recognise it.'

As Lucy talks, we can see that managing the demands of home and work is about more than time-management and organisation. It may seem obvious that Lucy needs help in the home, but recognising this is not a straightforward matter. Nor is it a simple matter for a mother to trust their baby to the care of someone else. These are situations that need continual monitoring, management and adjustment. Marion's son is now at secondary school, but the issues are just as real; working and being a mother still conflict. She talks of 'conflict', 'arguing strongly' for her right to do both, something none of the men we talked to had to do. This is complex, she is raising issues that cannot easily be handled by ideas of 'doing the best for my family', or 'knowing where to draw the line'. Marion has to recognise that she is also doing it for herself, and is comfortable with this. Nevertheless, the idea of putting herself first connects uneasily with notions of being a 'good mother'.

I think the biggest conflict is in time, the time that it takes. I still haven't resolved that – although

I've never been anything other than a working mother . . . and I've argued strongly that I should have a right to be both, to have both. That role as mother and that career role. I don't know that the two marry together that well, I really don't. There are times even now when, as I say, Josh's nearly thirteen, and even if I'm not actually doing school work, I'm pre-occupied with it. I mean, he is the focus, my sun and moon, but he could be forgiven for not knowing it sometimes, because I have another agenda. Now, on a good day, I say that he will look back, and he will be his own person, because he could see that I was my own person as well. I mean, my mother was never anything except people's mother . . . I'd never seen her as a person in her own right . . . I think it must help – it must benefit him in the end that his mother was a separate person, with a personality and a role and needs. But I don't know at what cost he will gain that insight.

Is this sustainable? Bolt-holes, burnout and babies

As managers describe the pressures of everyday life and the difficulties of fitting everything they want and have to do into their lives, one asks whether this lifestyle, with all its demands, is sustainable. At a broader level, there are questions of whether the changing patterns of work which we look at in Chapter 9 are temporary changes in organisational life, responses to recession and pressures to be competitive. In the public sector, is 'managerialism', with its emphasis on efficiency, cost-cutting and maximising use of available resources the product of particular economic or political moments? If external pressures change, will ideas and expectations of managerial work change or have we seen a shift in norms and expectations, a change in the 'psychological contract' whereby there is an accepted 'strategic exchange' of loyalty and security for 'interesting work' and opportunities to enhance 'portfolio' careers, with new skills and experiences (Handy 1978; Herriot and Pemberton 1995)?

Alternatively, it may be a matter of continuing to recruit the 'exceptional' people of the adverts looked at in Chapter 1. If individuals vary greatly in what they find reasonable or burdensome, should organisations be seeking those who 'thrive' on the challenges and opportunities they can offer? Or, will there be a growing supply of young, energetic, business school graduates, eager to take their turn? On the other hand, as Cooper et al. argue, are there individual costs to be taken into account – the ulcers, heart attacks, stress induced illnesses (1988)? Also, there are the increasing pressures on family life: divorce, possibilities of partners becoming less willing to support and tolerate the demands of organisational life, or dual career couples who find it increasingly difficult to make their lives 'fit' together in a satisfactory way. These individual crises have costs not only to the individual and their family, there are also costs to organisations in absence or the effects on work. A number of the people we spoke to drew on the argument that overworking is 'inefficient'. On the other hand, organisations' demands for creative, innovative managers may be at odds with working lives that leave little leisure time and little energy for outside interests and activities. Will people come to look back at such patterns of working life as counter-productive? It may be that the 'emergent managers' in our study are at a particularly difficult stage in their working lives. They are in the process of finding out whether they 'have what it takes' for managerial work, of adjusting and coming to terms with the demands that they face. Perhaps, with time, it will all be easier. Or, as Liza Potts put it, they may be looking for ways to 'have some of their life back', like some of the women managers in Marshall's study (1995), looking for a different kind of balance in their lives. Here, we go on to look at how they present their concerns for the future.

Escape routes and alternatives

At the moment, I haven't got any great desire to stop what I'm doing and go and live in a commune for instance, yes? Or I haven't got any great desire to pack it all in and – well, much as I'd love to move to Barbados and open a bar, you know ... So I think I've got the lot and I'm incredibly happy with that, yes.

We have already heard Dan Tracey talk of how he is 'on target' to fulfil his five-year plan of becoming a managing director of a company. We have also heard him say that he would review his plan if he found it was jeopardising family life, and the 'really important things' in any way. However, for the moment, he's 'got the lot' and intends to continue with his plan. Andrew Shepherd also remains ambitious. Going further in the bank may involve working in London for part of his career, but 'the hunger will need to stay, because it's going to be hard'. He's already thinking about how that will affect his family: 'Well, I'd travel, I'd live a long way out and travel. I won't inconvenience the family, inconvenience me.' So, Dan and Andrew remain ambitious. Both recognise that they may come to feel differently, they may lose 'the hunger', but for the moment, they plan for a future where work remains central, where they take on bigger jobs, bigger challenges.

However, other managers are less sure about how they see their future.

The thing I really worry about is, you know, getting to middle-age and like, really sort of cracking under the strain of it all. Because it is hard work, you know, and there is quite a lot of pressure. And I think it's good while you are young and you've got the ideas and the energy and stuff. But I have to say, I don't know whether I will be doing this job in sort of fifteen years' time, because I think it's the sort of job that you can burn out. I think if anything worries me, that's it. That I won't be able to cope with it when, you know, I haven't got quite so much energy.

Sally Vaughan looks around her marketing division and wonders what happens to all the people over forty. Only a few remain, in the more senior positions. She has seen people being medically treated for stress, or taking early retirement on grounds of ill health. The attitude is 'sink or swim'; 'you just couldn't hack it', rather than 'we're really sorry to lose you', although, 'the company obviously wouldn't overtly say that'. There is little sympathy from colleagues for 'whingers', 'everyone's just like, well, I'm sorry, but I've got twice as much you, so you don't say anything'.

Sally's 'escape route', if she faces 'burnout', is a career change, a move into lecturing.

I know people that are lecturers . . . they say that's very sort of stressful and high pressure. But I don't know, from what I've seen, it's nothing like what I do. [*laughter*]

Mary Rainey also plays with the idea of looking for 'an easier life', of taking steps 'backwards' and returning to 'hands on' nursing. She clings to the possibility of going back to nursing, if the pressures of her present job get too much. However, interestingly, she does not see this as a 'defeat': 'I know I've got it in me to do it'. Rather, she sees it as a tactic in her battle with all that she finds difficult about her present job. It would offer a 'rest from the hidden agendas', an 'emotional break', a chance to 'get myself together' and 'get my strength of character back ready for the next fight'. 'It's sort of like pulling your troops back and re-grouping.' So, the possibility of returning to something she feels 'very comfortable and very confident in' is a way of coping with the pressures of her current job. She is aware of how she draws on this, to help her deal with how she feels, day-to-day, in her work.

It all depends on how emotionally drained I feel at the time. Some days I think, be damned, I'll see you in hell before I resign or move into a different job. Then other days I think, I just can't face any more of this emotional stress and I'm going to go now . . . I saw a staff nurse job on the Isle of Wight and I was tempted . . . I was feeling really down, really fragile that day and it looked quite promising, a bit of sunshine.

However, Mary is conscious that the 'escape route' is not a real option, until her daughter finishes university, 'then I can think, well, bugger it. So long as it's a job that pays the mortgage and keeps a roof over my head.'

Earlier, Lawrence Young spoke of the need to be seen to be putting in something 'over the odds', of 'short-term pain for long-term gain', if he is to progress in the bank. However, in the hierarchical structure of the bank, he feels there is some choice about how long to endure the 'pain' of striving to get on. He sees people reaching a level they feel happy at, with 'your little branch out in Melton Mowbray, or whatever, and coasting through to retirement'.

After 'drifting around' after university, Charles Parker now feels he has reached a level where he has 'proved himself':

I'm 34 now – it's a terribly conventional way of putting it, and I apologise for this, but I do feel that I should be doing something of a certain status by now. Sounds a bit naff, but that's the way I feel ... So, in a way, it's like satisfying the aspiration and I'm pleased that I've done it, I've got there, I can do it, and it doesn't matter too much now ... It's something that's important to me. Obviously it's not important to everybody. I don't really know why. I suppose I'd a fairly conventional upbringing, maybe that's the reason for it. But I felt that I should be able to achieve something by a certain time and that's the way it was.

Charles describes himself as coming from a middle class background, 'I don't think I ever really left that. And if you see things in those terms, I don't think I've gone down and I don't think I've gone up.' So, in a sense, Charles has 'taken his place in the world'. Having fulfilled his personal aspirations and others' expectations of him, he now has a sense of greater freedom, he can choose to give it all up when he feels he's 'had enough of all this':

I never really wanted to get involved in all the sort of rat race stuff anyway – if I want to go and be something different, and set up a shop somewhere and, I don't know, travel around, or whatever you want to do, then I'll know that at least I managed to make it to a really sort of responsible position and I made a go of it.

Lucy Armstrong reflects on how she has come to change her longer-term view of the place of work in her life. She now holds open the possibility of giving up work at some time in the future as she weighs up the balance of 'quality of life'.

I'm forty-five and you know, I mean, it's a time when ... it becomes kind of more crucial, in a sense of the whole thing about balancing quality of life now and maybe quality of life later. You know, how long do I want to carry on working? It was never an issue for me, I thought well, I'll carry on working for as long as I can. I'm not sure whether I shall want to now.

Here, in different ways, we see how people present themselves with alternatives, that leave open and make 'emergent' aspects of their plans for the future. For Mary Rainey, these possibilities help her deal with her day-to-day feelings about herself and her work. For the others, identifying alternatives, for the longer term, seems to help make the present more acceptable – whether they choose to use them or not, they demonstrate ways in which they have some control over the demands of work on their lives.

Fitting in the baby

I don't honestly have a focus of where I want to be in ten years' time. And part of that is that little box I've got stored away, it's got children in it, you know. If I'm being totally honest. (Ellen Fitzgerald)

I want to have children, I want to have a family. You know, work is not the be-all and end-all for me. You know, I'm sure I will always work, but I couldn't have a family and do this job . . . I couldn't work the sort of day I work and then come back and be a loving mother! [*laughter*] I'd be a horrible mother! (Liz Carter)

I wouldn't say this to anyone at work, but I don't think I'm going to be doing it for the rest of my life because . . . there isn't really very much room for sort of a personal life, you know, a family, doing this sort of job. And the more senior people, especially the women, I mean, they don't have families or anything. You just couldn't possibly do it. (Sally Vaughan)

We've both got strong views about having a family. I've always maintained that if I had a family, then I should stay at home and look after that family. Because my mum went back to work when I was quite young, and I always wished that she'd been there for me when I came home. (Shirley Stitt)

Having children affects women's lives and careers. It disturbs the balance in 'dual career' families; it can produce what Bailyn (1980) calls 'slow burn' careers, women taking career breaks, or reducing their hours and commitment at a stage when their male colleagues are forging ahead and establishing themselves. Although professional and managerial women are more likely to return to full-time work while their children are young (HMSO 1991), we hear these ambitious and successful women having difficulty imagining how they would combine being a mother with their present jobs.

Ellen Fitzgerald debates the matter with herself:

If I was living twenty minutes from work, and you could employ a child-minder, a nanny or whatever, then yes, it would fit . . . I would like to think that I could switch off from the children, or the child, and put 110% into my work. But I don't think I could. That's probably back into my traditional upbringing – I think that the children would become the most important thing in my life. And if I couldn't give 110% to my career, my job, I wouldn't want to do it . . .
So it's like two things asking 110%!
Yes. It is. Yes, because I would want to be the best mother in the world, always there at the school play and nurturing and guiding, looking after children, being a housewife and things like that. And I would also want to be the career person . . . I know that people will debate it till the cows come home, and I could even fool myself into believing that I could do both – but I honestly don't believe the two mix.

Earlier we heard Marion Brown reach a similar conclusion, although she has always been a working mother, saying 'I don't know that the two marry together that well.' So, how do the women who, at present, have no children see themselves making it work?

None of them sees their organisation sharing the responsibility for making it possible. Ellen Fitzgerald says in the building society one would have to continue to achieve good results, 'but I know that if you're not giving 110%, then you won't'. Also, as a manager, she realises that having children can affect people's promotion prospects:

I know senior managers that are quite biased about women with children. Now I know and you know that, equal opportunities etc., they should never ask those kind of questions. But . . . people that I know would not give a woman a job that had got children. Because they would be concerned about where the children would go if they were ill.

Liz Carter foresees having to make choices and adjustments to fit work and family life together. She sees no part-time or job-sharing senior managers in the company at the moment:

There is going to have to be a compromise at some time in my life. But I'm happy with that . . . I love the company, I love the job . . . but I'm not hung up on staying with one company for the rest of my life and not developing my family life or whatever. I can see me having quite a few changes throughout my life. Sometimes the emphasis will be on family, and then I should think that it'll then move back to my job, so then I'll probably have a part-time job, which hopefully would be quite demanding. But I don't know whether there's a lot out there where the two can go together. And then going back full-time and focusing on progressing my career again.

Sally Vaughan is making exceptional progress in her marketing career. She has been told she has the potential to go a long way. She is now studying and taking opportunities to gain the broader experience she needs to go further. She is planning to move forward in her career. At the same time, she also anticipates 'some sort of career change', moving into lecturing or 'something that I could do part-time'. She has parallel plans or 'career strategies' in mind.

There is clearly much about Shirley Stitt's job that she finds stressful and difficult. Both times we met, she was looking at alternatives. Having a family is one alternative for Shirley, as she would give up work. She is looking at voluntary work as a way of meeting her need to explore new possibilities and also 'with a view to maybe doing it more seriously later on, once I'd had a family, you know'. She recognises that just staying at home 'would drive me to distraction' after a while.

Work is an important part of these women's lives; so is the possibility of having children. However, as they look at the future, they cannot see this combination working comfortably. They see no policies or models in their organisation that address their needs. They plan their futures assuming little or no flexibility from their organisations.

Alicia Coltrane actually had a baby in the interval between the times we met. The second time, she had only been back a fortnight after maternity leave, so was in the process of working out how to combine being a mother with a busy job. While she was away, the workload in her section reached a point where taking on another member of staff was viable, so Alicia has been able to reduce her working week by one day. Alicia sees this as just a lucky coincidence, 'it wasn't that I was able to negotiate my hours through the existing establishment'. Similarly, luck has it that her hours are fairly flexible, 'They need *me* to work flexibly . . . I work with a number of different voluntary organisations . . . therefore meetings are in the evenings.' In the past, Alicia has never taken her time back when she's been to evening meetings. Now, 'I might actually start thinking about how I manage my workload in order to take my time back. Because time in the evening is time away from my son and I want to be able to spend as much time with him as well as do a proper job when I'm at work.' So, the needs of the Housing Association fit, in some ways, with Alicia's needs, but more by luck than design.

Alicia's boss is sympathetic. He tells her to work from home, if ever she has problems with child care. However, Alicia says 'I don't think he really thinks about what that means . . . if I'm looking after my baby . . . I'm not going to be able to do any work . . . when he works from home, he goes and sits in his study and shuts the door.' Also, although he's sympathetic, 'it doesn't stop him giving you loads of work to do . . . I think he still expects you to do over and above your working week, which we all do.' So, Alicia's 'workaholic boss' is able to keep work and family life quite separate in a way she is not sure she will be able to. She is still working out how she is going to manage the demands of working and being a mother.

In their own jobs, the women managers talk of dilemmas about how to 'manage' women with children. Ellen Fitzgerald found 'it was like a country club, really, they just willy nilly would have time off if the children had got a cold or whatever'. Ellen decided they should take a holiday: 'you employ somebody to work for twenty hours, then I expect them to work for twenty hours'. However, she had 'quite mixed emotions . . . it depends which hat you're wearing.'

In the health service, there is considerable flexibility about the number of hours nurses work, but 'it would be what *we* need from *you*, rather than what you need from us'. Mary Rainey, as a manager, cannot give people the hours when they want them, 'there isn't a lot of slack', she has shifts to cover. Staff 'see what their needs are . . . they find it very hard to see it from the other side'. Diane Washington also finds it difficult to accommodate maternity leave or changes to part-time work and keeping the right balance of grades, specialisms and ensuring continuity of patient care: 'it's a bit of a nightmare' trying to accommodate everyone's needs.

So, it seems, women having children remains a 'problem', for individuals' working lives and for organisations. These women, working in large organisations, find themselves keeping quiet about 'the box' with the baby in it. They see little in the way of policy or practice to help them and are left to plan alternatives for themselves. 'Flexibility' is possible only where employees can match their needs with those of the organisation. We are far from the kind of career flexibility that Bailyn writes of (1993). As managers, the women we spoke to were aware of what mothers they employed might want and need, but were constrained in providing it. They are managing in a cultural and economic context in which customers and clients have priority of attention and in which costs have to be closely controlled. This is a key theme of our next and final chapter.

CHAPTER 9

MANAGING MANAGEMENT: EMERGENT MANAGERS IN A CHANGING WORLD

In this final chapter we shall set our selection of managers within the wider picture of which they are a part. We should perhaps first, however, remind ourselves that this selection of managers differs somewhat from what is normally seen in studies of 'what is happening' to managers. Study after study looks at the functionaries of large organisations operating in what we might call 'mainstream' industries or fields of administration. Studies tend to confine themselves either to a single industry or to a small sample of work organisation types. This is inevitable when the study adopts a case study or ethnographic style but it is often also the case when the study uses a survey/interview programme method. This is entirely reasonable, given the centrality of such corporations and activities to modern societies. Indeed, the present study covers people operating in such settings. But interest is not confined to such individuals as the one in our study who is in charge of training in a large construction company, the man who runs a branch of a large bank or the woman who manages the activities of a major hospital. Consideration is also given to people managing the work activities of a smallish school, a group of social workers, a building society office, a supermarket department, a bingo hall, a court, a pizza parlour, and a university department. This gives a much broader picture of managerial activities, and a fuller impression of the variety of settings in which such work occurs than is typically presented.

All of these work settings are part of a broader working world which is itself 'emergent'. We will therefore first give some attention to the nature of the working world into which our emergent managers are emerging and to how they are coming to terms with the type of work situation which is at the same time 'making' and 'being made' by them. And from this, attention is turned to what our investigation means for the notions of management learning and management development, allegedly crucial elements in the performance of modern employing organisations and for the 'psychological contracts' of individual managers. Finally, the focus is brought back closely to the personal thoughts and comments of the managers with whom we talked. We listen to the sort of advice that these individuals said they would offer to any readers of the proposed book who might themselves be emerging, or intending to emerge, as managers. The sort of advice given is looked at as a final indicator of the ways our managers, in their varied employment settings and stages in life, make sense of their past, current and continuing emergence as individuals with both a life identity and a set of work practices to manage.

Managing in a changing world: costs, customers and clients

A changing world of work

Managerial work in all the various settings that we have considered takes place in a particular economic and political context which has been taking shape for almost two decades. The political economies of industrial capitalist societies, because of their very nature, have always been characterised by swings, trends, declines and developments as drives for profit and accumulation interact with political and national interests, technological and ideological developments and with changing patterns of expectation on the part of people as citizens and as consumers. In recent years the whole pace of change has increased, not least because of the economic pressures coming from nations outside of the established western industrial world. Pressures of international competitiveness have meant that in countries like the UK efforts at the level of both state and commercial enterprise have increasingly focused on reducing costs and increasing the productiveness of all kinds of work activity. On the one hand there have been endless organisational or managerial initiatives designed to change the behaviours of employees at every level of the enterprise and, on the other hand, there have been numerous ways in which work activity itself has been restructured (Watson 1995c: ch. 8). An underlying principle of the emerging pattern is one that gives rhetorical priority to the requirements of the customer or the client of the work organisation, as opposed to the concerns of the organisations' own officers and workers. This has been as much a thrust in public sector thinking as it has in the commercial sphere, with many of the principles of commercial competitiveness and focus on what the organisation 'delivers' being carried over into public administration – to the extent, in fact, that the sector has attempted a degree of 're-invention' (Osborne and Gaebler 1992) and, as some would have it, 'managerialised' (Clarke and Newman 1993; Pollitt 1990).

These trends have had enormous implications for people employed as managers across both public and private sectors. They have offered both opportunities and threats. The greatest threat to the large swathe of so-called 'middle managers' who populate the middle levels of organisational hierarchies has simply been that of their being removed. Many have been removed as a result of a combination of top management's concern to reduce costs (to help 'competitiveness') and their concern to encourage enterprise and innovation among remaining managers who are liberated from the weight of hierarchy above and below them and empowered to take initiatives – again to 'further competitiveness'. At the heart of this discourse and its associated discursive practices has been the notion of 'delayering' organisations. This slicing through the managerial ranks has reinforced the poor morale and insecurity said to exist among many managers (Scase and Goffee 1989), an effect which can be reinforced among potential 'losers' by developments in information technology, 'lean production' styles of manufacturing management and 'business process re-engineering', whereby, as Scarbrough and Burrell put it, the aim is 'to polarise the distribution of knowledge and functions between an "educated" and "empowered" workforce and a much smaller group of corporate leaders, in whom concentrates power and discretion' (1996: 182). In spite of the clear evidence of large numbers of lost managerial jobs, there is evidence that delayering and downsizing may have 'reached its limits' (Warhurst and Thompson 1998: 18) and that efforts are now turning to recruiting and developing 'new managers', individuals who will bring 'new blood' to organisations and act as 'movers and shakers' (Mulholland 1998).

The prospects for managerial workers appear to vary from person to person and place to place. The restructuring of organisations clearly presents opportunities for fulfilment and personal development for some managers and this has been demonstrated in studies (Dopson and Stewart 1990; Watson 1994a). Yet these opportunities exist alongside the much more limited set of possibilities presented to some managers, as other researchers suggest. Mulholland (1998), for example, shows the 'movers and shakers' existing alongside the much less well-placed 'survivors' in the privatised utility she studied, and Newell and Dopson (1996) characterise the picture they saw in another corporation as a 'muddle in the middle'. A number of the managers we studied could clearly be compared to Mulholland's 'movers and shakers'. This is especially the case with the younger graduate managers like Liza Potts, whose employer was explicit about developing her cohort of graduates as a newer type of manager who would displace the older, less innovative, ones. The majority of our selection of managers cannot so clearly be characterised in this way, however. Nevertheless, we must note that the design of our study is such that we focus on people who are 'risers', rather than 'survivors' or managers stuck on a hierarchical plateau. Their 'emergence' has been an emergence into the new world of late twentieth century organisations and, as we now consider how they talk about and make sense of the changes which they see going on around them, we must recognise that they are part of this new world. They are

not the managerial functionaries of the old style bureaucracies who are
threatened with delayering and displacement.

Making sense of it all – and managing it

Across the variety of work settings that we have looked at, there are
some clear themes in the way our managers talk about the changes
which are going on around them. We used the terms 'managing in a
changing world' in all of our interviews and asked each manager what,
within this broad context of change, they saw as 'the most important
things that are influencing you in your job'. The answers to this
inevitably varied but they were typically framed within a discourse of
an increasing focus on customers or clients in the context of pressures
to reduce costs, either directly in order to compete with competitors in
the marketplace or, indirectly, as a result of state pressures on funding.
Managers in the public sector note other pressures from the state and
there is reference, from time to time, by managers in both sectors, to
broader trends in society. As we shall see, there is a general equivocation in the way the managers speak. Although some of these pressures
are experienced as worrying and, occasionally, excessively demanding,
they do seem to be awarded a degree of legitimacy. There is a comfort,
and even the possibility of inspiration, to be drawn by a hard-pressed
manager from a discourse which has at its centre a principle of 'pleas-
ing customers' or 'serving clients'. This is undoubtedly something
which the ideologues in senior management positions have been fully
aware of in encouraging the 'outward looking' and 'service ethos'
which their middle managers and employees in general are invited –
not to say 'challenged' – to draw upon.
    Ted Ellington says of his electrical goods company that 'It's just total
change, all the time, non-stop' and immediately moves into reference
to both customers and costs: 'We're trying to become more customer
focused, trying to take enormous amounts of cost out of the business.'
Ellington's acceptance of this is implicit in his use of the word 'we' and
there is enthusiasm in his voice as he explains that, 'We want people to
work smarter, we want to develop people to have new ideas and to
improve the organisation.' He calls this a 'totally new way of working'
and is keen to stress it is 'really happening'. When asked where he
believes the pressures to encourage these practices come from he again
goes back to the customers and costs principle: 'There are two really, as
I said before, one is cost, taking cost out of the business, to be competitive, and the other is improving customer service.' Typical of managers
– whether in the commercial or the public service sector – he does not
mention profitability of the business. He says that it is 'customer

service' which is 'the main driver'. But, in a typical way again, he immediately comes back to cost pressures: 'But, yes, cost is still very important, because we're in a very escalating cost type business. If you let it go, the costs just take over, and you become inefficient, because you can't finance it.'

What does all this mean for Ellington and his specific responsibilities for quality improvement? He is developing a 'relatively new core set up', he says, and this 'hopefully will give better service to the customers'. 'One-stop-shops for the customer ' are being set up which will lead to employees being trained to a higher level 'so they can deal with any query that you have, whether it's for service or accounts or whatever'. This will 'make things easier and better for the customer'. But everything is not straightforwardly bright and cheerful for everyone: thirty locations are to be closed as part of this 'improvement in service' to the customer. And 'how is all this coordinated?', we ask, and Ellington answers the question with one word, 'vision', before going on to explain that consultants were used to help develop this and that 'we transferred-in their learning and their knowledge so that we can take it forward ourselves'. 'Vision', it would seem, is not the inspirational near-religious thing it might at first sound like. It is part of a discourse transferred-in, in this case at least, from those key figures in management discourse propagation, the management consultants.

The managerial work that Ellington does involves bringing about a considerable amount of structural change to maintain the degree of competitiveness which is implicit in his talk of costs and customer focus. For a manager nearer to what she calls the 'sharp end', however, competitiveness is an immediately obvious fact of daily life. 'We have got so much competition', says Liza Potts, and illustrates in a boldly graphic way how managers in their daily life in a supermarket handle 'the realities of the marketplace':

Our jobs are made difficult every time Sainsbury's drops a pound of grapes by two pence. That causes us major paperwork – financial implications. Customers are affected, minute by minute, by what our competition does.
It really is as sharp as this?
Oh yes. People who shop in my store are affected strongly by the economic climate. They need to save every penny. Take the example of a produce manager. You order twenty cases of tomatoes that you'll sell. You then get an urgent e-mail that comes through 'Tesco's have reduced theirs by 20 pence a pound'. You instantly have to reduce yours to that price.
Always?
It's the company's policy: that we follow the competition (although it is a matter of opinion whether you should – I am not too sure that you should).
So you . . .
So you have to fill in the paperwork (you can't just reduce the price); you have to count stock; physically change the point of sale. It has to go through the system. Then your ordering is out of

the window because you find, say, you have sold twice as many tomatoes. This has a knock-on effect at the depot, which has a knock-on effect at the suppliers – who, of course, are trying to supply other retailers as well. And then the competitor puts the price back up and we have to go through all the same thing again. And this can happen two or three times a week.

The marketplace, however, is not just the high street. Sally Vaughan makes sense of what she sees happening in her pharmaceutical company and the way her marketing job is 'completely influenced by what's happening in the market' with reference to what she calls 'sort of macro-economic factors'. She points to such factors as 'the privatisation of health care systems in former Eastern bloc countries' and British government policies on such matters as 'retail price maintenance in pharmaceutical outlets'. She points to pressures coming from the 'environmentalist lobby' and from 'European Union directives regarding the types of packaging we can put our products in'. These things have to be coped with, but always within the constraints of costs and competitiveness. Ted Ellington made a similar point, explaining that his company respected ethical concerns about 'green issues'. They did things like 'recycling paper, making sure we do double-sided photocopying and avoiding CFCs like the plague'. This was not, however, being done as 'just a good gesture'. The company would not 'spend millions of pounds for no benefit' because 'it was not a charity'. There was concern about the environment because the company would want to avoid bad publicity; 'Everything is driven by commercial advantage', Ellington feels.

Other types of recognition of the market context of their managerial work come in managers' recognition of the pressures coming from potential business take-over. Harry Lyttleton, for example, points out that his chemicals company is a relatively small one and that 'in my industry the small players are being bought up by the large players'. This impinged on his own work by making him look at moving from product-focused factory arrangements to process-focused ones. The business needed to be a 'much more multi-product one' to 'cope with the competition'. Yet being very successful can make a company vulnerable in this way, as Mina Mangeshkar points out: 'These factors are always there. We're seen as one of the best run companies in our business – rightly and wrongly – and I think we are bound to get snapped up by a bigger fish.'

Julian Adderley relates the day-to-day pressures in his work to innovate to the extreme pace of change forced on any information technology company by what their competitors are doing and Lawrence Young explains that 'competition in the marketplace is driving all the changes that are taking place in the bank'. He points specifically to the 'low cost bases' of the 'streamlined building societies that are coming in and impinging on our market'. Things like this are 'always being cited in the bank' as 'the reason we must lose another twenty thousand staff or why we must redesign all our processes to make us efficient and save money'. We might note here that he talks about 'the bank' citing these reasons. He is not subscribing as readily to the 'official' discourse encouraged by the top management in the same way that Ted Ellington was. Where Ellington talks in terms of 'we', Young talks of 'they'. But when we turn to that source of concern to the bankers, the building societies, we find something very similar. Ellen Fitzgerald talks of the dominance of the 'competitive environment' and 'working to survive'. Costs have constantly to be 'driven down' so that 'we can offer competitive products'. 'Everything is purely costs' she says, switching back and forth between 'we' and 'they' and, indeed, using 'we' only with a degree of explicit caution.

Everything that's happening at the moment is purely for cost. So, where I am at the moment, they're changing the management structure, merging three layers of management, making people redundant, changing the roles and responsibilities of all of the managers. We're setting up a corporate side and a retail side, whereas before we'd all been one. They're just very drastic changes. *But who chooses how the competitive environment is to be dealt with? Who is in control?*

I think that we – and when I say 'we', it's very clearly our chief executive – we are in control of our own destiny, but we are being driven by market forces. We are not proactive, we're reacting to the competitive environment. But we are reacting in a very strong manner and trying to be ahead of the game all of the time.

And how does this directly affect you?

I am having to manage with very scant resources, and by resources, I mean money and that means people. Budgets are absolutely ridiculous, absolutely ridiculously tight. I can't even afford to pay – this is a very real example – the expenses of one of my office managers. She said to me, 'I've been to the meeting in Northampton, Ellen, and my business mileage adds up to this much, but I haven't put it through the budget.' And I said, 'Well why not?' And she said, 'Because we haven't got enough money for travel, and if I put it through the budget, you know, we're going to be really struggling.' And, I mean, this kind of thing is not on. We're getting a lot of customer complaints: 'Where are all the staff?', 'Why aren't other people serving?', 'Why isn't the telephone being answered?' The very real answer is that they're cutting staff. Staff are leaving that don't get replaced. Where my old branch used to have twenty-odd people in, for example, it's now got twelve.

Here is some real distress. There is no balking at the central discourse of competition and marketplace, however. There are very clear doubts, nevertheless, about the extent to which the top management ('they') are being reactive and 'driven' by market forces. Ellen Fitzgerald is very much experiencing the external world through the actions of others who are imposing changes on her. The top management – 'they' – are handling the changes in this way, as opposed to it being 'we' who are coping with challenges and pressures, as we hear at other times in our interviews. There is equivocation both within what our managers say and between different managers' accounts.

When we turn to managers in the public sector, we find it almost normal to refer to changes which are 'imposed' upon managers – whereas it is more typical in the commercial world for managers to see the pressures impinging on them more directly from the market environment. Jim Costello, a Civil Service executive, put it this way:

If you are a manager in the business world, you tend to see the market as inevitably *there*, if you see what I mean. But if you are in public service you, well I'm not saying you don't recognise that you are working in a market economy, but you have to be, sort of, forced to face the fact. You have to have the market forced down your throat. So you get the contracting in local govern-ment and wherever, you get the internal market in the NHS or you get the sort of market testing that a lot of us in the Civil Service have been put through.
A 'bad thing', I take it?
No, not necessarily. Well, yes, it often feels like you are regarded as a parasitic form of life rather than as a public servant and that big daddy (or 'big mummy' to get closer to the mark – as it was anyway) is saying, 'Stop feeding on the state and get out there and earn your own living'.
Was there any justification for this?
Well now, it's not as simple as that, is it? The parasite thing is ridiculous. But too many of us were running our departments for the sake of running the department – the Civil Service for the civil servants kind of thing. And it could so easily become the schools for the teachers, the hospitals for the doctors. And when I look at some of the local government people I know, well . . . They, like a lot of us civil servants, were really meant to be doing a management job. But we just did not think managerially.
By which you mean?
I mean, well I wouldn't have spoken in these terms before – calling it 'management' I mean.
[laughing] You've been 'got at'?
You could say that. No, not really. What I mean is, I was getting worried about how we were not really managing the resources allocated to us as efficiently as we might – really focusing on meeting public needs sort of thing. 'Value for money' always seemed to me to be a good principle. But it's taken all these changes – all this management and markets stuff – to really take it seriously. We've got to get away from what they sometimes call a 'producer mentality'. The money has got to be spent to maximise the quality of what we deliver – to the customer or whatever.
Are you happy with the word 'customer' in this context?
Not really. But there is a point to it. The public we serve are not customers in the same sense as in business. But there is still the point that we ought to focus on what we are there to deliver to the people who pay us.

Here is equivocation similar to that evident among our private sector managers. Changes are problematic in various ways, but they cannot, in another phrase of Jim Costello, 'be readily dismissed as a bad thing'. We hear something very similar from Marion Brown, the primary school head teacher. She identifies the main sources of change in education as 'resulting from external sources' and 'largely from central government'. She explains that 'A lot of the people I work with' resent the changes 'as an imposition'. However, she thinks that 'the breed of school managers that are coming up now – I wouldn't say that we were trained to deal with it, but I think that we *expect* to have to deal with it, in a way that I think our predecessors didn't have to at all'. It is perhaps significant that the term 'school *manager'* is used here – suggesting that, as with Jim Costello, a managerial discourse is not totally uncongenial, as it might have been with a more traditional head teacher or civil servant. The major 'external pressures' which Marion Brown's school has been under, albeit indirectly at present, are the requirements of the government's quality inspection body, the Office for Standards in Education (OFSTED). She says that, 'to be honest', there were various things that 'people could point the finger at in many schools pre-OFSTED'. Her school has not yet received an inspection but, as in every other school, it is always felt to be 'round the corner'. Although Brown 'spent two years saying, "We will not run this school to suit OFSTED" ', she nevertheless made many changes which were in accordance with their requirements. She introduced them because she felt they were 'philosophically sound' in their own terms, but admits 'with some embarrassment' that it had been 'quite helpful' to have 'an external agenda' to refer to. She believes, in fact, that OFSTED has 'formalised some good practice' and introduced some other procedures which 'might or might not be good practice'. Some of the changes which she has made, in this context, have been 'quite enormous' and she gives, as an example, the introduction of quite detailed and long-term planning of curriculum coverage, teamwork activity and teaching. This replaces the old-fashioned, 'plan on nothing more than a sheet of A4 paper'. The more detailed planning will please the OFSTED inspectors, she says, but it is what she believes should happen anyway – 'for the sake of the children and their education'. 'Bright people' in education always knew what was needed, she suggests, but it has taken 'external pressures' to bring them about to any significant extent.

When we turn to further education we find two of our managers speaking in not dissimilar terms. Lucy Armstrong, whilst stressing that many of the teaching staff in her college do not like the 'changes and new priorities' which are coming about, personally welcomes some of the changes. She refers in particular to the 'wider spectrum' of students which the college now serves. This puts pressures on her as the manager of support services but she believes that opening up further education to a wider range of students is something which 'needed to happen'. Lucy points out that this is a view that does relate to her managerial position and is not surprised that lecturers who have traditionally been concerned primarily with gaining high examination results with very able students will want to resist the 'broadening of the market'. Carrie Bley also recognises that her position as a manager – as the finance director of her college – influences her high level of sensitivity to the competitive position of the college. She observes that, in general in education, there is a 'competitiveness between organisations that is driving everything through'. She points in particular, however, to competition with the sixth forms of schools, who have the advantage of 'a captive audience'. The FE college, on the other hand, has to 'win' its 'A' level students. And the positive aspect of this is that 'it's made us think at lot more about the students'. Carrie uses the business language of competition and 'customers', but clearly connects this to a service notion of educational provision:

I think the focus on the student is fabulous and exactly where we should be. I think a customer-orientated service is what FE always should have been, and certainly wasn't as far as I'm concerned ten years ago. The attitude was, 'This is what's available, come in, sit down and do it.' I mean, I'm an FE product. I've been there and been FE'd and it wasn't a pleasant experience! I certainly wasn't looked after. I was just sort of there, signed up, did my bit, and went off.
And now?
Now, everything is personalised, lots and lots of care for the individual student, lots and lots of support, doing everything we can to ensure the student has a good experience. This is important because what we still find is that word of mouth is our biggest seller . . . So I think that's an incredible positive, from a service point of view, you know, somebody that truly believes in education for everybody, irrespective of age, and certainly second chance – which FE, again, is about, in my opinion. It's about giving people another chance who perhaps, for whatever reason didn't succeed at school. And I think the customer focus is phenomenal.
So you provide . . .
Yes, an example of something that we've got now that wouldn't have been in place ten years ago, is the crèche. We can take seventy children. We've got a full day nursery that can take thirty-five, where you leave the kids all day, proper lunch provided, all inspected by social services. There's incredible financial commitment there. It's there to facilitate some of our customers, and we do take a lot of mature women who are coming back to education for a second chance, who, if that wasn't available to them, wouldn't be able to be here. So all of those things, I think, are incredibly positive. I think the focus on the student is absolutely spot on.

By no means all our public sector managers were as positive as this. Jack Dodds, for example, spoke very negatively about the state pressure to 'maintain a quality output with a declining resource' in his university and, in contrast to Marion Brown, claims that the main effect of this is to *prevent* him engaging in any long-term planning. 'You do not know from year to year what sort of financial environment you will be operating in', he argues. The result is that short-term planning 'becomes the order of the day'. In spite of this, 'You try. You have contingencies and you try to have assorted schemes in mind to accommodate what you foresee as problems. But you don't really know how it is going to be resolved.' In a similar way, Tom Smith identifies the main pressure on his court management work as coming from the way the Lord Chancellor's office is constantly pushing to 'reduce costs'. Ron Scott, in the prison service, also talks of 'them always trying to squeeze a little bit more out of you'. But he also stresses that because the prison service is a 'kind of political dustbin' at the level of national politics, there are continual attempts to 'change direction' through the 'introduction of one management initiative or another'. He illustrates this:

Obviously the escapes from the top jails has not helped us one bit because that squeezes everything out of the system, just to cover – to bring down the KPIs.

KPIs?

The Key Performance Indicators which are set for us every year. One of these, when they first started, was to put complete sanitation in all prison cells throughout the country. Well, that KPI's been met, so they look for another Key Performance Indicator and one of them, obviously, is escapes from prison, so you've got to improve on your KPIs on that. So, you know, they're changing all the time really.

KPIs are the main pressure then?

Well, there's a strategic planning exercise every year. You've got to look at what they call the business plan, which is how the actual business is run, as a prison service, and the strategic plan, which is how that particular establishment is planning out for the next five years. So, you're doing five-year plans and trying to incorporate the Key Performance Indicators within that plan.

Again illustrating the discursive shift that seems to have occurred in the public sector, Ron Scott has little difficulty it would seem referring to the prison service as an 'actual business'. Yet he is clearly troubled by certain business-oriented trends when he refers to the *threat* of the prison being privatised and to 'the *threat* of market testing'. But the political pressures also have a more mundane, if no less stressful, effect on the work of the manager in the prison service. Scott gives the example of a situation where a prisoner somewhere in the country commits a crime whilst licensed to be on home leave. The result of this is, say, 'a national ban on prisoner release, on temporary licences'. What this means for the individual manager is that, 'It is you who has got to explain to a man who's been on home leave five times that he can't go any more. You have to do this, even though you fully know that you have never had a single non-return, or crime committed when on licence.' The manager then has to listen to people 'spouting off and blaming you' and 'tries to persuade himself that it is not really personal – it is really the system that they are blasting off against'.

'The system', as Ron Scott calls it, can change, of course, with changes in government or local authority. And where Ron points to national government influences, Colin Hawkins illustrates how changes at local level impinge on his work.

A couple of years ago, when I first started off in this job, it was very much a Tory type attitude of a purchaser–provider split, 'Be efficient, economic', all that. And then we had the Labour local government elected and they said, 'No, we don't want a purchaser–provider split.' So we're now in the process of trying to change our working relationships with the people that we've actually been working with. They're saying, 'We're not purchasers, you're not providers, we're all one large organisation.'

Local authorities can do this?

Oh yes, yes. They – the social services committee – are very clear that whilst a lot of good is coming out from the rhetoric, i.e. economy, cost and efficiency, they don't want the same sort of doctrine and the same sort of emphasis put on a capitalist push or what looks like Tory practices.

It is interesting to note here how Colin Hawkins observes the survival of a stress on costs and efficiency even where there is a change of political rhetoric. Managers working in the National Health Service made similar points, especially when they talked about a possible change of national government. They recognise that the NHS is a very politically sensitive aspect of life in the UK and see this as having considerable managerial implications for every branch of the service. As Betty Smith puts it, 'Whatever the government decides at the top filters down to us in General Practice and influences everything about the way we work'. Not only do major policies like those on 'fund holding' influence day-to-day managing but the government can, as she puts it, 'change things on a whim – and this can have quite massive effects on us at the bottom'. Other managers illustrate in a variety of ways the pressures which they experience as a result of national policies. Diane Washington, for example, was giving thought to the implications for her activities in her hospital of the 'locally negotiated pay and pay bargaining that's coming in'. She is particularly concerned about handling the problems of staffing when 'people who look to be doing what is essentially the same job in different units will get paid differently'.

The way national policies and priorities directly influence managerial work in the hospital itself is illustrated effectively by Jean Holliday who discusses the 'contracting process'. This, she explains, involves ' basically saying how many patients we can envisage we're going to treat, and then making sure we've got contracts that bring money in to treat that number of patients'. This is crucial because, 'if our contracts don't bring the money in, but the patients come in anyway, we're clearly going to over-spend'. Dealing with this is managerially very demanding and, for Jean Holliday, raises questions of principle as well as practicality. She talks about 'cancers and sniffles' and how, for her, knowing about such matters is 'what strategic management is'.

The situation gets very very complex because it's not just a matter of saying how many patients will we treat, because clearly it costs you a lot more to treat a cancer than it does a sniffle. So, you've got not just to be able to say how many patients, you've got to know how many sniffles and how many cancers. And that's, basically, what strategic management is. But this very system, albeit that it's fair and rational, will automatically bring in a managerial cost. Because you've got to know how many patients … if you're going to bring money in pro-rata to your number of patients, you've got to know what the cost of treating a patient is. And you've got to know not just what the cost of treating a patient is, but what the cost of a sniffle as opposed to a cancer is. Now this is all information that, up to 1991, we didn't have with any degree of accuracy. You're talking about major financial and major managerial systems which the government had no money to throw at. So, at the 31st March 1991, financially to the hospital, it didn't matter how many of our patients were cancers as opposed to sniffles. On the 1st April 1991, the day after, it mattered very much, how many were cancers as opposed to sniffles. But we hadn't got the financial and managerial systems in over-night. You're talking of, phew, probably five years, to bring those sort of systems in.

Has part of your work been bringing those in?

To bring the systems in, yes: the activity recording systems, the financial systems, the costing and pricing to come to terms with how much it costs us to treat a cancer as opposed to a sniffle; making sure that our activity recording systems differentiate cancers from sniffles. And that, if you're talking in terms of how much it costs to treat a cancer and a sniffle, given that you've got wards which treat both cancers and sniffles, you're then in to the business of whether the ward and the individual nurse know how much of her time goes on sniffles as opposed to cancer?

Yes, yes.

So you're talking of huge cost apportioning; you're talking of huge systems that'll take literally five years to develop. We're working on those systems with increasing speed. But there's a cost. Now, what will be interesting is what the ultimate cost would be or could be, because there's a cost that the health service is paying for the idea of making money follow patients. Might there be a cheaper way of doing it than all this activity recording etc., etc., etc? There might very well be.

And do you get involved convincing people at other levels in the hospital that the amount of effort that they have to put in to recording these kinds of activities is worthwhile?

Well yes, yes. You see – just to take further the example of the cancers and sniffles – as far as bringing the money in that pays the nurses, it's very important that we know how much it costs to treat a cancer as opposed to a sniffle. As far as the individual nurse on the ward, or the nurse manager on the ward, is concerned, what matters is the clinical management of the patients' care. What the nurses would presumably quite justifiably say is, 'How do you expect me to know – do you want me to walk round with a stop watch?' Do we really want a health service where nurses are expected to know how much time they spend on cancers as opposed to sniffles? Is that what we want? The system we've brought in is dependent on it. Is that what we want?

In this discussion, we get a powerful account of how one manager experiences the pressures of a particular political and economic context, bringing together notions of strategic management, the establishment of management information systems, the day-to-day relating to other staff and, finally, notions of what is right and wrong. She looks at the principles being applied to her area of work together with the managerial implications of these and ends up with the question, 'Is that what we want?' The analysis offered by Jean Holliday, and indeed other hospital managers like Mary Rainey, implies that it is not what anyone would want. Their views are probably well expressed in the words of two management consultants writing about the systems described by our managers. The internal market 'reforms' of the NHS, they argue, brought about 'command management, a high degree of centralisation, divisive competition and stultifying bureaucracy' (Coghill and Stewart 1998).

Management learning: 'sink or swim' versus integrated management development

When we look back at the way our managers spoke about their early experiences of managerial work, the variety of routes which they took into such work and the very limited extent to which they report clear and systematic preparation for it, we get an impression of a very 'hit and miss' approach to developing managers in the organisations which employed them. There was not a great deal of direct complaint about this situation, although one detects an overall sense of disquiet or, rather perhaps, a lurking suspicion that something more formal and systematic might have been done for them in shaping the organisational career that they were following. The repeated use of the metaphor of 'sinking and swimming' cannot be taken as a simple complaint that a lot more training, preparation or guidance should have been available in the organisations. Indeed there was an almost stoical acceptance that this was *perhaps* the way it had to be. To some extent this would be reasonable. In the first place, the nature of managerial work itself is far from clear, our managers' accounts would suggest. Management is indeed an *opaque* occupation, as we argued in Chapter 3, and thus is not something for which one can readily identify a clear training and development programme. Also, as we argued in Chapter 4, management is indeed – like swimming – a practice. Practising therefore, is perhaps the best way to develop it.

It may be that practice is indeed of the essence when it comes to developing practice. And it may be that 'small wins' in day-to-day problem-solving are as significant to learning as major breakthroughs in understanding at the individual level as well as at the organisational (Weick 1984; Weick and Westley 1996). But does that have to be the whole story? Indeed, we wondered, in Chapter 4, whether there are not better ways of helping people develop as 'swimmers' than simply pitching them into the raging waters and leaving it to the swimmers themselves to escape drowning. This raised the question of books, courses, mentors, university qualifications and training provisions. The potential which of all of these things have for individual and organisational performance, and indeed for managerial careers, is increasingly being understood as requiring some integration of management education activities, management development processes in organisations and the day-to-day work practices of the individual. This is recognised in the increasing attention being paid to *management learning*, 'the study of the management of learning processes, especially those which contribute to the practice of management, *including* both management education and development' (Fox 1997: 34–5). Interestingly, given our interest here in the notion of *emergence*, Burgoyne and Reynolds refer to management learning as 'an emergent field' and they see as central to it an emphasis on 'understanding the whole person as mediated through experience', this paying attention to 'more connectedness to daily personal and professional life and, in avoiding the passivity thought to be associated with more conventional educational methods, as offering managers more opportunity for development than seemed possible in focusing exclusively on the acquisition of knowledge and skills' (Burgoyne and Reynolds 1997: 18). This fits very well our concept of the individual as an emergent entity, a concept which also fits well with the influential writing on experiential learning and reflective practice in management and professional contexts by Kolb (1984) and Schön (1983).

The managers we studied do not appear to be benefiting significantly from such an integration of management education, management development and day-to-day managing experiences. On the whole, the managers did not talk about books, courses, mentoring and the rest as having made terribly significant contributions to their emergence from the 'training pool' of their early managerial experiences. Not only this, but when we raised the question in our interview of what they felt about 'new management thinking', they tended to refer to the type of principle we have seen in the preceding section of the present chapter – ones like customer focus and cost control. They rarely referred to any kind of management writing, whether of a 'respectable' academic type or from the category of fashionable ideas, fads and fashions and 'management guru' writings that academic analysts of management thinking have focused on in recent years (Huczynki 1993a, 1993b; Ramsey 1996; Watson 1994b). *Management knowledge* in effect, can probably be better understood as a form of 'cookbook knowledge' rather than as a science (Clegg and Palmer 1996: 4). If this is so, then we should come to terms with the fact that the best managers are likely to be like the best cooks. These are people who take into account what is written in the recipe books of experts but who, primarily, develop their own recipes through processes of trial and error and situated learning.

Inferences such as this are supported by what our managers said to us about their own experiences of emergence. The present study, taken on its own, however, cannot point to any policy conclusions with regard to how best to develop such a 'personal recipe' or 'situated learning' (Fox 1997) approach. The question of how formal management learning can more effectively be used to support and further the learning that occurs 'on the job' is a large and challenging one. The outcomes of our conversations with emergent managers could be read as simply showing that the world of work and its management are messy, muddy and muddled and that the way managers come to cope with having to make some order of this potential chaos is bound to be a similarly messy and muddled 'hit and miss', sink or swim affair. It might be inferred that this is how things inevitably have to be and that there is little point in trying to make management education, management writing or management development more relevant to managerial practice. However, people studying these matters on a larger scale do suggest that managers can be developed in a more systematic way than typically tends to be the case and that employers of managers should move in this direction. Snape, Redman and Bamber, for example, characterise the dominant employer approach as one of 'benign neglect' (1994: 11) and argue that more organisations should follow the lead of those who are going beyond this. They argue for a more 'strategic approach' to managing and developing managers, suggesting that 'organisations cannot afford to let their managers "sink or swim"; managerial performance is simply too important for this' (1994: 11). Such a view is supported by a major research study which compared management development practices in Japan and the UK (Storey et al. 1997). This systematic comparative study using research methods and methodological orientations rather different to the present one produces findings and arguments which can very helpfully be set alongside the picture being painted by ourselves and our smaller, but much more varied, selection of managers.

Storey et al. conclude that, insofar as there is a generic approach to management development in the UK, it is not one of neglect but one that lies 'in a "sink or swim" attitude to early career development, a reliance on specific performance targets, and a stress on the "ownership" of the career by the individual who then had to find a way through the internal and external labour market, drawing where relevant on an organisation's resources' (1997: 228). This description fits, almost to perfection, the stories that we hear from our own set of managers. But the Britain and Japan comparison that these authors make enables them to conclude that things do not have to be like this. In Japan, they show a much more integrated and systematic approach to the recruitment, training and career development of managers, something which they see as enabling Japanese employers to gain a much better return from their investment in their managers than do British employers. The British managers interviewed by Storey and his colleagues typically could not describe the training and development systems in their companies any more effectively than could our own informants. Yet the Japanese managers, at all levels, were able to do this. The managers in the British firms gave plentiful reports of training experiences, as did our own, but what 'tended to be lacking was awareness of where a course might lead and how it would fit in with a manager's career development', whereas the Japanese firms 'had integrated the idea of development into the whole way in which they operated' (Storey et al. 1997). Whilst we need to take great care in drawing inferences about what will 'work' in Britain on the basis of evidence of practices in Japan, this carefully presented comparative study does suggest that the situation spoken of by the managers in the present study is not the way it inevitably has to be. A degree of 'sink or swim', we would conclude, is as inevitable with the development of the manager as it is with the swimmer. But leaving a novice swimmer in a pool without a lifeguard to keep an eye on them or a coach to help them improve their strokes hardly seems desirable. And might not advice, preparation, guidance, training and education all be better integrated into a sense of the direction in which the swimmer is to travel – to the potential benefit of both the employer and the manager?

Managers and the employment relationship: 'jobs for life' or employability and the 'boundaryless career'

An attachment to 'sink or swim' management development practices, and indeed their tendency frequently to 'chop and change' development and training practices, is related by Storey et al. (1997) to a tendency in the UK to operate in a 'market-led' mode in which management development is a 'downstream' or 'second order' activity, being adjusted to meet inferred market changes faced by the organisation. This contrasts with the Japanese belief in 'the enduring value of growing managers in order to meet the changing character of market conditions' (1997: 207). And an associated contrast is that between the Japanese policy of the long-term integration of the manager's career into the corporation's development and the growing use by British employers of the notion of 'employability'. This is a concept of the manager's employment relationship with the organisation which has profound implications for the individual. It implies a major shift away from the traditional notion of the 'life career with the firm' for the manager. Instead, the manager is expected to work hard and loyally for the organisation with no expectation of a long-term career. The absence of the career security is compensated for by the employer's provision of training, experience and qualifications which they can 'take out' with them when their services are no longer necessary (Kanter 1983). Various writers in the USA claim that the restructuring of work organisations is making such a principle increasingly important. Individuals will more and more develop their personal careers entrepreneurially, taking their emergent expertise from labour market purchaser to labour market purchaser, thus actively shaping what Hall calls their 'protean career' (Hall 1996), Handy their 'portfolio career' (Handy 1989) or Arthur and Rousseau their 'boundaryless career' (Arthur and Rousseau 1996).

A shift in the direction of 'employability' and a boundaryless career and away from a 'job for life' would involve a considerable change in the 'psychological contract of the manager' (Rousseau 1995). Such a shift has been characterised by Herriot and Pemberton (1995) as one which puts a *transaction* based on mutual instrumentality in the place of a more traditional employment *relationship* – one which involves mutual trust and high levels of two-way commitment. This, we suggest, could create considerable problems for organisations as the employers of managers. Could they afford to rely on a largely instrumental relationship with their managerial staff? It may well be, however, that the claimed emergence of the boundaryless career is not well rooted in knowledge about actual organisational practices and changing labour markets (Nicholson 1997). And reading the research by Storey et al. (1997), or the earlier chapters of the present book, suggests that there are mixed signs when it comes to looking at what is actually happening. There are indications, on the one hand, that the employers want to develop their managers for a long-term involvement in the organisation. Yet there are also signs that the priority is for managers to prepare themselves and to 'get on with the job' as it presents itself now.

Managers speak very much in terms of 'owning their own careers' as opposed to sharing that ownership with the employer and seem willing to contemplate taking their acquired skills and experience elsewhere, when the time for this comes. This notion of an 'emergent career', as opposed to one carefully planned by or with an employer, may at first look like a sign of a trend towards the boundaryless or entrepreneurially shaped career. It is doubtful, however, whether this would be a wise interpretation. It is perhaps better understood as the pragmatic reaction of individual managers to employers who are not as attentive to the development of their managers as they might be. Indeed, we reiterate our question about whether the type of psychological contract that goes with the boundaryless career would provide the best framework within which the managers might cope and find fulfilment in the considerable challenges with which their employers face them. We would argue that attention must be given to the risk which is faced if too short-term and calculative an employment relationship between the employer and the manager is fostered, with all the implications for cynicism which that implies and all its implications for encouraging a short-term problem-solving mentality as opposed to an innovative, creative and developmental mental outlook.

Managing emergence: knowing the job, knowing yourself

Exactly how our managers' lives, careers and notions of 'self' will work out in the future is something that neither they nor we can predict. As human beings and as managers they will continue to 'emerge', in the light of the personal choices they make and the circumstances they meet. This is the case for all of us as managers of our own lives, whether or not we have an occupational role as managers of work activities in employing organisations. As a good proportion of our managers seem to suggest, there is a clear continuity between the management of one's personal life and the formal managerial work done in the organisation. This is once again apparent in the way our managers spoke when we asked what message they would offer readers if they were the author of this book or we enquired about the advice they would give to someone contemplating a managerial job.

In turning to the words of our managers here, we are keen to let them 'speak for themselves', insofar as this is possible. This whole book is the outcome of dialogues between us and our selection of managers and we would like to be able to say that we are simply providing a medium through which they can explain to interested readers how they have come to 'be' managers and how they are 'managing' their managerial roles. But we must not be too innocent about this.

The novelist, V.S. Naipaul, in his move away from the novel to what he calls 'non-fiction narrative' writes of his being a 'manager of narrative' (1998). This involves seeking out, organising and presenting the narratives of individuals with whom he talks about the various countries and beliefs he wishes to write about. It is a notion which appeals to us. Naipaul's books are, however, inevitably his creations. And the present book has been created by us, and not by the managers to whom we have spoken. Our personal values, concerns, theoretical interests and methodological leanings have shaped it. But the research process itself, inevitably and rightly, has developed these concerns and understandings. Nevertheless, we take a distinctive position which locates us alongside a range of other writers who are interested in *narrative* as a way of understanding human sense-making processes generally and organisational and managerial processes specifically (Boje 1991; Brown 1998; Czarniawska 1998; Mitroff and Kilmann 1975; Weick 1995, for example). On the basis of the narratives we have listened to and in the light of our own sense-making inclinations we have developed a particular set of arguments about how people become and develop as managers.

Our main argument is that the process of how people enter managerial work and 'learn to manage' has to be understood in the light of the individual's life, identity and biography as a whole. Because management is not a clear cut occupation with either an established body of knowledge and operating principles or a clearly specified set of tasks of the type which we might expect to see in other parts of a society's occupational division of labour, we have a difficulty when it comes to understanding how people make the 'transition' into managerial work and how they learn and develop (or are 'developed') when in a managerial post. To help improve our understanding of such matters, we have made central use of the notion of the 'emergent manager'. This is used, in part, simply to recognise that there is no obvious point at which one suddenly 'becomes' a manager and that even when the individual accepts the status or role of manager they will inevitably continue to learn about managing and will go on through their career to modify or develop their understandings and practices.

The concept of the emergent manager also has a *theoretical* significance, however. It is influenced by a particular way of thinking about human beings and the social world in which they operate. It was argued in Chapter 1 that we can most effectively improve our understanding of the human world in general and managerial activity in particular if we turn away from essentialist, representationalist or 'entitative' styles of thinking towards a more processual, relational or non-representationalist approach (pp. 17–21). Consequently, an 'ontology of becoming' (Chia 1996) was adopted and applied to managerial work in which people engaged in *managing* as a kind of work are seen as *making their worlds at the same time as their worlds are making them*. Managers are seen as involved in 'emergence' both in shaping their personal sense of 'self' and in shaping organisational work activities through 'organising'. Central to this are processes of learning. And this is learning *about life* and it is *learning through a lifetime*, as opposed to a specific 'management training' kind of learning. Our managers' accounts, we believe, clearly show that matters of identity and learning which go back into childhood or into pre-managerial work experience are vital to understanding how they 'manage to manage' in their current job and, indeed, will continue to manage and learn as their 'emergence' continues.

We would like to think that participation in our research has been of value and has helped the ongoing 'emergence' of the managers who spent time with us. In the interviews, of course, the managers were answering questions taken from our agenda rather than their own. And the resulting transcribed texts were analysed, 'cut up' and generally 'bashed' into the shape of a book that *we* thought would be of interest to readers. Nevertheless, we have striven not to 'over-manage' the narratives which emerged from our dialogues with our selection of managers. This has been a matter of moral judgement as much as one of social scientific or literary skill. We have attempted throughout to respect the integrity of these individuals and to manipulate their words only to the extent necessary to give our book sufficient clarity of narrative logic to make it coherent and readable. And we hope that we have respected the integrity of the people who helped us with the book. We hope that they will feel that we have honoured the accounts they gave us. In this spirit then, we attempt to give the 'last word' to the forty people who spent time with us and contributed to the study.

Very much in accord with the notion of emergence, as we have presented it here, manager after manager stresses the importance of taking one's time and gradually learning about managing, combining a process of trial and error learning with one of seeking information and guidance about the job from others. 'It's a gradual education and it's a slow process' which means that you have 'got to be patient', explains Betty Smith; 'Rome wasn't built in a day'. Like others, she relates such advice to the temptation which one faces when first moving into a formal managerial role of 'wanting to make things change, wanting to do it tomorrow' so that 'when it doesn't happen, you get frustrated'. Again, like many others, she emphasises the value of talking to people who 'know more than you about the job itself' or the organisation in general. Ron Scott expresses his very similar advice in terms of not 'trying to take over straightaway' but spending time to 'infiltrate, get amongst people and communicate'. If you go in to 'play the new broom' you will get people 'clamming up and opposing you from the start'. He also stresses, 'taking your time', 'finding out what everybody does' and getting to know generally 'how things operate'. The words of these two individuals are echoed time and again in the 'messages' and advice that our managers offer – regardless of their age, experience or background.

This advice may seem very simplistic, obvious and unsurprising. Indeed, it is. And the advice fits very well with all of those earlier accounts which compared new managers to novice swimmers – individuals struggling to stay afloat. But emerging as a new manager is much more of a social process than learning to swim – one listens carefully to others and establishes relationships as well as learning from both successes and mistakes. Relationships with experienced people from whom one can learn and with whom one can discuss one's work are obviously helpful. Equally important, however, are the relationships with those with whom one works more directly. Mina Mangeshkar puts this explicitly in moral terms, arguing that the manager is the one who 'sets the standards' in 'the environments where the people you are managing operate' and that 'high moral values' have to be instilled in order to gain the full commitment of people. This has to be done patiently and over time, with a lot of 'listening'; 'You have got two ears and one mouth, use them proportionately'. Mina emphasises the importance to this of 'knowing your own values' and 'mission in life' and this corresponds in part to Mary Rainey's principle of knowing 'what you want to be and where you want to go'. This is necessary if you are to 'face yourself every day in the mirror' and to get the respect of people; 'If you don't respect yourself in the way you work, nobody else can'. This then takes her on to her key moral principle which is to 'treat other people how you would like them to treat you'. As with other managers who speak in terms like this, Mary does not want this to be seen as a matter of being 'soft' or unambitious – you can 'get to the top without tramping other people under your feet'.

A common theme in the advice and messages offered is one of encouraging would-be managers to be sure that they know what it is they are undertaking – in terms of all the task pressures as well as the social and political ones. And it is especially important to be clear about one's individual strengths and weaknesses. As Colin Hawkins puts it,

I really think that you have to know yourself. I don't think anyone realises the demands that are going to be made on you personally, as an individual. You have to have the working experience, the knowledge, and some of the tools of managing. But most of all, I think you have to know your own strengths and weaknesses. I think your weaknesses will be found out in management, I really do. You can only hide them for so long. It's taken me a while to work through them all but I think I'm getting there.

Repeatedly we are warned of the dangers of the manager not developing a consistent view of how they are to be seen by others. This is a vital aspect of 'knowing yourself' and this is sometimes presented as a matter of *deciding* who you are, or, at least, how you are to be perceived. Carrie Bley explains that if she were writing the book,

I would talk a lot about perceptions, and how people's perceptions of you will change once you are a manager. I think that is the major difference. I think that it is key to accept and understand that your role is different and that you've got to play a slightly different part . . . I think there is a noticeable change when people move into management, not having been in that position before. This just knocks on to everything else really. And you've got to work at it – I mean you've got to decide how you want to be and what sort of messages you want to be sending. It might be that you've got to work incredibly hard to actually get that across. And it might be that you never quite achieve it. People's perception of the job, rather than you as a person, will outweigh any perception of you as an individual. You almost lose your individual identity as a person separate from the job.

Arthur Blakey tells us that this problem means that managing can be a 'rough ride' and that 'you have to take knocks'. It means that, 'You have to watch your own credibility', because 'one small thing and your credibility goes down the tubes'. It is what Arthur calls his own 'personal vision' of managing that you always have to be 'whiter than white'. 'You only have to say the wrong thing in front of someone, do the wrong thing, and it's all over', he warns. This implies the need for a considerable amount of self-discipline and, indeed, several managers use this very term. Kathy Westbrook, for example, speaks of 'self-discipline and motivation':

You've got to push yourself, you've got to keep reminding people who you are and where you are, and letting them know that you want to do this. They won't do anything for you unless you've let them know that that's what you want to do.

As several people say, you have got to be sure you want to do the managerial job. Mark Taylor talks this way and argues that it is vital that you decide that the job is 'what you really want' because there will always be 'grief'; the 'grief never goes away – you are always going to have to handle it'. Kathy Westbrook explains that this means that you have to 'harden up':

You have got to harden yourself, I think. I'm a naturally quite sensitive person, and I do get bothered about what people think about me. And really, you've got to start learning to shrug off what people think about you, because it all depends on the last shift they had. If it was busy, and horrible, then they probably hate you. And the next shift they have, they think you're wonderful, because it's calm and quiet, and everything's gone hunky-dory and they've made loads of tips. And you've got to learn that that's part of life, and it's the way you were when you were a waitress. You know, it's just the way it is. But you've got to learn to harden yourself up a bit, and discipline yourself. It's the only way you're going to succeed.

Another young graduate woman manager speaks in similar terms. Liza Potts says that she would not recommend managerial work to recent graduates who are 'not as strong as I am'. As she has done before, she relates managing at work to managing one's life. She argues that someone moving from a student life into a management career 'has lots of changes to go through – in themselves and in their personal lives'. They are likely to be used by an employer like hers as 'an agent of change' and 'if you were not strong enough to withstand that it would have a long-term damaging effect on you – you wouldn't cope'. This young manager is speaking in a way which reminds us of the discursive framing of modern management work which we saw in the job advertisements discussed in Chapter 1 – one which stresses the challenges to be taken up, in effect, by the 'right sort of person'. But what is this 'right sort of person'? Our study does not suggest that such a being can straightforwardly be identified. But it does suggest that to cope with the pressures which they face, the emergent manager has to be constantly learning, constantly adjusting and continuously developing the skills of a generally competent human being – a skilled social, political and economic actor. This perhaps helps us make sense of Liza Potts's final words of advice:

Realise that being a manager is not about being promoted and taking on a role and just getting things done each day. It is about who you are and how you approach life in all its different aspects. It is something that people who are not called managers do as well as those who are in a management job. Management is a way of thinking. It is a way of approaching the world that can't be taught.

BIBLIOGRAPHY

Alvesson, M. and Willmott, H. (1996) *Making Sense of Management: a Critical Introduction*, London: Sage.

Arthur, M.B. and Rousseau, D.M. (1996) *The Boundaryless Career: a New Employment Principle for a New Organisational Era*, New York: Oxford University Press.

Arthur, M.B., Hall, D.T. and Lawrence, B.S. (1989) 'Generating new directions in career theory: the case for a transdisciplinary approach', in Arthur, M.B., Hall, D.T. and Lawrence, B.S. (eds.) *Handbook of Career Theory*, Cambridge: Cambridge University Press.

Ashton, D.N. (1973) 'The transition from school to work: notes on the development of different frames of reference among young male workers', *Sociological Review* 21(1): 101–125.

Atkinson, P. (1990) *The Ethnographic Imagination*, London: Routledge.

Austin, J. (1962) *How To Do Things With Words*, Oxford: Oxford University Press.

Bahktin, M.M. (1981) *The Dialogic Imagination*, Austin, Texas: University of Texas Press.

Bailyn, L. (1980) 'The slow-burn way to the top', in Derr, B. (ed.) *Work, Family and Career*, New York: Praeger.

Bailyn, L. (1984) 'Issues of work and family in organizations: responding to social diversity', in Arthur, M.B., Bailyn, Lotte, Levinson, Daniel J. and Shepard, Herbert A. (eds.) *Working with Careers*, New York: Center for Research in Career Development, Graduate School of Business, Columbia University.

Bailyn, L. (1989) 'Understanding individual experience at work: comments on the theory and practice of career', in Arthur, M.B., Hall, D.T. and Lawrence, B.S. (eds.) *Handbook of Career Theory*, Cambridge: Cambridge University Press.

Bailyn, L. (1993) *Breaking the Mold. Women, Men and Time in the New Corporate World*, New York: The Free Press.

Barley, S.R. (1989) 'Careers, identities and institutions: the legacy of the Chicago School of Sociology', in Arthur, M.B., Hall, D.T. and Lawrence, B.S. (eds.) *Handbook of Career Theory*, Cambridge: Cambridge University Press.

Berger, P.L. and Luckmann, T. (1971) *The Social Construction of Reality*, Harmondsworth: Penguin.

Billig, M. (1995) *Arguing and Thinking a Rhetorical Approach to Social Psychology*, Cambridge: Cambridge University Press.

Boje, D.M. (1991) 'The storytelling organisation: a study of storytelling performance in an office-supply firm', *Administrative Science Quarterly* 38(4): 106–126.

Brown, A.D. (1998) 'Narrative, politics and legitimacy in an IT implementation', *Journal of Management Studies* 35(1): 35–59.

Burgoyne, J. and Reynolds, M. (1997) *Management Learning: Integrating Perspectives in Theory and Practice*, London: Sage.

Burns, T. (1955) 'The reference of conduct in small groups', *Human Relations* 8.

Burns, T. (1961) 'Micropolitics', *Administrative Science Quarterly* 6.

Carlson, S. (1951) *Executive Behaviour: A Study of the Workload and the Working Methods of Managing Directors*, Stockholm: Strombergs.

Carroll, S.J. and Gillen, D.J. (1987) 'Are the classical management functions useful in describing work?', *Academy of Management Review* 12: 138–151.

Chia, R. (1996) *Organisational Knowledge as Deconstructive Practice*, Berlin: de Gruyter.

Clarke, J. and Newman, J. (1993) 'The right to manage: a second managerial revolution', *Cultural Studies* 7(3): 427–441.

Clegg, S.R. and Palmer, G. (1996) *The Politics of Management Knowledge*, London: Sage.

Cleverley, G. (1971) *Managers and Magic*, London: Longman.

Coghill, N. and Stewart, J. (1998) *The NHS: Myth, Monster or Service*, Salford: Revans Centre for Action Learning and Research.

Collin, A. (1986) 'Career development: the significance of the subjective career', *Personnel Review* 15(2): 22–28.

Collinson, D. (1992) *Managing the Shopfloor: Subjectivity, Masculinity and Workplace Culture*, Berlin: de Gruyter.

Cooper, C.L. (1981) *Executive Families Under Stress. How Male and Female Managers Can Keep Their Pressures Out of their Homes*, Englewood Cliffs, NJ: Prentice-Hall.

Cooper, C.L., Cooper, D.R. and Eaker, L.H. (1988) *Living with Stress*, Harmondsworth: Penguin.

Cooper, R. and Burrell, G. (1988) 'Modernism, postmodernism and organisational analysis: an introduction', *Organisation Studies* 9(1): 91–112.

Czarniawska, B. (1998) *A Narrative Approach to Organisation Studies*, Thousand Oaks, CA: Sage.

Czarniawska-Joerges, B. (1993) *The Three-dimensional Organisation: a Constructionist View*, Bromley, Kent: Chartwell–Bratt.

Dachler, H.P. and Hosking, D.-M. (1995) 'The primacy of relations in socially constructing organisational realities', in Hosking, D.-M., Dachler, H.P. and Gergen, K.J. (eds.) *Management and Organisation: Relational Alternatives to Individualism*, Aldershot: Avebury.

Derrida, J. (1978) *Writing and Difference*, London: Routledge.

Dopson, S. and Stewart, R. (1990) 'What is happening to middle management?', *British Journal of Management* 1(3): 3–16.

du Gay, P. (1996) 'Making up managers: enterprise and the ethos of bureaucracy', in Clegg, S.R. and Palmer, G. (eds.) *The Politics of Management Knowledge*, London: Sage.

Edwards, D. and Potter, J. (1992) *Discursive Psychology*, London: Sage.

Fayol, H. (1916/1949) *General and Industrial Management*, London: Pitman.

Fineman, S. (ed.) (1993a) *Emotion in Organizations*, London: Sage.

Fineman, S. (1993b) 'Organizations as emotional arenas', in Fineman, S. (ed.) *Emotion in Organizations*, London: Sage.

Foucault, M. (1980) *Power/Knowledge: Selected Interviews and Other Writings*, Brighton: Harvester.

Fox, S. (1997) 'From management education and development to the study of management learning', in Burgoyne, J. and Reynolds, M. (eds.) *Management Learning: Integrating Perspectives in Theory and Practice*, London: Sage.

Gergen, K. (1992) 'Organisation theory in the post-modern era', in Reed, M. and Hughes, M. (eds.) *Rethinking Organisation*, London: Sage.

Gergen, K. (1993) *Toward Social Transformation in Social Knowledge*, 2nd edn, Newbury Park, CA: Sage.

Giddens, A. (1984) *The Constitution of Society: Outline of the Theory of Structuration*, Cambridge: Polity Press.

Giddens, A. (1991) *Modernity and Self-Identity. Self and Society in the Late Modern Age*, Cambridge: Polity Press.

Goffman, E. (1958) *The Presentation of Self in Everyday Life*, Harmondsworth: Penguin.

Goffman, E. (1961) *Asylums*, Harmondsworth: Penguin.

Grey, C. (1994) 'Career as a project of the self and labour process discipline', *Sociology* 28(2): 479–497.

Grint, K. (1995) *Management: a Sociological Introduction*, Cambridge: Polity Press.

Guest, D. (1987) 'Human resource management and industrial relations', *Journal of Management Studies* 24(5): 503–521.

Gulick, L. (1937) 'Notes on the theory of organisation', in Gulick, L. and Urwick, L. (eds.) *Papers on the Science of Administration*, New York: University of Columbia Press.

Gunz, H. (1989) *Careers and Corporate Cultures: Managerial Mobility in Large Corporations*, Oxford: Basil Blackwell.

Hales, C.P. (1986) 'What do managers do? A critical review of the evidence', *Journal of Management Studies* 23(1): 88–115.

Hall, D. (1996) 'Long live the career', *The Academy of Management Executive* 10(4).

Hall, D. and Hall, F. (1980) 'Stress and the two career couple', in Cooper, C. and Payne, R. (eds.) *Current Concerns in Occupational Stress*, New York: Wiley.

Handy, C. (1978) 'The family: help or hindrance?', in Cooper, C.L. and Payne, R. (eds.) *Stress at Work*, Chichester: Wiley.

Handy, C. (1989) *The Age of Unreason*, Boston, MA: Harvard University Press.

Harré, R. (1983) *Personal Being*, Oxford: Basil Blackwell.

Harré, R. and Gillet, G. (1994) *The Discursive Mind*, London: Sage.

Hassard, J. and Parker, M. (1993) *Postmodernism and Organisations*, London: Sage.

Hay, C. (1996) 'Narrating crisis: the discursive construction of the "winter of discontent"', *Sociology* 30(2): 253–277.

Herriot, P. and Pemberton, C. (1995) *New Deals*, Chichester: Wiley.

Hill, L.A. (1992) *Becoming a Manager: Mastery of a New Identity*, Boston, MA: Harvard Business School Press.

Hirsch, W. and Bevan, J. (1988) *What Makes a Manager?*, Brighton: Institute of Manpower Studies.

HMSO (1991) *General Household Survey*, London: HMSO Office of Population Censuses and Surveys.

Hochschild, A.R. (1983) *The Managed Heart: Commercialization of Human Feeling*, Berkeley, CA: University of California Press.

Höpfl, H. (1994) 'Learning by heart. The rules of rhetoric and the poetics of experience', *Management Learning* 25(3): 463–474.

Hosking, D.-M. and Morley, I.E. (1991) *A Social Psychology of Organising: People, Processes and Contexts*, London: Harvester Wheatsheaf.

Hosking, D.-M., Dachler, H.P. and Gergen, K.J. (1995) *Management and Organisation: Relational Alternatives to Individualism*, Aldershot: Avebury.

Huczynki, A.A. (1993a) 'Explaining the succession of management fads', *International Journal of Human Resource Management* 4(2): 443–463.

Huczynki, A.A. (1993b) *Management Gurus: What Makes Them and How to Become One*, London: Routledge.

Jackall, R. (1988) *Moral Mazes: the World of Corporate Managers*, New York: Oxford University Press.

Kanter, R.M. (1983) *The Change Masters*, London: Allen and Unwin.

Kolb, D.M. (1984) *Experiential Learning*, Englewood Cliffs, NJ: Prentice-Hall.

Kotter, J.P. (1982) *The General Managers*, New York: Free Press.

Legge, K. (1995) 'HRM: rhetoric, reality and hidden agendas', in Storey, J. (ed.) *Human Resource Management: a Critical Text*, London: Routledge.

Marshall, H. and Wetherell, M. (1989) 'Talking about career and gender identities: a discourse analysis perspective', in Skevington, S. and Baker, D. (eds.) *The Social Identity of Women*, London: Sage.

Marshall, J. (1989) 'Revisioning career concepts: a feminist invitation', in Arthur, M.B., Hall, D.T. and Lawrence, B.S. (eds.) *Handbook of Career Theory*, Cambridge: Cambridge University Press.

Marshall, J. (1995) *Women Managers Moving On. Exploring Career and Life Choices*, London: Routledge.

Mead, G.H. (1962) *Mind, Self and Society*, Chicago: University of Chicago Press.

Metcalfe, A.W. (1992) 'The curriculum vitae: confessions of a wage-labourer', *Work Employment and Society* 6(4): 619–641.

Mintzberg, H. (1973) *The Nature of Managerial Work*, New York: Harper and Row.

Mintzberg, H. (1975) 'The manager's job', *Harvard Business Review* July–August.

Mintzberg, H. (1987) 'The strategy concept', *California Management Review* 30(3): 11–32.

Mitroff, I.I. and Kilmann, R. (1975) 'Stories managers tell: a new tool for organisational problem solving', *Management Review* 64(1): 13–28.

Moir, J. (1993) 'Occupational career choice: accounts and contradictions', in Burman, E. and Parker, I. (eds.) *Discourse Analytic Research*, London: Routledge.

Mulholland, K. (1998) '"Survivors" versus "Movers and Shakers": the reconstitution of management and careers in the privatised utilities', in Thompson, P. and Warhurst, C. (eds.) *Workplaces of the Future*, Basingstoke: Macmillan.

Naipaul, V.S. (1998) *Beyond Belief: Islamic Excursions Among the Converted Peoples*, Boston, MA: Little Brown.

Newell, H. and Dopson, S. (1996) 'Muddle in the middle: organisational restructuring and middle management careers', *Personnel Review* 25(4): 4–20.

Nicholson, N. (1997) 'Review of Arthur and Rousseau, 1996', *British Journal of Industrial Relations* 35(3): 488.

Nicholson, N. and West, M. (1988) *Managerial Job Change: Men and Women in Transition*, Cambridge: Cambridge University Press.

Osborne, D. and Gaebler, T. (1992) *Re-inventing Government*, Reading, MA: Addison-Wesley.

Pahl, J.M. and Pahl, R.E. (1972) *Managers and their Wives*, Harmondsworth: Penguin.

Pettigrew, A.M. (1973) *The Politics of Organisational Decision Making*, London: Tavistock.

Plummer, K. (1983) *Documents of Life. An Introduction to the Problems and Literature of a Humanistic Method*, London: Unwin Hyman.

Pollitt, C. (1990) *Managerialism and the Public Services*, Oxford: Basil Blackwell.

Potter, J. and Wetherell, M. (1987) *Discourse and Social Psychology: Beyond Attitudes and Behaviour*, London: Sage.

Preston, D. and Hart, C. (1996) 'The trail of clues for graduates at Taylors plc' Paper presented at conference, *HRM: The Inside Story*, The Open University, Milton Keynes.

Putnam, L.L. and Mumby, D.K. (1993) 'Organizations, emotion and the myth of rationality', in Fineman, S. (ed.) *Emotion in Organizations*, London: Sage.

Ramsey, H. (1996) 'Managing sceptically, a critique of organisational fashion', in Clegg, S.R. and Palmer, G. (eds.) *The Politics of Management Knowledge*, London: Sage.

Rapoport, R. and Rapoport, R. (1976) *Dual Career Families Re-examined*, London: Martin Robertson.

Reed, M.I. (1984) 'Management as a social practice', *Journal of Management Studies* 21(3).

Roethlisberger, F.J. (1945) 'The foreman: master and victim of double talk', *Harvard Business Review* 23: 283–298.

Rorty, R. (1982) *Consequences of Pragmatism*, Minnesota: University of Minnesota Press.

Rorty, R. (1989) *Contingency, Irony, and Solidarity*, Cambridge: Cambridge University Press.

Rousseau, D.M. (1995) *Psychological Contracts in Organisations: Understanding Written and Unwritten Agreements*, Thousand Oaks, CA: Sage.

Salaman, G. and Butler, J. (1990) 'Why managers won't learn', *Management Education and Development* 21(3): 183–191.

Scarbrough, H. and Burrell, G. (1996) 'The Axeman Cometh: the changing roles and knowledges of middle managers', in Clegg, S.R. and Palmer, G. (eds.) *The Politics of Management Knowledge*, London: Sage.

Scase, R. and Goffee, R. (1989) *Reluctant Managers: Their Work and Lifestyles*, London: Unwin Hyman.

Schein, E.H. (1978) *Career Dynamics: Matching Individual and Organizational Needs*, Reading, MA: Addison-Wesley.

Schön, D. (1983) *The Reflective Practitioner*, New York: Basic Books.

Schutz, A. (1972) *The Phenomenology of the Social World*, London: Heinemann.

Sekaran, U. and Hall, D. (1989) 'Asynchronism in dual-career and family linkages', in Arthur, M.B., Hall, D.T. and Lawrence, B.S. (eds.) *Handbook of Career Theory*, Cambridge: Cambridge University Press.

Shotter, J. (1993) *Cultural Politics of Everyday Life: Social Constructionism, Rhetoric and Knowing of the Third Kind*, Milton Keynes: Open University Press.

Snape, E., Redman, T. and Bamber, G.J. (1994) *Managing Managers*, Oxford: Basil Blackwell.

Stewart, R. (1976), *Contrasts in Management*, Maidenhead: McGraw-Hill.

Storey, J., Edwards, P. and Sisson, K. (1997) *Managers in the Making: Development and Control in Corporate Britain and Japan*, London: Sage.

Taylor, B. and Lippitt, G. (1983) *Management Development and Training Handbook*, 2nd edn, Maidenhead: McGraw-Hill.

Turnbull, S. (1996) 'Emotional Labour in the HRM Driven Organisation – the 1990s Phenomenon? The Effects of Organisational and 'Feeling Rules' on Middle Managers' Paper presented at conference, *HRM – the Inside Story*. Milton Keynes: Open University Press.

Urmson, J.O. (1989) 'Truth', in Urmson, J.O. and Rée, J. (eds.) *The Concise Encyclopedia of Western Philosophy and Philosophers*, London: Routledge.

Vielba, C. (1995) 'Managers working hours', *Proceedings of the Annual Conference of the British Academy of Management*, University of Sheffield.

Warhurst, C. and Thompson, P. (1998) 'Hands, Hearts and Minds: Changing Work and Workers at the End of the Century', in Thompson, P. and Warhurst, C. (eds.) *Workplaces of the Future*, Basingstoke: Macmillan.

Watson, D.H. (1996) 'Individuals and institutions: the case of work and employment', in Wetherell, M. (ed.) *Identities, Groups and Social Issues*, London: Sage.

Watson, T.J. (1977) *The Personnel Managers*, London: Routledge.

Watson, T.J. (1994a) *In Search of Management*, London: International Thomson Business Press.

Watson, T.J. (1994b) 'Management "flavours of the month": their role in managers' lives', *International Journal of Human Resource Management* 5(4): 889–905.

Watson, T.J. (1994c) 'Managing, crafting and researching: words, skill and imagination in shaping management research', *British Journal of Management* 5(special issue): 77–87.

Watson, T.J. (1995a) 'In search of HRM: beyond the rhetoric and reality distinction or the dog that didn't bark', *Personnel Review* 24(4): 6–16.

Watson, T.J. (1995b) 'Shaping the story: rhetoric, persuasion and creative writing in organisational ethnography', *Studies in Cultures, Organisations and Society* 1(2): 310–311.

Watson, T.J. (1995c) *Sociology, Work and Industry*, 3rd edn, London: Routledge.

Watson, T.J. (1996) 'How do managers think? Morality and pragmatism in theory and practice', *Management Learning* 27(3): 323–341.

Watson, T.J. (1997) 'Theorising managerial work: a pragmatic pluralist approach to interdisciplinary research', *British Journal of Management* 8 (Special Issue): 3–8.

Watson, T.J. (1999) 'Human resourcing strategies: choice, chance and circumstances', in Leopold, J., Harris, L. and Watson, T. (eds.) *Strategic Human Resourcing: Principles, Perspectives and Practices in HRM*, London: FT Pitman.

Watson, T.J. and Harris, P. (1996) 'Human resources are strategic too: managerial career strategies, planned or realized', *Strategic Change* 5(6): 1–12.

Weber, M. (1968) *Economy and Society*, New York: Bedminster Press.

Weick, K.E. (1984) 'Small wins: redefining the scale of social problems', *American Psychologist* 39(1): 40–49.

Weick, K.E (1995) *Sensemaking in Organisations*, Thousand Oaks, CA: Sage.

Weick, K.E. and Westley, F. (1996) 'Organizational learning: affirming an oxymoron', in Clegg, S.R., Hardy, C. and Nord, W.R. (eds.) *Handbook of Organization Studies*, London: Sage.

Wittgenstein, L. (1953) *Philosophical Investigations*, Oxford: Basil Blackwell.

Wooffitt, R. (1992) *Telling Tales of the Unexpected: the Organisation of Factual Discourse*, Hemel Hempstead: Harvester Wheatsheaf.

AUTHOR INDEX

SUBJECT INDEX